Further Along the Garden Path

Further Along the Garden Path

Ann Lovejoy

Photography by Mark Lovejoy

MACMILLAN • USA

MACMILLAN
A Simon & Schuster Macmillan Company
1633 Broadway
New York, NY 10019-6785

MACMILLAN is a registered trademark of Macmillan, Inc.

Library of Congress Cataloging-in-Publication Data

Lovejoy, Ann, 1951–
    Further along the garden path / Ann Lovejoy ; photography by
Mark Lovejoy.
        p.   cm.
    Includes bibliographical references (p.   ) and index.
    ISBN 0-02-575585-4 (hc)
    1. Gardening. 2. Gardening—Calendars. 3. Gardening—
United States. 4. Gardening—United States—Calendars.   I. Title.

635.9—dc20   95-11939
                                                              CIP

For descriptions of photographs on page ii, see page 149; page iii, see page 101; page vi, see page 140; page vii, see page 108.

Printed in the United States of America

Design by Amy Peppler Adams, designLab, Seattle

In memory of Kevin Nicolay, who was a loving slave to the goddess Flora.

Contents

Introduction

This book is intended for novice gardeners who have learned the basics and are ready to travel further down the garden path. It offers a year-long course in garden making, presenting concepts and skills that will help both you and your garden grow. Instead of huge borders on sweeping estates, you will see pictures of small, personal, American gardens, most of them made and maintained without professional help. All the gardens shown are excellent role models for garden makers in any part of the country, but if you need more inspiration, look around. Most of these gardens are within a few miles of my house. It's amazing what you find when you begin to explore your own neighborhood and region. This book is organized by season, because that's how garden work is done. Short, specific chapters are grouped by month to guide you through the seasonal chores, garden planning and planting activities of the garden year. Some offer practical information and time-saving maintenance tips, others introduce important plant groups and families and suggest lastingly attractive combinations. At the end of the book, garden plans and planting diagrams demonstrate how to group plants beautifully and practically. The recommended plants are suitable for gardens in USDA Zones 4 to 6, with additional suggestions for both gentler and colder climates.

'Blue Parrot', an exotic parrot tulip, looks sensational in the spring.

Though the chapters are arranged by month, they must be interpreted with some flexibility. Whether you live in Kodiak, Alaska, or New Orleans, Louisiana, the basics of gardening (chores, design elements, cultural requirements, and so on) are much the same. However, the precise timing of jobs like mulching garden beds or preparing them for winter will naturally vary from the times I suggest. The truth is, no matter where you live, annual and longer term changes in weather patterns make it impossible to state with authority that any given chore should be done at the exact same time each year. Through observation and simple record keeping (the notes in your garden journal), each of us learns how to decide for ourselves when things need to be done. By watching the weather and assessing the progress of spring, you can figure out when the soil has dried out enough to be worked or when it warms up enough to plant. Learning to trust your own informed judgment is an important part of growth as a gardener. Eventually, your own garden journals become the most valuable and accurate source of advice you can find anywhere, because they contain the fruit of your own direct experience. In the meantime, however, it's helpful to have some guidelines, especially when it comes to garden design. For many of us, this is the most intimidating part of garden making. Rather than turning the design process over to someone else, why not experiment with giving shape to your own taste? If this seems risky, it's only a small risk, for gardens are flexible and plants are forgiving. If something fails to please you, most changes are easily made. Remember too that a professional design can also fail to please you and costs a good deal more. Happily, the design process breaks down readily into a number of related topics, any of which can be mastered by an interested amateur. Explore them at leisure, then implement them as time and weather allow. Take pleasure in the process and you will find even more pleasure in the result. We have more connection to gardens we make ourselves, for they reflect our personal taste, needs, and values.

Creating pleasing color combinations and artful arrangements of compatible plants is a similarly personal process. Again, however, some solid guidelines can help you paint satisfying garden pictures with your favorite plants. Since your basic skills are firmly in place, secondary skills such as unobtrusive staking, grooming, and pruning will lend polish and depth to your plantings. Cultural pointers help you place plants appropriately and encourage healthy plant communities, thus reducing the gardener's workload.

Whether you are creating your first real garden or renovating a neglected older one, you can have terrific fun doing it. After all, the garden exists to please and nourish you, the gardener. If we become slaves to the garden (or to ideals of garden perfectionism, gardening starts to feel like work. It is work, of course, but at its best, gardening is peaceful, healthful, and therapeutic work. Because garden making is a lively art, it is sometimes messy, as any creative process must be. Relax. Enjoy the process as much as the product. If you haven't already, you will soon discover that there will never really be a final product. Fortunately, the more of a gardener you become, the gladder you will be that there is only and always a garden in progress. For lifelong, bone-deep gardeners, nothing could be more satisfying—or more fun.

The glorious blossoms of the classic shrub rose 'Graham Thomas' perfume the garden with an irresistible fragrance.

JANUARY

Before the Beginning

Assessing a Garden Site, Old or New

The hardest part of garden making is the very beginning. You know you want to make a garden, but you aren't quite sure how to get started. Perhaps your lot is barren, stripped of everything but grass and beautybark. Maybe the yard was once a lovely garden but is now an overgrown mess. Most likely it presents the common combination of rough grass, elderly foundation plantings, and frumpy shrubs. In each case, the trick is to find the garden in the setting, just as sculptors find the statue in the stone. Before you buy a plant or set shovel to the ground, take the time to observe and to record, to dream and to analyze. Thoughtfully done, these four preparatory activities will help you discover what you want from your garden, as well as what you can actually have.

Begin by carefully observing your setting. The more you know about the piece of land you will be working on, the better informed your choices. To begin, make a simple map. (It may be rough, but should be accurate in proportion.) Draw in the house, patio, driveway, and garage, as well as major features like entry path, steps, walls, and fences, and large trees and shrubs.

Winter doesn't seem so bleak when the garden holds plenty of plants with interesting shapes, textures, and colors. Whitewashed bramble, *Rubus cockburnianus*, ruddy dogwood, *Cornus alba* 'Sibirica', and tussocks of *Carex morrowii* 'Variegata' combine attractively at the Washington Park Arboretum in Seattle.

This small urban garden feels nestled amidst trees and shrubs which are actually on neighboring lots or across the street. This is what is called a "borrowed view." (Garden of Doug Bayley, Seattle.)

Indicate orientation to the sun, and show any sloping ground or changes of level. Leave a little space outside the property line and mark any great views or problem areas. Once you have a fairly accurate rendering, make several working copies and store your master somewhere safe (you really don't want to do this twice).

Use the map like a journal to record pertinent observations: Where does the wind come from in each season? Where does the winter sun fall? Where is there summer shade? Is there a quiet corner? Are there areas that never get wet, or places where water pools after a rain? Is the soil heavy clay or light sand, or a combination of types? Are there views or noises you want to screen out? Is there a tiny glimpse of distant mountains or a twinkling cityscape that might be effective if carefully framed? Evaluate neighboring properties as well, for nearby trees or hedges can become backdrop or focal points for your own vignettes. While

compiling physical characteristics, keep track of how each area is being used. Record the paths of the garbage man and the meter reader as well as your own trips with groceries. Where do you tend to sit outside? Where do the kids play? Where does the dog sleep? All these observations will influence planting as well as architectural plans.

Look at everything. Look out of each important house window to identify areas that will be constantly in view, and mark these as places to group evergreens for strong winter interest. Look very closely at any mature shrubs before removing them, for potential beauty is often concealed by neglect and bad pruning. Tatty foundation plantings may be transformed into terrific perimeter hedge plants, instantly providing a sense of enclosure and maturity. Give any standing trees the benefit of the doubt, for some things only time can buy; once gone, they can't be replaced in a day or even a decade. If they are mangled by poor pruning, there may seem nothing left to save, yet many trees can be restored to beauty by sensitive reshaping, and the judicious removal of hacked or crowded lower limbs often reveals a graceful canopy. The uncertain gardener can consult with a designer who specializes in restoration and renewal of older gardens. Ask for recommendations at your favorite specialty nursery, or call plant societies in your area for advice on finding knowledgeable, responsible tree trimmers and shrub pruners.

On wet days when it's too miserable to wander outside, sit down with whomever else may be intimately involved with this future garden and do some dream work. Exercise your imagination, creating visions of your inner garden. What do you see? Are you enclosed in greenery or encircled with flowers, basking in sun or sheltered by trees? Do you smell roses and jasmine, soothing herbs, hot pine sap and lemon blossom? Do you hear bee buzz or bird song, water music or a gentle wind susurating through tall grasses? Does it feel country simple or romantically opulent? Is it welcoming or stimulating in ambiance, casual or formal in design? Your garden can evoke any of these impressions easily once that becomes your conscious goal. Ignore for the moment the limitations of your yard and list all the features your dream garden offers: bower and barbecue, hammock and hot tub, fountain and Frisbee lawn, fragrant vines and vegetables. As your dream garden comes into focus, write down each detail. Having dreamed your dreams and assembled your facts, return to your map and analyze. Now you must figure out how to combine the actual with the possible, the reality with the dream. Eyes refreshed by fantasy may find new possibilities in that dreary passageway between the garage and the kitchen door: What if it were trellised, hung with ivy and baskets of shade flowers, a cobbled path of smooth stones running between

mosses and ferns, the quiet broken by the trickle of a wall-hung recirculating fountain? That boring back gate might become an arbor hung with sweet peas, grapes, and evergreen clematis. Evict the garbage can from that dusty, sun-baked corner and turn it into a rose-draped bower where you can sunbathe in privacy. The sunny but sterile front lawn could be a green haven, with eye-level hedges blocking out street noise while allowing in plenty of light for an herbal tea garden, a pocket of salad vegetables, and a little cutting garden full of long-lasting flowers. The wasted few feet behind the garage can hold the compost bins, a tiny tool shed, or a folding potting table, while the wheelbarrow and garden chairs can be hung on pegs to stay dry beneath wide eaves. Every tiny space and odd angle has its potential purpose; think about the way ingenious boat owners coax a multitude of uses from a very limited space.

Put all this together, and your garden plan will practically make itself. Vegetables and roses, garden bench and compost bin will all find their allotted space, directed by your solid understanding of your site. Those who know their requirements as well as their territory can save themselves a good deal of heartache by choosing the right plants for each position. Even novices will be able to outline specific needs to a knowledgeable nursery person; when you can say, "Sell me a narrow evergreen that likes dry shade and won't exceed ten feet at maturity," you will be steered toward appropriate selections. While some dreams may prove too grandiose for one small yard, scale back a bit and you will find that satisfying compromises work themselves out. Where a pond won't fit, a reflecting pool will similarly wed the garden to the sky. Perhaps your borders won't stretch to the vanishing point, but if well planned, a single mixed border strip can still provide you with color and scent throughout the year.

The best way to achieve the garden of your dreams is slowly, for time is the gardener's best friend. If you simply must have some flowers right away, choose a manageable space and pack it full of fast producers. Take as much pleasure as you can wring from this little patch of bloom, but give the searching process at least equal time. Recognizing both your own expectations and your property's limitations are the keys to making a living garden that succeeds on your terms. Don't grudge the time it takes, for this initial investment pays handsome dividends, beginning with clear guidance in garden planning and continuing with multiple garden pleasures (and the absence of common problems) for years to come.

Even tiny gardens can afford room for a miniature reflecting pool. Check marine supply houses for long-lasting, sturdy plugs to permanently seal drainage holes in pots or containers. (Little and Lewis Water Gardens, Bainbridge Island, Washington.)

Winter Sweets

Early Bloomers for Year-Round Gardens

When deceptive January thaws convince us that spring is already here, the return of its sudden frosts or sullen rains can make each week feel two months long. At this time of year, we gardeners need tangible tokens that renewal is indeed at hand to fend off our gloom. Fortunately, it doesn't take much to convince us that all will soon be well: a spray of fragrant flowers, some fuzzy catkins, or a few green leaves are enough to balance out the gray doldrums of winter. Every garden, however new or small, needs an off-season performer or two to provide just such a midwinter boost. Happily, wistful gardeners can draw upon a surprising number of winter delights to ease the wait for spring to be reborn.

Where snow remains deep through the tail end of winter, woody plants will prove to be the most practical. Since most gardens have room for just one or two larger plants, it's important to choose trees and shrubs that are attractive all year round. All candidates should have a pleasing natural shape that needs little pruning. The best will remain compact in maturity, enjoying good health under average conditions. Once chosen, large-scale plants must be placed with an eye to the future so they don't obscure wanted views, run into power lines, infiltrate sewer lines, or shade the vegetable garden as they grow. All these things considered, any of the following will provide their winter sweets for many years in exchange for minimal care. Indeed, most prefer benign neglect, wanting only an annual feeding mulch to keep them fit and productive. Naturally, the year they are planted, all will need the same tender care any young plant should receive; plenty of water during a hot summer, their ground space kept free of competing weeds and grasses, and a thick mulch to keep the roots cool and moist. Once established, though, most are as carefree as any living thing can be.

In our front yard, a western willow, *Salix scoulerana* (Zone 7, to 30 feet) always produces its gigantic, silken catkins in time for our youngest son's birthday in mid-January. The umbrella-shaped tree is decked in summer with tapered oval leaves, leathery dark green on top and furred with gray beneath. Though this species is not especially hardy, our native pussy willow, *S. discolor* (Zone 2, to 20 feet), can grow almost anywhere, opening its silvery pussies in late winter. Upright and narrow in the best forms, it can also be rangy and overly casual in habit. Since cuttings of this or almost any willow root at light speed in a glass of water on the kitchen windowsill, when you see an especially good-looking pussy willow, beg a few stems and make your own plants. Young, flexible shoots at least the thickness of a pencil can be rooted indoors in winter, or in spring they can be stuck straight into the ground to root and grow. Indeed, after a bad windstorm, we gathered up broken branches that were as big around as a man's arm and a good ten feet tall from our pussy willow and shoved them into the sodden ground all over the property. Every one of the pieces took root and is now a thriving tree.

These are both plants for big places, but an elegant Japanese shrub, the rose-gold pussy willow, fits more easily into the average garden. *Salix gracilistyla* (Zone 5, 6 to 12 feet) has finely textured, pewtery foliage and a graceful, upright habit, mak-ing this a good mingler in beds and borders. The striking catkins appear in late winter, emerging like wet kittens from tight blackish sheaths. They soon fluff out, their long gray fur starred with gilded and rosy anthers. Its cousin, *S. g. melanostachys* (Zone 5, 6 to 12 feet), boasts dusky, charcoal-colored catkins spangled with ember red anthers. Too dark to have much garden effect, these stunning black pussies are best admired indoors in table arrangements. Left unpruned, either form of *S. gracilistyla* makes a large, arching mound, but since this willow takes kindly to pruning, you can gather all the branches you like for decorative purposes without harm. Indeed, the plant will remain more compact and cleaner in its lines if cut back to stubble every few years, and the pussies will be larger than ever the following few years (do this hard pruning in late winter). Very easy to please, rose-gold pussy willow tolerates practically anything but utter drought and deep shade, but it grows best in sun and needs no extra fertilizer if given ordinary garden soil with good drainage. Virtually all nursery stock is from male, catkin-bearing plants, but occasionally very cheap "bargain" plants turn out to be female. Again, if you see a good, productive plant, beg a few bits to take home and you can root your own quite quickly.

Where space permits, the autumn Higan cherry, *Prunus subhirtella* 'Autumnalis' (Zone 5, 15 to 30 feet), makes a wonderful addition to a garden. Unpruned trees have a graceful, open canopy, twisting branches, and pale, reddish gray bark with a satin-matte finish that glows quietly against the snow. In winter, their handsome silhouette is a strong asset, even at an early age, for these trees (and most of their *P. subhirtella* cousins) are quick to develop the individuality and character of maturity. 'Autumnalis' begins to open its semi-double, soft pink flowers in fall, as the name suggests, usually after its tapered green leaves (now turned soft

Rose-gold pussy willow, *Salix gracilistyla,* is a practical choice for small gardens. Pair it with evergreen grasses like *Carex morrowii* 'Variegata' to make a memorable winter vignette. (Washington Park Arboretum, Seattle.)

cherry that is pruned hard (or brutally hacked at, as is regrettably common practice) has multiple wounds which are gateways for infection. Indeed, cherries are not good choices for compulsive pruners, but are perfect for those who practice benign neglect.

Their light canopy allows the gardener to underplant Higan cherries with small shrubs, bulbs, and perennials. It is important, however, to choose companion plants from amongst the many sturdy, self-reliant woodlanders that do not want supplemental summer water or rich soils, since either may set up problems for the cherry. The glossy, holly-leaved Oregon grape, *Mahonia aquifolium* (Zone 4 with protection, 3 to 6 feet), evergreen privet honeysuckle, *Lonicera pileata* (Zone 6, to 3 feet), and winter daphne, *Daphne odora* (Zone 7, to 4 feet), are all good Higan cherry partners, as are tall sword ferns, *Polystichum munitum* (Zone 5, to 3 feet) and green hellebores, *Helleborus foetidus* (Zone 4, to 2 feet). Even without company, the sight of a well-grown Higan cherry, its gray limbs misted with delicate pink blossoms, during a soft snowfall in November or March is unforgettable.

Established gardens may not have room for any more trees, but even smaller gardens will have space for one or two of the shrubby off-season performers, all of which are steady contributors during the warmer months as well. Among the very best is Chinese witch hazel, *Hamamelis mollis* 'Pallida' (Zone 5, 15 to 30 feet), a slow-growing shrub that can become very large over time. In summer, witch hazel has big, shield-shaped leaves that take on sizzling sunset colors in autumn. In winter, its furry twigs are trimmed with thready little scraps of flowers in yellow and amber, not showy but powerfully fragrant. In mild years, it may bloom from December until March, and even in cold years it can generally be counted on

gold) have fallen. They will continue to open in flushes straight through a mild winter, finishing off with a flourish in early spring, still well in advance of the foliage. The flowers are followed in summer by a scattering of small, black fruits, better enjoyed by birds than by humans.

Though cherries in general are short lived and prone to myriad diseases, the Higan cherries are long lived and healthy. This is especially true of unpruned (or very lightly pruned) trees, for any

to open a few flowers during any warm spells, beginning to bloom in earnest by late winter. Though there are more colorful forms, such as the hot red 'Diane' and the coppery orange 'Jelena', none are more fragrant than this Chinese species. In the coldest parts of Zone 5 (and into Zone 4, with protection from wind), an American hybrid, 'Arnold Promise' toughs out prolonged, hard frosts better than the others do, losing fewer of its large, deep yellow flowers to sudden cold snaps. Any of the witch hazels will grow happily in full sun, where their splendid autumn color is most prolonged, but they also grow well in partial or filtered shade, coloring attractively and blooming just as abundantly as in sun.

In the smallest gardens, a witch hazel relative, *Fothergilla gardenii* (Zone 5, to 4 feet), might replace its outsized cousin. Compact and shapely, this remarkable little native shrub has long been appreciated in England, but is less planted in its own backyard. Though not so early a bloomer as witch hazel, its ivory, bottle-brush flower spikes appear well before its bold, rounded foliage. In the form, 'Blue Mist' (Zone 5, to 3 feet), the big leaves are glazed with a shimmer of blue-gray that makes it an excellent mixer amongst perennials, which show up delightfully against their glimmering backdrop. The curious, bristly flowers are poignantly sweet smelling, and the plants' autumn color is often spectacular. This is even more true of a bigger species, *F. major* (Zone 5, 6 to 9 feet), which has similar flowers and foliage.

Wintersweet, *Chimonanthus praecox* (Zone 7, 6 with protection, slowly 12 to 15 feet), is a tall, fountain-shaped shrub that fills the garden with its potent scent of spiced honey. The translucent, twisting little flowers are pale yellow touched with maroon, popping open singly or in small clusters at each leaf node on the slim, naked stems. In summer, its gleaming, dark green leaves make a

pleasant backdrop for perennials, and later on, its modest autumnal display, green and gold mingling in quiet confetti, gently enlivens its corner of the yard. Clearly, this modest creature isn't the first shrub one would choose to plant, particularly

Chinese witch hazel, *Hamamelis mollis*, brightens late winter with its thready yellow flowers. Their intense fragrance fills the garden on warm, still winter days. (Washington Park Arboretum, Seattle.)

knowing that it may take six or seven years for a young plant to begin to bloom. However, where there is room enough and patience, it is a treasure that can transform a dreary, gray day into a taste of spring.

Winter jasmine, *Jasminum nudiflorum* (Zone 5, 2 to 15 feet), is a sunny, happy sprawler which can tumble over a high wall or bank or be tied upright to cover trellis, fence, or house wall. At the far range of its hardiness, it needs a protected nook, away from biting winds and sheltered by early morning sun (which can blast frozen buds) to do its best. Anywhere it grows, its fresh, Irish green stems look glossy and healthy even in the depths of winter, despite their lack of leaves. These are narrow and very dark green, divided in lacy threes to make a filigree of foliage in summer. The slim golden trumpet flowers begin to open as early as November where winters are gentle, continuing in fits and starts clear through till spring. Elsewhere, a few buds will swell and burst into bloom during each thaw, but the full flush of bloom will be delayed until late winter. On still, sunny days, a faint trace of the wild familial perfume can be detected at close range, but though winter jasmine can't offer us the heady, exotic scent of its summery cousins, its glowing good looks are reward enough in these bleaker months. If late frosts threaten to blast opening buds, a light cloth (an old sheet or shower curtain) can protect them even from sudden arctic blasts. The cloth can be left in place for weeks without harm, to be removed when the weather improves. Since winter jasmines take up so little ground space and remain attractive through the summer, they can be planted liberally throughout the garden, decorating doorways, encircling windows, festooning garage and back fence alike. This way, their thick golden columns and trellised fans add a good deal of winter cheer to the quiet seasons, and if the flowers are frozen on some plants, others may remain unscathed.

First Flowers
Snowdrops and Snow Crocus

For many an ardent gardener, it becomes a minor point of pride to have something in bloom or berry on any day of the year. This is hardly a challenge from April through October, but when winter slows the sleepy garden to a standstill, the choices narrow a good deal. However, a hardy handful of early bloomers will brighten the late winter garden, undaunted by frost. Even an inch or two of snow can't dampen their exuberance, and heavier falls will only set back their emergence a bit. While winter-blooming representatives can be found in nearly every category of plant, from trees to ground covers, among the earliest and most willing performers of all are the snowdrops and snow crocus. Though they are classified among the minor bulbs, this rating refers strictly to stature, not worth. Small they may be, yet frigid temperatures can only delay, never defeat, these sturdy troopers.

If your garden is only just beginning to show signs of life, make note now of bare spots that could be brightened by a sunny splash of crocus or a handful of silvery snowdrops. Skip ahead in your garden journal and leave yourself a reminder to add some of these dependable die-hards to your autumn bulb order. (Add a little sketch to indicate where to plant them; gaps that seem obvious now may well be invisible then.) Minor bulbs are most effective when planted with a lavish hand, so think in terms of dozens or hundreds rather than fives and tens. Happily, such extravagance comes relatively cheap; a hundred snow crocus cost ten or twenty dollars, depending on kind, while common snowdrops are only a bit higher.

Unlike big border tulips, minor bulbs are sound perennials that will reappear each spring indefinitely. Indeed, many are quick multipliers when their modest needs are met. Happily, this is seldom difficult, for most want only plenty of light and water from winter into mid-spring. The trickiest part of their care comes after they have faded from view, for once dormant, these little bulbs must rest dry and undisturbed. Blended into ordinary garden beds, they are apt to rot from excess water, or get spaded up during autumnal transplanting operations. Too diminutive to make much of a show on their own, they gain impact from proper placement with appropriate companions. Both crocus and snowdrops can be added lavishly to shrub beds, which are seldom disturbed, and they will gleam out all the brighter if surrounded by evergreen ground covers such as *Vinca minor* (Zone 5, 2 to 4 inches). Bouquets of the robust hybrid snowdrop, *Galanthus plicatus* x *nivalis* (Zone 3, to 6 inches), will burst like tiny fountains through loops of *Vinca minor* 'Burgundy', with its wine-red flowers, while lavender *Crocus sieberi* (Zone 3, to 5 inches) sparkle between strands of *Vinca minor* 'Flore-Pleno', its doubled, rather purple-blue flowers winking up at the winter sky. Mosses, sandworts (*Arenaria* species), and low-growing perennial ground covers such as creeping thymes, prostrate veronicas, and baby's-tears (*Helxine* species) are also suitable companions for the diminutive bulbs of winter, keeping them free of mud yet never stealing center stage. The little bulbs may also be judiciously mixed into beds of drought-tolerant perennials that receive little summer water. One can also strew them thickly beneath hedges and along paths, thread them in wide ribbons beneath deciduous trees, and lace them around border backbone shrubs, where they make pretty pools of color in the duller months.

Both snowdrops and crocus look lovely spangling the lawn or meadow, but if they are to naturalize, their turf can't be mown until their foliage withers and seed ripens. Since this occurs some-

Snowdrops are most effective when planted in generous groups. These are intermingled with early-flowering snow crocus against a backdrop of evergreen *Carex comans* 'Bronze Form'. (Garden of Daphne Stewart, Bainbridge Island, Washington.)

Scores of delightful early-flowering crocus are sold as snow crocus. Among them are many fine forms of *Crocus chrysanthus* like white 'Snow Bunting' and yolk-yellow 'E. A. Bowles'.

can manage it. (A dry afternoon in November or December is ideal.) This leaves the turf tight and trim right through the winter, so the flowers show up nicely, rather than straggling up between long tangles of grass.

In mild winters, snowdrops often appear hard on the heels of the New Year, their tightly sheathed buds poking through frosty ground, curving on slim necks before opening their white wings at the first hint of thaw. The common snowdrop, *Galanthus nivalis* (Zone 3, 4 to 6 inches), is charming in its simplicity, with a grace and clarity of form that is masked by the heavy, ruffled skirts of its double form, 'Flore Pleno'. If you look closely at a snowdrop, you will discover that the three outer petals have the substance and texture of slubbed silk, while the finer-textured inner petals are marked on their fronts with green fish or hearts and neatly penciled with green inside. To emphasize their understated charms, set clumps of snowdrops between evergreen ferns, tuck them into trails of silver-flecked ivies, or cluster them beneath winter-blooming witch hazels (*Hamamelis* species). For all their delicacy of modeling, snowdrops are impressively tough. On a cold morning after a hard frost, the clumps seem melted to mush, yet a few hours later, the warming sun revives them and they rise again, crisp and fragrant.

Snowdrops are easy to please in garden settings, where they need no special care other than protection from errant shovels. They seem equally happy in sun or shade, and though they emerge earlier in light, sandy soils, they also thrive in heavy ones. In England, one can find many named snowdrops, selections and hybrids chosen for variations of form, color, or bloom time, and at least a dozen species. Though few of them are available here, it is always worth checking bulb catalogs for varieties like 'Mighty Atom' (Zone 4, to 6 inches), a robust, big-winged beauty, or the extra-early species,

time between the end of April and Mother's Day, ardent lawn mowers must exercise patience. Go ahead and trim up the lawn as early as you like; just leave the grass around the bulbs alone for that extra week or two. Unless they are left alone to ripen off in peace, they can't store up the energy they need to make next year's flowers and foliage, and will soon dwindle away altogether. It helps to give the lawn a last, rather short haircut as late in autumn as you

Galanthus elwesii (Zone 4, to 6 inches), with its dark green markings. If you can't find what you want, ask for it at local nurseries and garden centers—in writing, if necessary—for we gardeners represent a lucrative market, and once our wants are recognized, they are usually met.

Snow crocus are a group of small but early-blooming species that often beat their big Dutch hybrid cousins into flower by as much as six or eight weeks. Most are multi-flowering as well, boasting six or eight blossoms from each bulb. All of the following are hardy to Zone 4 unless otherwise noted. They are tough little things, and most of them are worth trying even in colder areas, choosing sheltered, sunny spots in which to trial various species. Well-drained soil and the reflected heat from house walls or rocks can also boost their hardiness quite a bit. Often, crocus losses are due to sodden summer soil rather than winter frost, and surprising improvements in longevity can be achieved by giving them enriched but fast-draining soils. If you garden on clay, try improving a suitable area by digging in lots of coarse sand or fine grit as well as compost. Place the bulbs on a pad of grit a few inches deep, and cover their necks with coarser grit to encourage prompt rain run-off. (Bulbs with wet necks may suffer collar rots which eventually destroy the entire bulb.)

Squirrels are also common culprits where crocus vanish rather than multiply. To discourage these merry pranksters, scatter a thin layer of smelly naphtha-based moth flakes over the bulbs as you plant them, renewing them once or twice if the autumn is very rainy. Usually squirrels confine their attentions to newer plantings, leaving established beds relatively unscathed. If you can keep the varmints at bay for a few seasons, your crocus plantings may increase enough that the loss of a few bulbs won't be noticeable.

In my garden, golden *Crocus chrysanthus* (4 to 6 inches) blooms during every thaw from late January into March. Tucked between the paving stones of the terrace, the tiny bulbs produce increasingly fat clusters of bloom. It is amazing how quickly these early flowers, nestled amongst bumps of moss and running thymes, attract the first bees, sleepy bumbles who drone quietly from cup to cup, butting their square heads deep into each flower. *Crocus chrysanthus* is a variable species with many colorful forms in shades of yellow, orange, and cream as well as blues, lavenders, and purples. Sweet-scented 'Blue Bird' is the tender blue of a rain-washed sky, while 'Violet Queen' is Easter-egg purple with a slate eye and red-gold stamens. Boldly striped 'Advance' displays a lively combination of bronze and thundercloud purples when closed on gray days, but when the thin winter sun coaxes it open, pure sun yellow spills from its deep cups. The fragrant, buttery petals of 'Cream Beauty' are faintly feathered with bronze on their backs, while sun-yellow 'Gypsy Girl' has bright, brassy stripes that call out the copper in partnering, grassy clumps of evergreen *Carex comans* (Zone 6, to 18 inches) Dapper little 'Lady Killer', clean white, heavily barred, and brushed with midnight purple, combines strikingly with black lab violets (*Viola labradorica* 'Purpurea', Zone 3, to 2 inches) and tufts of black mondo grass (*Ophiopogon planiscapus* 'Nigricans', Zone 6, to 6 inches) or white winter heather (*Erica carnea* 'Springwood', Zone 5, to 1 foot).

Crocus sieberi (Zone 3, to 3 inches) is the hardiest of the group, its gold stars gleaming up through the coarse corn snow of late winter like lost pennies. It has blue-and-lavender or mauve forms as well which run like bright embroidery through mats of creeping thyme or sedums at the border's edge. Of these, 'Tricolor' is outstanding,

its lavender-blue flowers lightened with cloudy white at the throat and glowing with fluffy gold stamens at the heart. *Crocus ancyrensis* (to 3 inches), the golden bunch, is a snappy, tangerine-colored species that emerges in bright bunches like tiny bouquets between the flagstones of path and terrace.

Perhaps the most prolific multiplier is *Crocus tomasinianus* (4 to 6 inches), which will quickly colonize border or lawn if allowed to ripen seed as well as foliage. Tommies, as they are affectionately known, run from lavenders to purple-blues in nature, making them good company for blue- and purple-flowered lungworts (*Pulmonaria* species) and the mauve and misty purple Lenten roses (*Helleborus orientalis*, Zone 5, to 18 inches). Tommies also come in named varieties, among them the grape jelly–colored 'Whitewell Purple' and 'Ruby Giant', a vinaceous red. Tucked between pink primroses and rosy hardy cyclamen, any or all of these will give your garden a lovely late winter lift.

Harnessing the Force of Nature

Coaxing Early Bloom from Spring Shrubs

When the sleeping garden lies blanketed with snow, a jar full of sun-yellow forsythia offers a mute but joyful promise of approaching change. Vases of purple, pleated hazel leaves or tender green willow wands are living balm to spirits battered by sleet and gray skies. Fortunately, such balm is easily come by, for many early-blooming woody plants will put on a command performance, indoors and (more or less) on your schedule. Which plants will cooperate and when the gardener should begin the persuasive process depends on a given garden's microclimates as well as its climate zone, but there are a few faithful performers that can be coaxed into winter bloom almost anywhere. With practice and experience, you can develop a long list of persuadable plants that will keep a steady succession of flowers and foliage on your table from January until spring awakens the garden once again.

The winter solstice marks the changing solar tide of the year, and as the days lengthen almost imperceptibly, buds swell along with them. My children and I pick bare brown forsythia stems each Christmas day as part of our midwinter ritual. Forsythia's willingness to bloom prematurely makes it an ideal plant with which to discover the delights of what is usually called forcing, the process of inducing indoor, preseasonal blossom from spring- or winter-flowering shrubs. Placed in a sunny kitchen windowsill, the forsythia stems will begin to bloom within ten days to two weeks, depending on the severity of the current winter. As soon as those first twigs come into flower, we pick another bunch of stems which blossom a day or two quicker than the first. We repeat this cycle until the buds on our shrub are showing color, almost ready to bloom naturally, and our last batch of indoor forsythia coincides with the shrub's full flowering.

Here in the Pacific Northwest, our Zone 8 winters are often mild, but the time required to force forsythia varies remarkably little whether temperatures plummet or not. In colder regions, the forcing schedule for this and other plants will differ from mine by days or weeks. To develop your own schedule, cut a few forsythia stems for

Small but determined, *Crocus tomasinianus* spreads into impressive colonies over time. This area of lawn must be left unmown until the foliage and seeds are ripe, usually in late May. (Garden of Daphne Stewart, Bainbridge Island, Washington.)

the house each week in January and watch what happens. Yearling growth produces only leaves, so look for older stems that carry both rounded leaf buds and narrower flower buds. As spring approaches, these last reveal themselves clearly, elongating and standing out from the stem at a slight angle before assuming their ready-to-open droop. Each time you cut fresh twigs, look for changes in bud size and shape as well as bark color. By the time the sap rises and the slumbering shrub awakens, your eye will be trained to notice the many small indications of spring's arrival and you will be able to select blossom-loaded stems infallibly. As the forced flowers open and fade, record the results of each batch in your garden journal. Do this for every kind of plant you experiment with, and over the years you will amass a body of specific information that will prove both fascinating and enormously helpful should you ever want to force flowers for a special occasion.

Though any forsythia can be forced, my favorite is a Chinese species (the first to be grown in America), *Forsythia suspensa* 'Sieboldii' (Zone 5, to 10 feet), with pastel rather than brassy flowers. Its trailing stems make it an excellent choice for the top of a bank or wall, where its sheets of bloom and glorious red-gold fall foliage are well displayed. The *F.* x *intermedia* hybrids (Zone 4, 8 to 10 feet), more upright and less leggy, are better choices for small gardens. Where space permits, it is pleasant to grow several contrasting forms, perhaps the chalky yellow 'Primulina' and the splashy golden 'Spectabilis' with its large and eye-catching flowers.

So-called white forsythia, *Abeliophyllum distichum* (Zone 5, to 6 feet) does resemble its popular cousin (both belong to the *Oleaceae*, the olive family). Its shell-pink buds and ivory bells are small but profuse, opening in advance of the oval, tapering leaves. Though root hardy, it does not always flower well in colder areas because the

flower buds are formed in autumn and may be damaged by hard spring frosts. If you have waited in vain for this shrub to bloom, try harvesting an armload of branches in midwinter. They may take a month or more to flower, but flower they will.

Japonica or quince has suffered many name changes and the sturdy, large-flowered shrub our grandmothers grew as *Cydonia japonica* is now *Chaenomeles speciosa* (Zone 4, 6 to 15 feet). Though most hybrid forms remain compact, the species becomes very large in time, its thousands of cupped, coral-red blossoms attracting squadrons of hummingbirds over its prolonged flowering period. The huge old shrub in my garden blooms with the early single tulips, but cut stems can be convinced to do so far earlier. We begin gathering stems soon after New Year's, and within three weeks, the first marblelike buds pop open. Quince flowers on old wood, which may be thick and woody and not inclined to take up water well. If the outer bark is peeled off the last few inches of stem and the leaves are removed as they open, most stems will remain in flower for close to a month. Forced quince blossoms are often lighter in color than their outdoor counterparts. Forced on a sunny windowsill, coral flowers become pastel salmon. If forced in our dimly lit cellar, the same flowers will be near white. Dwarf border quinces bloom a bit later outside and take correspondingly longer to come into flower as cut stems. The sprawling, almost prostrate *C. s.* 'Jet Trail' grows vigorously even in dry shade and proves an abundant bloomer indoors or in the garden. *Chaenomeles* x *superba* 'Cameo' (Zone 5, to 3 feet) is similarly diminutive but upright in form, and its pinkish, terra-cotta–colored flowers become a cloudy, porcelain peach when forced.

Not all early bloomers are so quickly forced: Flowering currant (*Ribes sanguineum*, Zone 6, 8 to 12 feet) picked on New Year's Day won't bloom until late February (though stems picked a month later will bloom only a few days after that first bunch has opened). Woody stems of camellia, rhododendron, or magnolia can be forced as well; though the glossy new foliage will open promptly enough, tight flower buds may wither or rot without opening. To be safe, wait until the buds show color, for they then will open reliably (if only a few days earlier than the mother plant). Many fruit trees can be forced from tight bud, though they will take their time about opening. For an early March wedding one year we forced masses of gnarled old apple and pear twigs to fill the house with their fragrant foam. A sudden string of unseasonably hot days rushed them toward bloom, so they were banished to a dark, cool shed to retard their progress. Just before the wedding, snow and hard frosts hit the area and the buckets of bloom spent several days around the wood stove catching up again. The struggle ended in triumph, but it was not an experience I care to repeat. These days, I content myself with gleaning budded up twigs from limbs blown off our ancient trees during winter storms or tossed aside when we prune in February, letting them open at their own pace.

True winter bloomers may seem illogical forcing candidates but when brutal weather postpones or threatens their blossom, it is well worth bringing in branches or twigs to enjoy indoors. Wintersweet, *Chimonanthus praecox* (Zone 7, 8 to 12 feet), may take up to seven years to produce its twisted, translucent little flowers, but their romantic, evocative perfume makes the wait worth while. Witch hazels, especially the showy Chinese species, *Hamamelis mollis* (Zone 5, 8 to 12 feet, or very slowly to 30 feet), open scented, skinny ribbon flowers of yellow, tawny orange, or cinnamon red from late February into April, but picked stems will bloom as early as January. Sweet

box, *Sarcococca hookerana* var. *humilis* (Zone 5, 1 to 3 feet), is a glossy little evergreen with insignificant, greenish white flowers that fill the cold winter air with the mingled smells of honey and vanilla. Winter honeysuckle, *Lonicera fragrantissima* (Zone 5, 6 to 8 feet), offers similarly unimpressive flowers, creamy green and small, which are as delicious to the nose as the name suggests. Each of

Forced forsythias can decorate the house anytime around the winter solstice. Here, branches picked on December 12 are in full bloom for the winter holidays.

The pleated purple fans of a handsome hazel, *Corylus maxima* 'Purpurea', will open months ahead of schedule indoors. Twigs picked as soon as the buds begin to swell in January will be open within a few weeks.

hazel, *Corylus maxima* 'Purpurea' (Zone 5, 10 to 20 feet) and copper beech (*Fagus sylvatica* 'Atropunicea', Zone 4, slowly to 90 feet). Neither leaf is very long lasting in well-heated areas, but daily misting keeps them from drying out in warm houses, and both hold nicely in cooler rooms out of direct light. These big leaves are even more fun to observe than flowers, for they pop out enchantingly from their tight wrappers, expanding into graceful ovals, pleated and goffered. Textured like wild silk, their tiny hairs catch the light so they glimmer with a pewtery bloom. Golden streamers of weeping willow, *Salix babylonica* (Zone 6, 25 to 60 feet), can be gathered anytime after the New Year. They will open in a week to ten days, their tender green a lovely accent amongst flowers. Silky gray pussy willow catkins can also be coaxed open by those hungry for a taste of spring. Many other foliage shrubs are persuadable, such as golden ninebark (*Physocarpus opulifolius* 'Dart's Gold', Zone 3, 8 to 12 feet), cutleaf elder (*Sambucus canadensis* 'Acutiloba', Zone 4, 10 to 20 feet), and blue arctic willow (*Salix purpurea* 'Nana', Zone 4, 6 to 12 feet), so anything with a pretty leaf is worth trying.

Once you have selected and cut some likely stems, you can arrange them at once and watch their buds unfold or set them aside to develop, arranging them when they approach their peak. All will be improved in looks and longevity if the stems are conditioned first thing. Even stems which spend their first indoor weeks out of sight, either in the sun porch or shut away in a dim basement, will benefit from careful preparation before the forcing period begins. Really, this preparation begins with your secateurs or clippers, which should be kept very sharp so that the bark is not pulled and stems are cut clean, not crushed. Like cut flowers, cut stems can dry out quickly

these candidates for forcing boast surprisingly potent perfumes—one or two small twigs can scent a small house delightfully—and their cut stems can be persuaded to bloom in the dead of winter. Daphnes, viburnums, and sweet olive (*Osmanthus fragrans*) may similarly reward indoor trials.

Foliage can sometimes be forced as well as flowers. I have had good luck with both purple

even on a cool day, so carry a bucket of slightly warm water out to the garden and plunge stems immediately after cutting.

Next, take those bare brown stems and strip any buds that will be submerged in vase or container off the lower ends. Put the branches into a deep basin of warm water and recut their underwater ends a couple of inches higher up the stem. (Dry and oil your wet secateurs before putting them away to prevent rust spots.) Green, flexible stems can be cut at a sharp angle to assist water absorption but older wood requires sterner treatment if it is to enjoy a long indoor life. Before you recut woody stems, peel off a few inches of bark above the place where you are going to recut them. Next, the stem ends can be recut straight across, then split up the middle for about an inch with a sharp knife (a rose budding knife works nicely). According to various schools of thought, the woody stems of magnolias, camellias, and rhododendrons should then be dipped in boiling water for 10 to 20 seconds or smashed with a hammer to encourage them to take up more water. (I can't imagine either process being encouraging, but they are so universally advocated by flower arrangers that I pass them on for your consideration.)

If the weather has been unusually cold and the buds are not very far along, plunge flowering stems up to their necks in warm (never hot) water. Don't soak buds that are well swollen or show color, how-ever, for they may bloat and discolor or rot. If foliage plants such as hazel and beech are picked in deep winter and show very tight buds, they will rouse faster if entirely submerged and soaked for several hours (use the bathtub if you are working on a large scale). A warm bath will also persuade tightly budded forsythia and quince to open several days sooner than usual. Young, supple stems may take up quite a bit of water within an hour or so, but hard, woody ones with hard, closed buds can be left for half a day without becoming waterlogged.

If you are forcing plants before arranging them, check their water level every day, changing the water if it becomes murky. Most forced flowers bloom better and longer if their leaves are removed as they open to reduce the competition for water. Once arranged, continue to add fresh water daily as needed, but if the vases or containers are well cleaned after each use, changing the water daily is unnecessary and merely rumples the flowers. Some people add a teaspoon of glycerine to the water, especially in leaf arrangements, for it makes the leaves supple and can prolong their vase life.

This year, when the garden lies locked in winter's frigid embrace, your frost-rimmed windows can be decked with a spattering of pale blossoms smelling of spring. Keep on cutting; even if the stubborn snow piles up in grimy heaps that won't retreat, your personal spring can arrive on schedule.

FEBRUARY

Garden Rooms

Enclosure from Fence, Trellis, or Hedge

Gardens are as diverse as the people who make them, varying enormously in style, size, and atmosphere. Different as they are, the best gardens have in common a certain presence; each is a distinct place in its own right, not just an adjunct to a house. This quality comes mainly from what designers call enclosure. Gardens that are sheltered from the world, whether by walls, hedges, shrubberies, or fences, become places of retreat that offer people a closer connection with the natural world. Since the earliest historic times, enclosed gardens have been treasured as green havens of peace and serenity. Enclosure need not be a barricade, but is created by anything at all that divides us, even illusion, from the bustling streets. In English and European gardens, the barriers are apt to be picturesque old walls and ancient sheared hedges. On this side of the Atlantic, we tend to prefer picket fences and low hedges, neither of which is quite inclusive (or exclusive) enough to create the proper effect. Indeed, the English garden writer Penelope Hobhouse says frankly that enclosure is "the most important element in garden design," and one which North Americans are slow to adopt.

Crocus are the lions of winter, braving frost and bitter winds to bloom amid the tattered leavings of summer.
True harbingers of spring, their fragile-looking buds are undaunted by snow or hard-frozen ground.

Hand-crafted fences and gates like this one, built by Joey Shelton, not only enclose a garden, but may be considered as art in their own right. (Garden of Ashlee Owen, Seattle.)

sure starts to seem a bit more interesting. If you genuinely like the wide open look of American lawns, you can certainly continue to enjoy it, but a few modifications will give you more useful options as well. That seldom used front yard, now a monument to weed-'n'-feed, could become a low, rippling tapestry of dwarf evergreens, handsome all year round yet requiring little upkeep and no toxins at all. With that sop to convention, the backyard could be screened into two or three enclosed areas where you and your family can sunbathe and garden and enjoy an al fresco meal in peace and privacy.

If the backyard is very small, it makes sense to choose the slimmest possible privacy barriers and to preserve as much open space as you can. Even in tiny gardens, however, one or two separate places—perhaps the narrow side yard, or the patch behind the garage—can be split off to provide you with several garden rooms, each with its own particular purpose, ambiance, or style. The idea of garden rooms is not strictly literal, but a useful device, helping us understand how to divide up our lawn space into distinct areas that may serve different needs or simply have a particular feeling. Look around the yard with new eyes and try to imagine how various parts could become garden rooms. At this stage, they may well not be rooms with a view of anything in particular, but that is easily rectified. If that sunny, open area were screened off from neighbors and road with fencing, trellis work, or a slim hedge of columnar junipers, a small paved seating area might house a table and chairs, suddenly becoming a lovely place to enjoy a book or a cup of tea. Low, running hedges (or again, trellis panels or fences) can similarly screen off smaller rooms to hold the children's sandbox and play yard, the dog run, or the compost heap. You don't want to cut up all your space in a series of bitty little green boxes, but by group-

Americans favor open yards, perhaps divided from neighbors by a split-rail fence or a waist-high row of privet, but we prefer the school of landscaping that makes it clear we have nothing to hide. The flip side of this openness is that we enjoy very little privacy. When you tire of the neighbors knowing exactly what's sizzling on the backyard grill, how your tan is coming along, and that you spent Saturday in the hammock listening to baseball instead of mowing the grass, the idea of enclo-

ing the trash can holding area, the compost, and the tool shed together, you can confine the less scenic parts of the garden to one area, which is then shielded from view.

Even underused and neglected parts of the yard can take on new life if imaginatively treated. A skinny side yard might become a quiet green room just big enough to hold a bench. Walled with contained bamboo or clambering ivy, floored with polished beach stones, mosses, and ferns, street noises muffled by a wall-hung recirculating fountain, this neglected, useless space could be transformed into a meditative retreat. A sunny side strip screened with trellis panels can hold a sunbathing chaise longue, its walls draped with heat-loving jasmine and fragrant climbing roses. If all you have is a passageway, turn it into a covered walkway and store your tools and garden supplies under its sheltering roof.

Most of us have to stretch our imaginations a bit before we can envision enticingly enclosed garden spaces which are also practical and affordable. The English garden writers are always telling us firmly that we must build more garden walls. Here, however, walls are very expensive and not always things of beauty. The fortunate folk who garden where local rock is plentiful, lovely, and inexpensive can indulge themselves in granite walls, slate terraces, basalt steps, and all sorts of delights that the rest of us can only admire in books. However, it is worth remembering that even desperately ugly cinder block walls can be hidden beneath creepers and climbers or cascading evergreen shrubs. Harshly colored new brick can be painted with buttermilk to encourage moss and gentle the uncompromising color, which is compatible with absolutely nothing that grows. Brick or even concrete walls will also hold a lot of plants, especially if strong eye-bolts have been set into them at regular intervals. These can be threaded with heavy wire into a sturdy grid to support climbers and leafy creepers. Even humble homemade walls made of broken-up concrete sidewalks can be beautified by tucking lots of catmint, sweet alyssum, and valerian into their cracks. This is easiest to do when the walls are being made, but can happen long afterward, if a gardener is determined.

Hedges make lovely green walls that could enclose all or part of the garden, creating shelter and privacy in one swoop.

However, hedging has several significant drawbacks, beginning with time and expense. The dignified hedges we admire in English and European gardens are often centuries old. The large plants necessary to create instant enclosure are very expensive, and smaller ones will take five to seven years to reach adequate height to be useful. Most hedges require a good deal of ground space as well, particularly big thugs like laurel and copper beech. The faster-growing plants often recommended for hedging usually require clipping several times a year to look presentable, and many are short lived, passing quickly through triumphant maturity into decaying senescence.

Hedging is still a magnificent option where there is plenty of room, time, and money, and the lucky gardener who enjoys all these can choose amongst many delightful kinds of hedging. Informal hedges of bushy barberries or columnar evergreens such as arborvitae don't need regular pruning at all, and may be combined with fencing to offer immediate privacy. Naturally upright evergreens can be mingled with deciduous shrubs as well, adding spring bloom and fall color to winter interest and summer framework. Low, room-dividing hedges within the garden may be planted of evergreen boxwood (*Buxus microphylla*, Zone 5, to 3 feet) or dwarf conifers. Semi-evergreen privet honeysuckle (*Lonicera pileata*, Zone 6, 2 to 3 feet), feathery, deciduous dwarf Arctic willow (*Salix purpurea* 'Nana', Zone 3, to 5 feet), or tidy little *Spiraea* x *bumalda* 'Lime mound' (Zone 3, to 3 feet) are also handsome, useful interior hedging

Handsome fencing makes a strong design element, giving the garden shape and definition. Openwork barriers of this sort can divide the garden into various areas or rooms without blocking light and air. (Garden of T. R. Welch, Woodinville, Washington.)

plants. Where space is limited, short trellis panels (or long ones set on their sides) can be set into wooden frames and covered with clematis and honeysuckle or set with sweet peas and raspberries. These make very attractive little dividers which are useful as well.

Privacy screening can be had at once with solid fences, which can be designed to complement the architecture of home and neighborhood (or, if necessary, to disguise the same). Wooden fences can be elegant or baroque, depending on your inclination, skills, or pocketbook; and whether plain or painted, wood makes a lovely backdrop for plants. Where zoning rules restrict fences to certain heights (often five or six feet), smaller panels of trellis work may sometimes permissibly be added to cap off a wooden fence, adding further screening without violating the code. Such panels may also be combined in series to form openwork walls or visual baffles within the garden. If you are stuck with a fence you don't like, try painting it a muted, blending shade of sage or olive green, or disguise it behind an interesting assemblage of trellis fans, wheels, and arches. Any fence can be hung with rolls of woven bamboo screening, which is surprisingly durable and long-lasting even in rigorous climates. Sturdy chain-link fences, unlovely as they are, can look quite handsome when woven with long, flat cedar strips and draped with climbing plants.

Most of us end up employing some combination of all three kinds of enclosure elements in our gardens. To avoid a patchy, haphazard look, try to establish some commonality between the various ingredients. For instance, if the front yard is fenced with white pickets and the back area is enclosed with solid boards, painting both fences the same color will make for a more unified look than having one natural wood and the other painted. If tapestry hedges are chosen, signature combinations of key plants, repeated several times and in various parts of the garden, will create visual consistency and coherence. Similarly, identical trellis panels can be placed vertically in some areas and horizontally in others, rather than choosing different patterns, shapes, and sizes for each situation. In very small yards, bold simplicity is the key to restful, attractive garden design. Larger gardens can encompass far more variety without difficulty, yet even where space is no object, repetition of important elements—fences, arbors, trellis, or plan groups—is unifying and comforting to the eye.

The idea of garden rooms can be interpreted as closely or loosely as you like, depending on the site and your own predilections and pleasures. It can be great fun to find the rooms hidden within your garden, just as the sculptor finds the statue within the stone. In very little gardens, such rooms may be suggested rather than fully enclosed but it is worth trying to develop several distinct areas wherever possible. When we can see the entire garden at one glance, there is nothing to explore. A curving path whose end is unseen lures us onward with the promise of more to come. A hedge or fence interrupted by gate or door (whether genuine or mere subterfuge) gives a garden that vital element of mystery which imbues it with a presence and a distinct life of its own.

Trellis panels and fences provide instant privacy at relatively little cost. If climbing plants are encouraged to scramble through them, they can also baffle a good deal of street noise.

Roses of Winter

Tough and Sturdy Hellebores

Evergreen perennials are not always truly worthy of the name, for quite a few pass the winter as miserably as cats in snow, their ragged leaves furling with distaste in the cold. Merely retaining foliage over the winter is not enough to qualify a plant as a winter beauty. Hellebores, the so-called Christmas or Lenten roses, rank among the choicest, holding their looks in all but the worst weather. Handsome in leaf, often dramatic in form, these lovely toughs enrich the winter garden, brightening the shady reaches of the border back. Well placed and properly sheltered, hardy hellebores staunchly withstand hard frosts and are undaunted by anything short of several feet of snow. They bloom earliest where winters are mild and brief, but even in the colder regions, their lustrous foliage and swelling buds bring life and promise to the chilly garden. The sight of a colony of glowing, wine-red hellebores spreading beneath the underskirts of a weeping crabapple lingers long in memory. Even a single plant can contribute strongly to a winter vignette of evergreen ferns and dwarf rhododendrons. Nestle the group amongst larger shrubs, place them to receive afternoon sun in winter and light shade all summer, and your handiwork will reward you all year round in exchange for very modest annual care.

The best known hellebore is the Christmas rose, *Helleborus niger* (Zone 2 to 3 with wind protection, to 18 inches), which has been grown in English and European gardens for hundreds of years. The large, deeply lobed and divided leaves look something like peony foliage, and their rich, deep green gleams out dramatically against snow or frosty ground. Cupped and green-eyed, the 2-inch white flowers are like single roses. Nodding at first, they turn upward as they mature and are pollinated (as do most hellebore flowers). Their petals have the texture of wild silk, and each starry blossom is spangled with a fizz of thready golden stamens. In a protected and favorable garden spot, Christmas roses may begin to flower in late fall, continuing in bursts throughout the winter. Unless you live where winters are mild, you aren't guaranteed flowers at Christmas, despite the common name, yet it has been known to bloom in December in Massachusetts. In very cold regions, Christmas roses are more apt to produce a few flowers in late fall, followed by a full complement of blossoms in late winter or earliest spring. It's worth experimenting to find just the right microclimate to suit it, for this hardy winter bloomer is very reliable when satisfied with its conditions.

Lenten roses, a hybrid group called *Helleborus orientalis* (Zone 4, 12 to 18 inches), bloom a bit later. These robust plants hold several large flowers on each long stem, running from greenish whites through creamy pinks to rich, ruddy purples, and often attractively freckled with wine-red

spots. In my Zone 8 garden, the first bells open soon after the New Year, but in colder climates, they are more apt to flower from March to May. Newer hybrids, both English and North American, display a delightful expansion of the family range. Larger blossoms with broader, rounder petals are favored, but a few breeders are introducing narrow, starry flowers as well. Some look as black as a chunk of coal and a few approach clear red, while others are salmony rose, buttery yellow, or near green. Patient gardeners will find them quite easy to grow from seed, which is a good way to get a large quantity of these still-scarce hardy perennials. They appreciate the same conditions as Christmas roses, and thoughtful placement may similarly coax them into earlier bloom, so give them a sunny, protected site to receive their best efforts.

One of the oldest garden hybrids has been circulating for years as *Helleborus atrorubens* (Zone 4 to 5, 12 to 18 inches). This charmer is increasingly available from specialty nurseries under various names, most of them containing *atrorubens* in some manner or other, but it is sometimes listed simply as 'Early Purple'. Whatever the name, it will have very dark, divided foliage which is all but evergreen, since the new leaves come on in late autumn just as the old are passing away. The flowers look dusky burgundy in shade, but wandering shafts of winter sun awaken vivid ruby tints in those dark petals, which age to a curious but attractive greenish bronze. Here in the mild Northwest, this hard worker flowers from November through March, napping under the snow during harsh weather, then reappearing with renewed vigor as the frost or snow retreats. It often flowers around Thanksgiving in upstate New York and central Ohio, though in Katharine White's cold garden in New Brooklin, Maine, it rarely bloomed before mid-January. I am especially fond of this plant for reminding me of a very dear friend who gave it to me when we first moved to this garden. She got it, years ago, from her mother's garden, where it had been growing all her life. Such plants are often called heritage plants, because they are so intertwined with the history of our country and gardens alike. Whenever I look at my ruby hellebore, I think of Pat and her mother and the unknown gardener who brought the mother plant west with the wagons, and the still earlier woman who carried it tucked amongst her luggage as she traveled across the sea from England.

Statuesque Corsican hellebore, *Helleborus lividus corsicus* (Zone 5 with protection, 14 to 18 inches), is prized by flower arrangers, who covet its remarkably beautiful foliage. The trifoliate, spiny-toothed leaves are gray-green, softly marbled, and glazed with a pewtery sheen, setting off the creamy green flowers to perfection. This lustrous, glossy plant is quite hardy and remains quite showy through the winter if given substantial, consistent protection. This may come from any combination of evergreen shrubs, large rocks, walls, or fences, but it is vital to the looks of this big plant, for in exposed positions it is inevitably frost burned and damaged by wind. In my garden, a small colony of *H. lividus corsicus* is contained beneath the sheltering arms of a large weeping birch tree, accompa-

Lenten roses, *Helleborus orientalis*, open their nodding bells of pink or rose or white very early in the year. The satiny flowers last well in water if picked before they are fully open.

The green, burgundy-rimmed bells of *Helleborus foetidus* have a delicate, wilding fragrance, especially in the collector's form called 'Miss Jekyll's Scented'.

nied by compact rhododendrons and evergreen honeysuckle, *Lonicera pileata*. Here, out of the wind and snow, the hellebores hold their ivory-green bells high above the dappled foliage, beginning in late winter and continuing through the spring. Well mulched with shredded leaves and manure, they produce numerous seedlings to replace the mother plants as they grow tired.

A tall fir or magnificent maple could shelter liberal stands of *Helleborus foetidus* (Zone 3, 18 to 24 inches), a strapping species which boasts mag-nificent fans of long-fingered, ink-green foliage. Its drooping sheaves of ice-green blossoms begin to open in midwinter, but never quite manage to finish, remaining primly furled even after fertilization. Since each plant can achieve the size of a bushel basket in just a few years, these big beauties need ample spacing to do themselves justice. In a small garden, a single plant makes an attractive focal point for a little winter planting, but where space allows more generous use, one can arrange very showy groups of this hellebore with tall sword ferns, glossy daphnes, and witch hazels. This species is fairly short-lived, and like most of its cousins, resents division. Fortunately, it is a prolific self-sower, providing a steady supply of seedlings for replacements.

The twin keys to success with hellebores are to satisfy their cultural needs as closely as possible and to provide adequate shelter from wind and hard frosts. Hellebores are happiest in dappled shade and neutral soils, preferably moisture retentive but well drained. To approximate this, open tight clay soils with coarse grit and plenty of humus. Sandy ones can be loaded with compost and further enriched with hydrophilic polymers such as Broadleaf P4 to provide little reservoirs for thirsty hellebore roots. A thick, weed-suppressing mulch of shredded bark or chopped straw is beneficial in all cases. Acidic soils can be sweetened both with pH-buffering compost and a dusting of agricultural lime. Hellebores do best with moderate feeding, preferring a slow, steady diet to sudden seasonal boosts from chemical fertilizers. A spring feeding mulch of aged manure, alfalfa pellets (the kind fed to dairy goats), and cottonseed meal will keep them sassy all summer, and may be repeated in early autumn if the soil is poor. In late fall, trim away any tired old leaves, cutting close to the base of the crown but taking care not to damage any flower buds, which may already be forming. Give each plant a snug winter muffler of shredded leaves or chopped straw, tucking in a few smelly mothballs to keep mice from wintering in the mulch. Where slugs roam free, a circle of sharply gritty diatomaceous earth acts like an armed guard all winter and isn't washed away by rain—this substance protects hostas and other high-risk delectables as well.

Often, a good deal of the hellebore foliage is still healthy-looking in fall, but by late winter it gets rather tatty. Keep watch over your plants, and as soon as you notice flower buds emerging from the crowns—which may happen as soon as January or as late as March, depending on your climate and the harshness or mildness of the year—cut all the old leaves away, again taking care not to nick the new foliage buds as you do. If any leaves show black streaks or patches on them, your plants may have black spot, a fungal disease similar to that experienced by roses. The cure is the same in both cases: remove affected foliage and either burn it or bag it for the trash (never compost diseased foliage or the problem may be perpetuated). The preventive spray favored by rosarians works quite well on hellebores, too. Fill a gallon jug with water, add a tablespoon of baking soda and a few drops of liquid dish soap (to make the stuff stick). Shake it up, then spray it on the new leaf buds. When the leaves emerge, spray again, covering tops and bottoms alike. It will wash off, unfortunately, so you may need to make several applications, but it does help.

Proper placement is as vitally important as any cultural practice, for hellebores need both room to breathe and protection from drying winds. Though tolerant of drier soils once established, they don't appreciate severe drought or active root competition. Few if any will thrive if planted smack against a tree trunk or set too close to a strongly growing shrub or hedge. The shelter of an overhanging tree works wonders blocking wind and catching sharp frosts, but be sure and place your hellebores in deep soil pockets toward the outskirts of the tree shadow (the area shaded by the canopy of branches). If you can provide a sunny, sheltered corner, some taller shrubs to break the wind, and compact, neighborly dwarf evergreens for closer company, you have every chance of success with these delightful creatures.

The dusky bells of *Helleborus atrorubens* often begin to open in November and continue well into spring. This heritage plant is also called 'Early Purple'.

Bulb Buddies

Perennial Companions for Early Bloomers

In many gardens, the first flowers to brave the cold are bulbs, whether tough little snow crocus and snowdrops or species tulips from the steppes of Turkmenistan and hardy dwarf daffodils with names like 'February Gold' and 'March Sunshine'. Small and short-stemmed, these early blossoms are easy to overlook in the still shaggy beds and borders of the winter garden. Planted in timid twos and threes, such bulbs are charmingly unexpected rewards that brighten the late winter task of readying the garden for the arrival of spring beauty. Planted more generously, in tens and twenties, if not fifties and hundreds, these diminutive bulbs gain significant impact, spilling through mulch and rotting leaves in rivulets and pools of living color.

Welcome as they are in any setting, early bulbs shine far brighter when given supportive companions. Dwarf border shrubs, especially evergreens, can create both backdrop and context for them, while evergreen or winter-blooming perennials keep them closer company. Early-blooming woodland and meadow flowers such as primroses and hellebores, trilliums and epimediums are among the most obvious candidates, and while gardeners in mild winter areas may assemble the broadest palette, a hardy handful will perform with verve even in the colder parts of the country.

It's great fun to arrange pretty partnerships, but in any season, plant combinations must be based on more than bloom time and color. Both (or all) of the chosen plants must grow well in tandem if they are to share the same piece of ground, so it helps to match cultural needs as closely as possible. This can seem impossible, because many bulbs prefer full sun and good drainage, while their perennial partners are apt to want summer shade and damp feet during active growth. Fortunately, such seemingly incompatible needs can be met by choosing a planting site which offers appropriate seasonal variations. Many early bulbs which need full winter sun can live happily beneath deciduous trees and shrubs, open to the sky in winter yet providing summer shade for their woodland perennial companions. Such sites also offer the ample moisture bulbs require during active growth, from late autumn through late spring, while presenting significantly drier soils (for which many woodland perennials are well equipped) during the bulbs' summer dormancy.

You also need to consider the mature size and growth habit of each plant, for these are long-term combinations, not temporary alliances of bedding annuals and bulbs. In most color combinations, the main players have equal roles. With little bulbs, perennial partners must emphasize, not dominate their easily overwhelmed companions. Tiny snow crocus and dainty dwarf tulips should be matched with clump-forming perennials, rather than busy spreaders that will soon crowd the bulbs to death. This is even true with what seem to be well-matched thugs: although fat, cobalt blue spikes of grape hyacinth, *Muscari armeniacum* (Zone 3, to 6 inches) are delightfully echoed by the china-blue bells of creeping comfrey, *Symphytum* 'Hidcote Blue' (Zone 3, to 1 foot), after just a season or two, the grape hyacinth—itself no slouch at reproduction—will be swamped by the taller creeping comfrey. We have to be ready to intervene, removing chunks of the comfrey each year in order to allow the luxuriant grape hyacinth foliage plenty of room to ripen properly.

In the garden, as elsewhere, good relationships are harmonic but not static. The best give off visual sparks; imagine cloud-eyed cups of *Crocus chrysanthus* 'Blue Bird' shining above sheets of golden Scotch moss, *Sagina subulata* 'Aurea' (Zone 4, to 1 inch), backed by clumps of starry little blue spring beauty, *Hepatica americana* (Zone 3, to 6 inches). Picture apricot pink 'Sweet Lady' tulips (*Tulipa kaufmanniana*, Zone 3, to 6 inches) nestled in their own sage and burgundy foliage in front of a rosy hellebore (*Helleborus orientalis*, Zone 5, to 1½ feet) and bushy little heathers, *Erica carnea* 'Springwood Pink' (Zone 5, to 10

inches). Such groupings work best when the plant partners are compatible, the bulbs are grouped effectively, and the perennials are intermixed in judicious proportions.

The smallest bulbs, tiny crocus, scillas, and grape hyacinths, are best showcased by low companions such as periwinkle (*Vinca minor*, Zone 5, 4 to 6 inches). Tidy little 'Miss Jekyll's White' makes an airy carpet that won't smother delicate snowdrops, while lustier forms like the yellow-variegated periwinkle, *V. m.* 'Aureo-marginata', and the white-edged *V. m.* 'Argenteo-variegata' will weave festive wreaths around taller daffodils and tulips or the big Dutch crocus. Though not the showiest of plants, periwinkles are ardent bloomers that often produce a few brave blossoms even under the snow. Many are semi-evergreen, and their glossy new leaves make pretty mudguards for small bulbs, keeping their delicate petals clean and fresh despite lashing spring rains. An evergreen wood sorrel, *Oxalis oregana* 'Wintergreen' (Zone 5, to 4 inches) is another good bulb companion, making an open carpet easily penetrated by snowdrops or crocus. This form of the northwestern native species sends up lavender-pink flowers, rather than the usual white, above red-backed, cloverlike leaves.

Common primroses (*Primula vulgaris*, Zone 3, 3 to 6 inches) are also early risers, and their crinkled, leafy rosettes are often full of sunny yellow buds by late winter. They like the same conditions as most other woodland wildflowers, appreciating light or dappled shade and plenty of humus in their soil. They make pleasant company for golden avalanche lilies, *Erythronium* 'Pagoda' (Zone 4, to 1 foot), and dwarf double narcissus, 'Rip van Winkle', which look like fluffy yellow pompoms. Hybrid primroses, *Primula* x *polyanthus* (Zone 3, to 6 inches), come in a cheerful rainbow of colors which can be mixed and matched with dozens of early bulbs. Soft blends of pink and purple primroses can encircle patches of nodding checker lilies (*Fritillaria meleagris*, Zone 3, to 10 inches), echoing their tender, tweedy mauves

Starry little Turkish tulips, *Tulipa turkestanica*, bloom above a patch of Grecian windflowers, *Anemone blanda* 'Blue Shades,' in early March. (Author's garden, Bainbridge Island, Washington.)

and lavenders. Blue and white primroses make fetching dust ruffles for sunny yellow winter aconites, *Eranthis hyemalis* (Zone 3, to 6 inches), or the ivory stars of Turkish species tulips, *Tulipa turkestanica*. Lipstick-red primroses look great paired with short species like scarlet *T. linifolia* and the wide, flaring flowers of *T. greigii* 'Red Riding Hood'.

Like primroses, the violet family gets off the mark very early, and winter weeders may discover tricolored Johnny-jump-ups (*Viola tricolor*, Zone 4, to 3 inches) glimmering between golden bunch crocus, *Crocus ancyrensis* (Zone 4, to 4 inches). Sweet violets, *Viola odorata* (Zone 5, 4 to 8 inches), release their sweet old lady fragrance very freely on the cold winter air. Even the foliage and stems are scented, and their slightly soapy odor clings to your hands when you free the little plants of old leaves and mulch at winter's end. The murky black leaves and dusky flowers of black labs, *V. labradorica* 'Purpurea' (Zone 5, to 3 inches), look smashing with deep blue Siberian squills or double snowdrops, as do strands of golden grass, *Milium effusum* 'Aureum', its broad yellow blades shining like sunlight in the shade. A fitful perennial (Zone 5, to 1 foot), its small clumps fade away in wet winters but each spring dozens of its offspring return, their lemony coloring proclaiming their parentage from first emergence. (This is nice, because most ornamental grasses look exactly like weedy grasses when young; I am always reclaiming their seedlings from the compost pile when I belatedly realize that those tender green shoots really did belong in the garden.)

The sprawling, evergreen blue spurge, *Euphorbia myrsinites* (Zone 6, 6 inches to 2 feet), never looks untidy and little bulbs can be set closely around its small, tap-rooted crowns. Its striking, steel-blue foliage is arranged in overlapping scales that run down long, lax arms, ending in fat lemon and lime flower heads which bloom from late winter into spring. This European spurge needs the same sunny, well-drained position that such early daffodils as 'February Gold' and 'March Sunshine' do. Later in the season, the euphorbia's muted blues and greens will accord nicely with pewtery 'Blue Aimable' tulips or the near black tulip, 'Queen of the Night'. So, too, does its cousin, the redwood spurge, *E. amygdaloides* 'Rubra' (Zone 7, to 20 inches). This semi-evergreen species seeds itself into both sunny and shady corners, but is easier to establish in partial shade, where it makes upright clumps, its stiff arms clothed in whorling, rounded leaves of an inky green suffused with red. It blooms in March or April, but its dull green flowers are so small that this event is easily missed. However, in or out of bloom, its dark foliage makes wonderful company for smoky red tulips like 'King's Blood' or the coppery flowers of *Tulipa batalinii* 'Bright Gem', both of which may blossom in February or March.

By late spring, the borders are filling fast with summer-blooming beauties. While neither browning bulb foliage nor the sometimes rather frumpy remains of their early-blooming companions make a handsome setting for these coming attractions, their awkward stages must be tolerated. Both bulbs and woodland perennials need to dry out undisturbed (this means no braiding or early dismissal of their leaves), but you don't have to watch the entire process. Half-ripe leaves can be gently tucked beneath a light, deep mulch. Better yet, later arrivals like leafy daylilies and tall asters can be placed so that they screen the retreating plants from our view. It's important to allow them plenty of room, however; bulbs in particular resent being overcrowded even when they are dormant. Tucked away into shallow pockets at the border back, these earliest players can bow out unnoticed, making room for the prima donnas of summer. If we honor their contribution with spring offerings of compost, mulch, and adequate breathing room, both the bulbs of winter and their accompanists will brighten our gardens for many years to come.

Cutting Comments
Prudent Pruning for Health and Good Looks

Even in winter, a sunny day can insistently lure eager gardeners out of doors. Once there, however, the brisk breeze reminds us that the vernal equinox which marks spring's true arrival is still several weeks away. Fortunately, most early garden jobs provide enough mild exercise to keep us warm despite the chilly wind. Late winter is the traditional time to prune fruit trees, for instance, and is also a good time to do some careful, selective pruning of other garden trees. Pruning is a favorite way to let off steam or reduce cabin fever, but too often the result is only therapeutic for the human. The uncomplaining tree is left both unsightly and unhealthy, setting up future problems for all concerned. If past pruning experiences have been less than successful, this year, before hauling out the saw and having at a victim that can't fight back, take a few minutes to consider exactly what pruning is supposed to accomplish.

Stand in front of the tree you plan to work on and run down this short checklist, adding other pertinent questions as they occur to you. Are you trying to control disease or repair storm damage? Is the goal to let more light and air into the garden? Do you want to reduce the tree's canopy, remove lower limbs to free up ground space, or thin some higher branches to create lighter shade? It often helps to write down your goals if they are multiple or complex, so you don't lose sight of

them in the heat of pruning frenzy. It is also useful to make a simple sketch of the tree, erasing limbs on paper to see the effect before performing irreparable chain-saw surgery.

Remind yourself as well of all the positive functions the tree performs already. Does it screen out an unattractive view or noisy neighbors? Does it shelter plants, or baffle traffic sounds and block street dust? Do the kids climb it, or is it simply a beautiful, sculptural garden element? With all these positive attributes firmly in mind, you can now decide what kind and amount of pruning or limb removal will accomplish your primary goals without impairing or outright destroying the tree's valuable contributions. Don't be hasty in reaching for the saw, though; there's still more to consider. Look at the tree again to discover and appreciate its natural shape. The pruner's overall aim should always be to retain and emphasize that fundamental form. This is one reason why tree topping is never the right approach. Never. If for some reason a tree can't be pruned without disfigurement, better to remove it entirely and start again. This time you can make a more deliberate and appropriate choice before planting, selecting a tree that will mature to the size and shape you want.

Most of us get in trouble when we trim our trees casually, without really thinking about what will happen next. If a branch offends us, we pluck out the bit that we find immediately annoying. When trees sucker from the base, or produce water shoots, those straight, tall new stems which line older branches, reaching for the sky, our usual reaction is to chop away what we don't want and hope for the best. The tree usually responds by producing a nine-headed Hydra of new shoots at the site of our hasty cut, creating a vicious cycle of ugliness and destruction. Happily, both hope and help are at hand. The best book I have ever seen on the topic is a recent one called *Pruning: A*

ABOVE: Lacy-leaved *Dicentra formosa* is an excellent companion for early-flowering bulbs, as are primroses and hellebores. (This silvery purple plant is a natural hybrid seedling of *Helleborus torquatus*.)

OPPOSITE: Tough and adaptable, *Erythronium* 'Pagoda' is a splendid hybrid form of our native dog-tooth violet or avalanche lily. This one is partnered with plump spikes of grape hyacinth, *Muscari latifolium*.

When pruned by a gardener with a light hand and a sensitive eye, trees have graceful, distinctive shapes. This flowering plum is placed near enough to the house that it softens the hardscape (architectural elements) without overhanging windows or roof. (Garden of Obi Manteufel, Bainbridge Island, Washington.)

Practical Guide, by Peter McHoy (see the appendix). It not only discusses tools, timing, and techniques, but offers unique illustrations of the seven basic types of pruning, both for trees and for garden shrubs. Before and after shots of actual plants are accompanied by detailed drawings that thoroughly illuminate each kind of cut. This section alone would be worth the price of the book, which will quickly pay for itself in the hands of those with Savage Saw Syndrome. (If even three or four woody plants survive unscarred thanks to the information it offers, the book has done its job.) McHoy also includes an illustrated encyclopedia of trees and shrubs, with clear instructions for how and when to prune each one.

Sometimes a badly mangled tree doesn't have a natural shape anymore. In such cases, it is often kinder to remove it entirely and start all over. This is seldom a job for amateurs, unless you have

excellent insurance and distant (or exceptionally tolerant) neighbors. For tree removal, or, indeed, for any large-scale tree surgery, the wise gardener calls in professional help. However, finding help should never be a casual process. If your favorite fine nursery can't recommend a reliable, artful pruning service, read carefully through the listings in the phone book. For starters, ignore any ads which advertise tree topping; this is not a practice advocated by educated professionals. Look instead for mention of membership in the National Arborist Association or the International Society of Arboriculture. Look too for certified arborists who offer consultations (sometimes, but not always, for free). Set up an appointment, show the job appraiser your checklist (the goals that the pruning or removal should accomplish), then listen carefully to what is said about your tree(s). If your concerns are not reflected back to you, seek out another service. Another good way to learn what you will be paying for is to ask not just for verbal references but for addresses of satisfied customers who are willing for you to visit and see the kind of work that has been done by the company in question. It may take several tries to locate a service that suits both your needs and your aesthetic values, but all this forethought will reward you for years to come if the result is a handsome, healthy tree. What's more, no amount of sorrow and regret can replace a limb or a tree that is damaged or lost because of careless or improper pruning.

Once you find the right people to do your bigger jobs, ask if you can watch them work. Many good tree surgeons will gladly explain exactly what they are doing and why. Watching an artistic pruner in action is highly instructive, and such lessons are far cheaper in the long run than ambitious experiments that cost the life or health of a mature tree (not to mention the pruner). Skilled arborists are frequently qualified to do fine pruning as well, so it can't hurt to ask whether they might be willing to demonstrate proper pruning of any shrubs you find difficult to work with. Such a lesson will prove a bargain at almost any price if you come away understanding the principles behind good pruning and are able to keep your garden in good trim in the future.

Trouble with shrub pruning is usually due to excess of zeal. Shy bloom is a common complaint, but nothing can bloom when all its buds are sheared away each winter. What's more, few shrubs adapt well to relentless reshaping into cubes or lozenges in the name of neatness. Neatniks should avoid exuberantly shaped forsythias and quinces in favor of compact, naturally shapely conifers, dwarf maples, and rhododendrons, none of which need more than the lightest of pruning to retain their good looks. If control seems to be the overriding issue between you and

your shrubs, try using another mental checklist before slicing and dicing. What do you want your shrubs to look like? Is there any possibility that they can look that way without your assistance? Do you really like the shrubs you are growing, or would you be happier with something else that better approximates your ideas about beauty? Incompatibility is as big a problem between plants and people as in any other relationship. The nice part is that you can go your separate ways with no recriminations. Give incompatible shrubs to friends who really like them and feel free to make fresh, more appealing choices in your own garden.

As with trees, the basic purpose of shrub pruning is to maintain or improve the looks and health of the plant. The simplest kind is called hard pruning. Root-hardy, summer-blooming shrubs like butterfly bush (*Buddleia* species) and bluebeard (*Caryopteris* species) can be cut hard in late winter, all stems trimmed off above the bottom two pairs of leafbuds, which are usually within a few inches of the ground. New shoots will appear as spring arrives, creating a shapely and flower-filled bush. Where you want more height from such a shrub, you can trim stems higher up, leaving a taller woody framework of stems to resprout. With suckering shrubs like lilac or crowded old hydrangeas, the object is to open up the heart of the plant, allowing in light and air. First, remove all branches that are weak and spindly. Next, cut away any that are crossed and rubbing on each other. If the oldest stems produce the fewest or smallest flowers, remove them as well. Now cut back any stems that are markedly longer than the others. Once the shrub is well balanced, you can prune lightly each year to maintain the shape you like.

Shearing—clipping back the new growth evenly to create a smooth, usually rounded shape—is appropriate for shrubs like boxwood,

heathers and heaths, shrubby veronicas (*Hebe* species) and dwarf arctic willow (*Salix glauca* 'Nana'). With flowering shrubs, simply removing the old flower heads may be enough to restore the desired shape and size. In other cases, you may want to cut deeper, but try not to remove more than half the old growth, and never cut back into old wood (the bare, brown stems) unless you are sure that plant will resprout. If in doubt about what should be done, take a good, hard look at the plant and find its natural shape, then do what seems logical. Timing—deciding when to prune— is less important than deciding how to prune. Most authorities recommend autumn or winter pruning for trees, but quite a few garden shrubs can be sheared either in early spring or late summer. Some excellent gardeners (notably Christopher Lloyd, the well-known English garden writer) agree that the best time to prune is when you notice the job needs doing. Indeed, most experienced gardeners always have their clippers at hand, ready to snip an errant twig the minute they notice it.

A good pruning handbook makes such trial and error unnecessary. Borrow a selection of such books from the local library to see which is easiest for you to follow before plunking down your money, though; pruning books abound, but are not all created equal. If book learning is not your style and professional help is too expensive (good help often is), consult an experienced gardener whose garden you admire. Don't be nervous about asking for help; gardeners are as ready to pass along information as plants. The only recompense most of us ask is that you, in turn, pass on all you can. Such a possibility may seem unlikely when you are just starting out, yet surprisingly quickly, you will find yourself with both plants and knowledge to share as you travel further along the endless garden path.

ABOVE: Tightly sheared shrubs look appropriate in orientally influenced gardens. However, unless done with attention and skill, such hard pruning can be permanently disfiguring.

OPPOSITE: Selective thinning of entire limbs creates an open canopy and lighter shade beneath the boughs of mature trees. Those of us who don't do our best pruning when balancing on small ladder rungs are well advised to find skilled professional assistance when coping with large trees like these.

MARCH

Keep It Simple
Laying Down the Lines

As winter wanes, the itch to begin gardening grows stronger. Any day now, it will be mild enough to start digging in earnest. At last the plans we drew and dreamed over during the winter can be realized. The transition from fantasy to reality can be tricky, for no matter how carefully you measure your distances, your plans won't translate exactly from paper to ground. Partly this is because available garden space grows during the winter, fed by longing and imagination, then shrinks like a pricked balloon come spring. Then, too, exaggeration is an inseparable part of the planning process. Don't worry if you realize things aren't working out exactly as they did on paper; they really never do, even for professionals. When you run into difficulties, stay flexible and adapt freely, keeping as close to the spirit of your plan as possible, even if the details are a bit different.

If the conversion really seems hopeless, take time to walk your property again, relearning its realities. Once back in tune with the site, you'll find it easier to fit your design to the facts. It's worth spending some extra time over this

Lenten roses, *Helleborus orientalis*, ring out the end of winter and proclaim the imminent arrival of spring. By March, their freckled bells are no longer drooping but beginning to turn upward as the fertilized flowers form their fascinating, inflated seedpods.

When generously proportioned paths are first laid out, they usually look far too wide. However, once their bordering plantings fill out, there may no longer be room for two people to walk comfortably side by side. (Garden of Robert Freitag and Jason Devinney, Bainbridge Island, Washington.)

somest you've ever seen, but it's wiser not to pledge your troth too hastily. Better to recognize that the spot you've chosen for the arbor is a wind tunnel before, rather than after, the installation of a significant amount of lumber. It will save a good deal of heartache (and expense) if you know for certain that the terrace or patio will remain reliably sunny both early and late in the year. Seating areas that are clogged with moss and filled with lanky plants straining for the distant light are hardly a lift to the spirits, especially if they represent a serious investment. Once such matters are confirmed, you're almost ready for action. First, however, give your ideas a trial run before committing them to the earth.

It is generally recommended that garden beds and paths be laid out with sticks and string. When it comes time to dig, it's well worth adopting this time-consuming technique, which will keep your lines straight and true. However, at this stage, it's far quicker to outline your proposed garden beds, paths, and patios with flexible garden hose, particularly if you aren't completely sure about the shapes you want. Mow the lawn (if there is one) so it won't hide the hoses, then snake them out into the lines and curves of your design. Some people can look at the hose lines and picture the actual garden they imply without effort. Others are reminded of the aftermath of a fire sale. If you have trouble imagining how the garden will look, buy some inexpensive plastic drop cloths (the thin kind used by house painters) and lay them out over the proposed beds (or lawn and paths, if that's easier). Now scrutinize your handiwork thoughtfully and see if it looks harmonious and nicely balanced. If not, try simplifying your plans. In small gardens, especially, less is definitely more; the simpler the lines, the stronger the design. An unbroken sweep of grass (however tiny) makes a cramped space seem larger and more gracious.

stage of implementation, for although most plants can be moved many times with relative ease, few architectural features are so obliging. Think of it as the dating period; the plan may be the hand-

Even in large gardens, lawns that are interrupted with lots of fussy little planting beds will look choppy and restless. It helps to consider what different kinds of lines and patterns do to and for plants. Smooth, uncluttered lawn and fewer but generous beds will set off colorful combinations and foliar tapestries, just as an understated frame supports the painting it surrounds. Squiggly lines and fancy shapes call attention to themselves, as do very bold lines and dramatic combinations of surfaces. Indeed, so potent can these elements become that the plants become subsidiary. I am always annoyed when I notice a tendency (especially prevalent in books by architectural designers) to refer to nonwoody plants as "infill." This seems like a dismissive, slighting term that minimizes the importance of a plant's role in our gardens. Often, indeed, no specifics are offered; "with an infill of perennials," they say sweepingly of each bed, as if it hardly mattered what bits and pieces were tossed in to finish things off. Good lines and good bones—the woody plants that frame the garden—are certainly very important. However, to those of us who love our plants, all of them, in every combination, are worthy of endlessly satisfying research and consideration.

To make the most of all your plants, their beds should be as big as you can comfortably manage (in terms of weeding and so forth), while remaining appropriately in scale with the garden overall. The question of scale is really one of proportion; a huge house on a tiny lot might need bold, simple plantings involving very large, dramatic plants to keep house and garden in balance. When a tiny house sits on a big lot, you might create intimate, complex plantings near the house, getting simpler and larger as you move toward more public areas. Most urban gardeners find themselves trying to cram a lot of dreams into quite a small area. Whatever size the house may

be, if your lot is only 35 feet wide, a very simple, generously proportioned planting will look most attractive. You might opt to flank a 20-foot-wide carpet of grass with twin borders 7 feet across. If you prefer nonsymmetrical beds, you might make one 10 feet deep and the other 5 feet deep. Either arrangement would look ample and suitable in scale with the lot, offering a decent-sized planting

Small gardens are often scaled down to reflect their ground space rather than the house and neighboring trees. This tiny urban garden is designed with refreshing boldness of vision and proportion. (Garden of Doug Bayley, Seattle.)

area while preserving enough lawn to evoke visual serenity. A larger lot, perhaps 120 feet wide, could boast 20-foot borders on three sides and still have plenty of room for hedges and lawn. No matter what scale you are working on, keep your lines as plain and unembellished as possible without being spartan about it. In very small spaces or when your design is formal, straight lines are generally the most effective. If you prefer softer shapes, keep in mind that long, gentle curves are soothing to the eye, while abrupt, meaningless ones are distracting.

Once your lines are laid down in pleasant places, you are ready for commitment. Now you can set up those stretches of string and sticks that keep your hands true to your vision. Stout sticks some 2 feet tall work nicely, and if your shovel tends to wander, lace them with two rows of string, one a few inches above ground level, the other near the top of the stakes. Move around to view your handiwork from various angles so any wobbling will betray itself before you dig. When your eye is satisfied, start making your cuts. A heavy-duty steel edger can set the line very true, even in rough meadow grass. The best shovels for sod cutting have flat or shallowly rounded blades—rounder blades will give you a series of scallops rather than a good clean edge. If your turf is decent (and often if it isn't), you can cut it lengthwise into ribbons some 18 inches or 2 feet across. When you're done, roll them up, peeling them away from the ground and slicing tough roots as necessary to leave the bare undersoil. These turf rolls can be used elsewhere, or may be composted by stacking them sides-together in mounds. Set the first ones grass-side down, pile the next ones on green-side up, then grass-side down again, and so on. Cover the whole business with black plastic, and this time next year they will have become coarse but crumbly compost. This rolling up of the strips is a neat trick, but doesn't always work. If your space is large and the grass recalcitrant, shred the beds with a tiller, leaving a narrow strip of grass which you can later trim down to an attractive edge.

When the beds are cleared, you can amend the undersoil, adding plenty of humus. Aged animal manures, rotted sawdust mixed with cottonseed or soy meals (to replenish nitrogen), and chopped leaves are all excellent soil conditioners. Seed and kelp meals add nitrogen and trace minerals, while a dusting of agricultural lime sweetens and neutralizes acid soils. You can work this material into your soil in two ways, one excruciating, the other a piece of cake. I used to faithfully double dig all my beds, trusting tradition despite the cost to my back, because what was good enough for the redoubtable gardener Gertrude Jekyll was good enough for me. As Gertrude no doubt knew, double digging is far easier when somebody else does it. Since the underpaid and indefatigable garden boys so prevalent in Victorian England are no longer around (they probably all died of their exertions), I did my digging myself. I am willing to bet that Gertrude never even tried this stunt, or she would not have been so insistent about getting the soil well worked to a minimum of two feet below the surface. In any case, when I learned that Graham Stuart Thomas, the famous English garden writer, no longer considers this back-breaking torture necessary, I gratefully adapted his method, which works wonderfully. Just layer on the amendments, mulch the beds well with shredded bark or more finely chopped leaves, and leave the whole business for the worms to mix. When you do begin to plant, dig generous holes and mix their contents well. The rest can meld and mingle at its own rate, without any fussing from you.

Whichever method you choose, the amendments you add must depend on the nature of your soil. Sandy, light soils can use all the humus you can muster, in the form of compost, chopped

This miniature country garden is a comfortable place for both people and plants. Its simple lines are restful to the eye, while the easy flow of color and architectural detail maintain interest. (Garden of Lindsay Smith, Bainbridge Island, Washington.)

leaves, and aged animal manures. Even sawdust can be used if heavily dusted with cottonseed or soy meal—otherwise it robs the soil of nitrogen as it breaks down. Clay soils also need humus, but will be improved by coarse sand or fine grit to keep the soil from locking up in summer. To find out what else your particular soil will benefit from, contact your county extension service agent for specific regional information. The same department may offer free advice through a Master Gardener program as well, a wonderful resource for advancing gardeners in search of appropriate information. (Also see the appendix for books on the topic.)

These brisk, breezy days are better for active digging than thoughtful planting, but quite soon soft spring winds will break up and scatter winter's tattered gray clouds. At first tentative, but almost daily gaining strength, gentle March sunshine

soaks into the soil, releasing the intoxicating earth perfume, pure essence of growing things awakening in spring. Well-balanced and harmonious, those new beds await planting. What better gift could spring offer?

Lovely Lungworts

Garden Pulmonarias

Gardeners are often accused of being addicted to plants, and there is some truth to that. Learning to please plants, then watching them thrive is indeed a compelling pleasure, one that leaves you wanting more. However, unlike other addictions, plant dependency improves character. Spending hours and days among plants has been demonstrated to soothe human nerves, to reduce stress, to improve health. Furthermore, something about plant companionship clearly makes people more generous, optimistic, and good-humored than is normally the case. If we gardeners have a fault (and I suppose we must), it is greed. Not only are we driven

A recently introduced lungwort, *Pulmonaria* 'Roy Davidson', has beautifully mottled leaves that remain attractive long after the powdery pink and blue flowers have faded. Its companion here is the creeping dead nettle, *Lamium galeobdolon* 'Hermann's Pride'.

to acquire more and more wonderful plants, but we can't bear to let the garden slumber in peace. Garden addicts are constantly searching nurseries and catalogs for plants that will help extend the gardening season early and late. Others may toss in the trowel soon after Labor Day, but not garden addicts. As autumn lulls the borders to sleep, we groom and rearrange the best of the late bloomers, stretching just a few more weeks of glory from the fading borders. We contrive cozy winter corners for our precious off-season blossoms and poke through mounds of snow and fallen leaves to find the very first flower of the New Year.

Since I garden in a warm section of Zone 8, cold weather gardening might seem a simple task. Even here, however, plants that perform reliably during the colder months are hardly common, and additions to the modest list are always welcome. Spotted lungworts (*Pulmonaria* species) deliver as solidly in colder climates as in the maritime Northwest, yet they are surprisingly uncommon in American gardens. As a group, these herbaceous perennials offer a long succession of bloom at a time when flowers are sparse. The first—or last, for whether they are very late or very early bloomers is rather hard to say—of these blossoms often grace the breakfast table on Christmas morning. Red-belled and cheerful as a robin's breast, *Pulmonaria rubra* (Zone 4, to 1 foot) is known as Christmas cowslip in England, where the ruddiest, earliest, and largest forms have been selected for centuries. Rosy 'Redstart' looks great under holly, while 'Salmon Glow' blooms the color of smoked salmon, a brilliant match for coppery 'Princess Irene' tulips and bronzed grasses (really *Carex* species). Other lungworts—pink and purple, blue or white—come quick on the heels of the late winter bulbs and remain in flower until spring itself has lost its first freshness. The best of them keep on performing, their speckled and spotted foliage adding a dash of flash to the green tapestry of summer.

Smaller and less aggressive than related herbs like comfrey or borage, garden lungworts vary in growth habits. While none exceed 2 feet in height and most are decidedly shorter, some are clump formers, often slow to increase, others spread more rapidly from multiplying crowns, and the rest have creeping rhizomes which pour slowly into thick carpets across a woodland floor. Native to alpine meadows or lowland woods, lungworts perform best in shade, preferring cool situations and soils that don't dry out too much in summer. This, coupled with their informal appearance, makes them look comfortably at home in shady gardens, running in broad blue ribbons beneath rhododendrons or hydrangeas. Though delightful in full flower, these plants are best placed where they will be prominent in spring but unobtrusive in the summer, perhaps tucked beneath deciduous shrubs or ranged at the back of a deep border along with spring bulbs.

Most lungworts flower from late winter well into spring, their little bells dangling in profuse clusters above the emerging leaves. Often the buds and flowers present tweedy mixtures of blue, purple, and pink, some in pastel blends, others bolder. A few have blue flowers—but to say "blue" is not enough; this is like saying the sky or the sea is blue, for lungworts bloom in a full palette of blues, from skim milk through clear celeste to periwinkle and cobalt. Those that bloom in vivid, Mediterranean blues will intensify the dusky, receding colors of black tulips or tall purple Persian fritillaries and balance the singing yellows and potent whites of spring. Quieter lungworts gentle with age into dim pinks and purples which complement delicately tinted tulips, narcissus, and primroses.

Unfortunately, the most commonly grown species, *Pulmonaria angustifolia* (Zone 3, 8 to 12 inches), is among the least attractive. Its untidy foliage is a dull brownish green and its pink buds and brilliant blue flowers are usually groveling in the mud, thanks to lax, lanky stems. Fortunately, Jerry Flintoff, a Seattle plantsman, recently introduced a splendid form which he named 'Benediction' to honor Loie Benedict, a lifelong gardener in whose wonderful garden the plant was found. 'Benediction' is compact and shapely, with large, intensely blue flowers held on strong 8-inch stalks over softly spotted leaves. Like its less favored cousins, 'Benediction' is a fast spreader that will make a glowing sapphire carpet beneath a sunny forsythia or rosy flowering almond.

Flintoff's best known introduction was discovered in the garden of Roy Davidson, a renowned Seattle gardener who has himself introduced a number of garden plants. *Pulmonaria* 'Roy Davidson' (Zone 3, to 10 inches) produces masses of powdery blue flowers above broad, ribbony leaves that are sprinkled like the Milky Way with star dust. Instead of turning ratty as summer approaches, as lesser lungworts do, 'Roy Davidson' produces a steady supply of new leaves all through the year. In spring, the spangled leaves look fresh as paint. In the heat of a dry August, they remain amazingly attractive, good enough for a front-line position in the border. By autumn, the plants are in need of a discreet trim, but clip away the tired old leaves and a host of new ones are already in position, ready to set off masses of colchicum or late-blooming asters. Where winters are mild and open, *P.* 'Roy Davidson' is an outstanding addition to the winter garden, its generous clumps brightening any shady corner.

A long-leaved lungwort, *Pulmonaria longifolia* 'Bertram Anderson' (Zone 3, 8 to 12 inches), is

Beloved by generations of cottage gardeners, *Pulmonaria saccharata* 'Mrs. Moon' is often found in older gardens. In my garden, she has happily carpeted an overgrown shrubbery for some fifty years.

droughty, light soils, so give him extra helpings of compost and aged manure in late winter and again in early summer to keep his long leaves lush.

One of the oldest lungworts, *Pulmonaria saccharata* 'Mrs. Moon' (Zone 3, to 1 foot) is sometimes discovered in mature gardens, appearing as tangles of overgrown shrubbery are cleared away. A quick worker, it survives even droughty conditions, though suffering dreadfully from powdery mildew. Given decent garden soil and light shade, this willing spreader will make a pretty tapestry rug under shrubs or old fruit trees, but is not robust enough to compete effectively in wild gardens without annual intervention. 'Mrs. Moon', an old cottage garden plant, carries flurries of warm pink flowers fading to purple and blue above smallish, freckled leaves. A handsomer form, 'Highdown', has rounded, stippled leaves and rich blue flowers, but sulks unless grown in neutral or sweet soils that do not dry out in summer. The recent interest in making white gardens brought a couple of white-flowered lungworts out of retirement. Both *P.* 'Alba' or 'Sissinghurst White' (a form favored by Vita Sackville-West) offer clean white flowers clustered above broad leaves which are themselves neatly spotted with droplets of silvery white. Both forms make good company for white dog tooth violets (*Erythronium* species) or white snakeshead lilies (*Fritillaria meleagris* 'Alba'), but they can take a year or two to settle in and seldom increase quickly. They demand humusy, sandy loams and display an annoying tendency to rot in heavier clay soils. A handful of grip or coarse builder's sand at planting time helps to open tight soils, which pleases these prima donnas.

Lovely as a well grown lungwort may be, an unhappy one can quickly become unsightly, its leaves browned and curling or disfigured with powdery mildew. To prevent spring beauties from

one of the probable parents of 'Roy Davidson'. It boasts narrower, strappy leaves dappled with silver, the spidery rosettes a delightful counterpoint to the pleated fans of lady's mantle (*Alchemilla mollis*, Zone 3, to 1½ feet) and buxom hostas. 'Bertram Anderson' blooms in mid-spring, its blossoms a saturated blue-violet that sets off 'Apricot Beauty' or 'Kings Blood' tulips. A modest clump former, Bertie's multiple crowns can be prey to mildew in

lapsing into midsummer liabilities, lungworts must be given the conditions they crave right from the start. In general, they prefer moist or retentive soils and shady sites, though they can tolerate a fair amount of full sun so long as their roots never dry out. Pulmonarias do not hide their wants and will quickly signal their displeasure with leaf scorching or brown leaf curl in excessively sunny situations or with powdery mildew in droughty ones. Since garden shade is usually cast by trees and large shrubs, the shaded sites they prefer are often infiltrated with woody roots that compete successfully with young, newly planted or shallow-rooted perennials for available moisture. To give lungworts and other woodlanders a proper start, their planting site should be amended with compost and other humus-based soil conditioners, as well as a water-storing polymer or hydrogel. (Choose polymers that are at least 94 percent copolymer for best and most lasting benefits.) If summer heat and drought invite mildew despite these precautions, a close shave and a light feeding mulch of compost, watered in with a restorative dose of manure tea (brewed from 1 part aged manure to 20 parts water), will stimulate a flush of new growth which will hold its looks well into winter. In improved soils, the combination of a hydrophilic polymer at the root zone and an annual spring feeding mulch of compost mixed with alfalfa pellets (the kind commonly fed to farm animals) may eliminate midsummer flops altogether, but in poorer conditions, this feeding-and-mulch treatment should be repeated several times through the year to keep soil and plants in good heart.

While few nurseries or mail-order catalogs carry more than a handful of lungworts, all of the above are commercially available in the United States, and more named garden forms are to be found every year. Since lungworts are quite easy to grow, an increased demand for these lovely plants should quickly produce a more abundant supply.

Make Beautiful Dirt
Readying Beds and Borders

When we first moved to our present garden, the old farmyard was a wilderness of blackberries, brambles, and nettles. What once had been a lawn was a rough meadow, crisscrossed with dog runs and kennels. Goats had been penned in the aging shrubbery, and ponies were grazing freely in the old borders. The result was pretty unsightly, but we felt sure that where so many animals had spent time, the ground must be enriched by their leftovers. Apparently, however, these animals gave less than they got, for what we found when we began to make the garden was not fluffy loam, softened by generations of cow pies and horse puckies, but sterile blue clay, too hard to open without a pickaxe. (I later learned that we had elected to begin making the garden in the old car-park area, saturated not with animal by-products but with generations of noxious drips and exhaust fumes.)

The next cheery discovery was that the well which had served this old farm for generations was not deep enough to serve more modern folks. A well-preserved Maytag wringer-washer out in the cookshed explained our predecessors' conservative approach to laundry, as did the complete lack of closets within the house. What with two muddy kids, the dogs, and the garden, we put quite a strain on the system. By August, the well finally gurgled dry, just as the temperature soared. My newly transplanted garden was in shock and so were we. Looking around, we realized that our nearest neighbors had just installed (literally) a tree farm and were watering round the clock.

Several new neighbors had arrived as well, and together we were using more water than the shallow aquifer could supply. We soon hooked the house up with a local water company, using the well just for the garden. That helped, but the situation wasn't really resolved.

The solution to both the water problem and the dirt problem turned out to be the same. Indeed, the solution is the key, the heart, perhaps the very soul of gardening. It is, in fact, the best garden advice I know. This is it: Make Beautiful Dirt. The idea seems too modest to have such powerful repercussions, yet adopting it will positively change your garden as no other single factor can. Many of us are gardening in used dirt, tired dirt, dirt that has given its all long ago. The gardener who turns nasty dirt into beautiful, healthy soil is rewarded by a healthy garden and disease-resistant plants. In healthy gardens, plants can thrive without chemical assistance or toxic interventions. It's that simple.

Looked at in those terms, it no longer seems like too much trouble to make endless supplies of compost and to feed the garden not with chemical fertilizers but with soil-building amendments. By feeding the soil, we give our plants everything they need to grow well on their own. Naturally, there are always a fussy few plants—like hybrid tea roses—that demand more from us, but the majority of garden plants, from trees to ground covers, actually prefer to eat beautiful dirt.

Beautiful dirt has a secondary advantage which is nearly as persuasive as the first. Farmers and gardeners talk of soil that is in good heart, meaning that it is nutritious and shows a good balance between water retention and drainage.

Such soils conserve moisture better than unimproved dirts. Make beautiful dirt, top it off with a good, thick mulch, and you will find that your plants are better equipped to handle drought. This means you can water less frequently, something all gardeners are considering these days. In my own case, when we began making our present garden, the heavy clay retained water nicely. However, it drained so poorly that I lost depressing numbers of plants to root rots and fungal problems that I had never encountered before. Now that the border soil has been improved, most of my plants thrive all summer on just a single monthly watering. (Don't discount this because I live in the rainy Northwest; our climate is what's called modified Mediterranean, which means summer rains are rare. The modified part means that summer sun is also rare, but that's another story.)

No matter where you live or what kind of soil you are working with, the object is to promote living, actively healthy dirt. Pick up a handful of garden soil and squeeze it. If it smells cleanly earthy and faintly sweet and crumbles nicely into fluffy, evenly sized bits, well, congratulations. You are fortunate indeed, for you have loam, an often ideal soil type that can be sandy (it will feel gritty) or clay-based. If it is very loose in texture and crumbles into tiny bits, you have sandy soil. If it pours out of your hand like water, you have sand: consider the charms of gardening in containers. If your dirt stays in a clump with your fingerprints clearly showing, you have clay-based soil. If it gloms into a hard ball you can lob unbroken over the back fence, you have my kind of clay. Each soil type has strengths and drawbacks, and all can be made to support thousands of kinds of plants, but

This excellent form of *Pulmonaria saccharata* commemorates Vita Sackville-West's restored castle and garden in its name, 'Sissinghurst White'.

all will do the job better with encouragement. (We'll get to that in a minute.)

Besides their basic textural qualities, soils can be acid or base (alkaline) or nearly neutral (around 7 on the pH scale). Most plants grow best in neutral or slightly acid soils (with a pH between 6 and 7), so if you are struggling to get plants to grow in what looks like perfectly good dirt, get a pH kit at the local nursery (they are inexpensive and reusable) and test your soil. My blue clay tests at about 5.6, which is fine for azaleas, rhododendrons, blueberries, and other acid lovers but not so good for many perennials. There's no point in fighting nature, so I grow a lot of plants that like heavy, acid soils. However, there are plants I really want to grow that won't be happy unless I help them out a bit, so when I feed my beds and borders, I add agricultural lime to the areas where these plants live.

It's important not to use hydrated lime, which is what you want for the outhouse or mixing cement. Agricultural or dolomite lime is longer lasting and also contains some magnesium (plants need trace minerals just as we do). On my heavy clay, I have to add lime each spring, using about five pounds of lime to sweeten a hundred square feet of garden and bringing the pH up from 5.5 to 6. A friend who gardens on sandier soil adds half that amount, while loamy soils need a middling amount. Don't expect to see immediate changes, for this is a leisurely process. Test again each spring, adding lime again if your pH is still not where you want it. After a few years, you will get a better sense of how much lime your soil requires to keep it in the neutral zone.

It's easy to get caught up in formulas for success, but remember that gardening is not an exact science. Thousands of plants enjoy moderately acid situations, so your garden soil does not have to be exactly neutral to be serviceable. East of the Cascade Mountains, where my parents live, the soil is on the alkaline side. They add quantities of buffering compost and aged manure to their beds and borders to neutralize the soil. Thousands of plants also grow happily in mildly alkaline soils, so in such cases, frequent, generous amendment is all the intervention necessary.

These details of soil composition may seem boring, but they become more important when we realize a curious fact. Our soil is alive. Though we can't see them (just as well, really) the soil is crawling with tiny microorganisms which contribute forcefully to the health of our plants. Earthworms are valued for their role in soil building, but a huge team of invisible partners—a vast clan called microlife, which consists of microrizhae, soil fungi, and bacteria—do more good and get less credit. Their job is to predigest the nutrients locked in the soil and feed them in a more accessible form to our plants. In Sweden, farm families set out saucers of porridge each night to feed the Tomten, benign little troll relatives who watch over the farm while the family sleeps. Similarly, gardeners have to take these tiny soil builders on trust, feeding them and appreciating their help without ever seeing them face to face.

Fortunately, feeding microlife is very easy. These little creatures prefer to eat decaying organic compounds (as in compost, aged manure, and so forth), but where that is in short supply, they make do by cannibalizing each other. Soils with low humus content don't support plant life well, because when microlife is in short supply, plants can't readily access the nutrients they need. The obvious way to set things straight is to provide plenty of humus, not just once but on a regular basis. The point of all the soil boosting and amendment we do is to make beautiful dirt so we can enjoy beautiful gardens. Not so wacky after all, hmm?

So how do we go about making beautiful dirt for our plants? The basics, everywhere, are the same. Plant roots need both water and air, so we aim for soils that are retentive yet open in texture. Heavy clay soils can be lightened up with humus (compost, aged sawdust, or manure), then opened with grit or coarse sand to keep them from locking up like adobe in the dry summer heat. Sandy soils need all the humus they can get, delivered on a regular and continuing basis. The easiest way to provide large quantities of humus is to blanket the soil twice a year, in early spring and late fall, with a 2- or 3-inch layer of compost mixed with bone-meal and other nutritional amendments. Few of us are about to dig up an established garden just to improve its soil, but this kind of blanket mulching is quite easy—just take care not to smother the crowns of your perennials. Soil improvement is an ongoing project in most gardens, and some part or other of the process can be worked on in any season. Indeed, much can be accomplished simply by fortifying the planting spot each time you add or move or divide a plant.

Though we have shoveled our share of dirt in our day, we now use a leisurely (or lazy) gardener's technique to create new beds. Once the sites are

Short stakes mark the resting crowns of perennials, which must not be smothered when the annual spring mulching takes place. Here, pit-washed dairy manure covers the Northwest Perennial Alliance Border at the Bellevue Botanic Garden in Bellevue, Washington.

chosen, we cover them (grass and all) with a layer of slim, twiggy sticks (birch twigs are ideal) topped with a thick (2- or 3-foot) pile of coarsely blended dry leaves and green grass clippings. The twigs let in air and water and keep the piles from becoming anaerobic—without air, compost can be the nastiest green slime, stinking and revolting. Add air, and a miracle of garden alchemy occurs; stinking green slime is transformed into sweet-smelling, crumbling black gold. The softer materials rot down fairly quickly, encouraged by armloads of garden greenery gleaned in weekly grooming sessions. Beds started in spring are ready to turn in fall. By then, the grass has rotted away and the skinny twigs disintegrate under turning fork or tiller tines. If the compost is still rough, it will finish breaking down over the winter. We dig or till the new beds, setting their edges clearly, then blanket them thickly with our usual amendments—lime, a handful of kelp meal (for trace minerals and elements), a thin layer of cottonseed or soy meal. If I am ready to plant, I just mix up each planting hole, leaving the rest undisturbed. Planted or not, we top the whole thing off with 6 to 8 inches of bark or straw mulch. Over the winter, the worms do the mixing for us, and by next spring, the new beds are either plantable or already going strong.

Make beautiful dirt, and your plants will make themselves beautiful. The deep manure mulch shown earlier has been transformed. (Northwest Perennial Alliance Border at the Bellevue Botanic Garden in Bellevue, Washington.)

One popular soil builder that is no longer in favor is peat moss. In practical terms, dry peat is difficult to wet, responding best to hot water or lengthy soaking. Peat-based potting mixes are lightweight, which is good if you are carrying the pots around, but less good when plants are rocked by wind (their roots often tear). Once dried out, peat-based mixes are demons to rewet (hot water would cook the plants). Peat is a remarkably poor mulch, drying to an impervious, water-shedding (rather than water-conserving) mat in no time. It isn't really much good in composts, either, adding little nutritive value to the soil as it degrades. On top of all this, greenhouse workers who come in frequent contact with peat moss are now warned to use respirators and gloves, for it harbors tiny unfriendly bacteria that can cause serious lung infections, among other things. Last but not least, peat is only a renewable resource in glacial terms. It takes hundreds of years for natural peat to accumulate in bogs, yet we strip it away so fast the bogs simply can't replenish themselves. (In the same way, a mesquite plant big enough to make barbecue charcoal for twenty chickens may be three centuries old.) Some things just aren't sensible trade-offs, and peat appears to be one of them.

While planning out your garden beds, save room for a nursery bed as well. The nursery bed is a haven where new or young plants can wait while the garden takes shape. You can save a lot of money by buying inexpensive small plants and growing them in the nursery bed. This is where we tuck divisions and tender seedlings, giving them plenty of room with no crowding. By the time you're ready for them, all will have gained in size and rootball and be able to hold their own in more competitive border situations. Nursery beds also give you the chance to learn your plants' habits, discover what they will do over time, and how they look in autumn and winter as well as

spring and summer. The nursery bed can also be the artful gardener's storage cupboard. Other fine artists keep supplies ready at hand, and so should we, for plants are the materials of our art and our craft. When you find a plant that intrigues you, with fascinating leaves or glorious flowers, don't hesitate to buy it just because you aren't sure what to do with it. Those who hesitate often lose, for a lovely unknown is likely to be snapped up by some other ardent gardener. If you have a nursery bed, you can hold new treasures there until you decide where they may best grace your garden. I feel it is our duty to advance artful gardening by keeping our nursery beds as well stocked as our kitchen cabinets (which is to say, jammed with staples as well as interesting newcomers). It's a tough job, but....

Rites of Spring
Preparing for Active Duty

As lashing spring rains wash away winter's grimy leftovers, the mixture of snow crystals and fresh, running water turns to silver tea, a revitalizing spring tonic for wakening plants. As March roars in, the thousand chores of spring await eager gardeners, who dash out to perform them between downpours. Perhaps chore is the wrong word; our present occupations are more like preparations for a splendid, ongoing party than like chores, a word that implies boring drudgery. Gardeners, the luckiest people on earth, can scarcely be considered drudges. Who else gets such delight from a handful of crumbling, sweet-smelling earth, rich and ready for planting? Who else sees perfect happiness in a large mound of manure? Each year, we take active part in miracles of transformation as the tiny seeds we sow become vegetables, herbs, fragrant flowers, even trees. If winter robs us of beloved plants, spring catalogs present endless opportunities to acquire many, many others, each more tempting than the last.

The anticipation of such wonders spices our preparations with pleasure even when a certain discomfort is involved. Digging in the drizzle with icy rivulets sneaking down one's spine can definitely be daunting. Evenly scattering heavy globs of sodden manure over drenched borders without harming emerging plants requires a good eye, a steady hand, and a very strong arm. A vigorous pruning session can leave us aching in back and shoulders for weeks.

The secret to carrying out the most demanding garden work is to take a tip from spring weather and change often. Work hard but briefly at heavy digging or tree pruning, then transfer your attentions to the seed flats and transplant trays, mixing in some brisk lawn trimming or light shrub pruning. If you spend twenty minutes stooping, follow it up with an activity that requires stretching, such as tying clematis or honeysuckle strands to trellis or arbor.

It also helps a good deal to be appropriately dressed for action. After ruining more good clothes than I ever thought to own, I have finally trained myself to change into combat gear before entering the garden in mud time. I am always relieved when I visit other gardeners and see that they, too, dress for garden success with striking, if not exactly attractive, results. I favor old sweats with pockets for foam knee pads added on, a heavy canvas jacket with deep pockets that hold tools and twine, and a baseball cap (Mariners or Red Sox) to protect my head from thorns. You don't have to match these sartorial depths, but if you don't make yourself comfortable before engaging in active duty, you will make yourself sorry afterwards. The first principle here is practicality. Wear loose, warm clothing that you don't mind getting dirty. If you don't like knee pads, use a rub-

ber kneeling mat to keep your knees from getting coated with cold mud. Tightly woven cloth like canvas lets thorns and clinging twigs slide away, unlike softer weaves which are easily snagged. If you don't like hats, try a scarf or ear warmer; if your head is warm, the rest of you stays warmer too.

The comfort of your hands is vitally important. When leather or cloth gloves are saturated, they can make your hands feel like ice cubes. Inexpensive rubber dishwashing gloves keep hands really dry on damp days. A shake of talcum powder absorbs sweat and makes tight gloves, which are easier to work in, slide off effortlessly. If your feet get cold, try buying a larger size of garden boot than usual and layering your socks, starting with silk liners and adding bulky socks of wool or booties made of the fluffy polypropylene blends that skiers and climbers wear. Put all this together and you can probably hire out as a scarecrow anywhere in the country. If dowdy dressing hurts your pride, remember that many of the most famous English gardeners look far, far worse than this in their garden gear. (We have the pictures to prove this assertion!) Remember too that no sacrifice is too great when beauty is at stake. In this case, it just happens not to be our own beauty.

Once suited up, we can reduce preparation pains even more by taking five minutes to do some warm-up stretches before setting foot in the garden. Loosen up your joints—knees and ankles, hips and waist, shoulders and neck, elbows and wrists—with slow, circling motions, moving first in one direction, then the other. Next, stretch your legs, leaning gently toward the floor to loosen up tight back muscles as well. Running in place, skip-rope jumping, or a few mild jumping jacks all boost your circulation nicely. Now you can grab your gloves and tools and hit the dirt without paying for the unaccustomed exercise with backaches and muscle strains. No matter how young and fit and active you are, a few minutes spent limbering up are worth your weight in Tiger Balm or Ben-Gay™, for gardening has a mysterious way of involving muscles that are called upon by no other form of exercise (indeed, muscles we didn't know we had). If gardening is your preferred form of exercise, make that ten minutes of warm-ups. It may seem a silly bother, but the combination of light exercise and frequent job-swapping improves both performance and stamina and can spare you a lot of unnecessary pain.

I used to spend a lot of time planning out in advance what I wanted to accomplish with each garden session (or each dry period). Now I plan provisionally, knowing I will inevitably get side-tracked by a hundred details that needed prompt attention. I head out, shears in hand, to tackle the overgrown kerria hedge. Once there, I notice the slugs enjoying the young hosta shoots underfoot, so I round up a few beer bottles, filling each with an inch or so of flat brew in which the young slugs will blissfully drown. I scatter a handful or two of diatomaceous earth about the plants as well for immediate protection. Returning to the hedge, I find seedling blackberries infiltrating the kerria shoots. I fetch my toothed iron farmer's knife to root them out, but a few pulls on those thorny stems sends me back to the house for my heavy leather linesman's gauntlet gloves. As I return to the garden, I notice several flats of seedlings are flooded, so I carefully punch in a few more drainage holes with the farmer's knife. As I move the flats, I find that the autumn-potted primrose divisions nearby are thrusting roots out the bottoms of their pots. As I transfer these ardent creatures to larger pots, I am reminded that a friend wants divisions as well, so I carry the now-empty small pots and some fresh soil over to the mother plant. She looks sad and soggy, so I clear away the

Many of the garden year's first chores require muscles that haven't been used for many months. Doing a few warm-ups before spending long hours tossing manure and compost will result in fewer aches and pains afterward.

choking winter mulch and wet leaves, move a few small neighboring coral bells further apart and generally prink the bed a bit. As I straighten up, a branch of the big quince overhead pokes me in the ear, so I get the folding saw and begin reshaping the elderly shrub, a task I accomplish a bit each year to avoid shocking the plant into producing thousands of suckers. I remove most of the pesky lower branches, making room for younger, more floriferous limbs. As I make my way around the shrub, I see that several roses need new hoops after the buffets of winter.... At some point, I end up back at the kerria hedge, with time to trim and clean out a few more yards of its length before the next distraction appears.

I once believed what many books insist: that consistent, logical, linear application is the best, indeed, the only way to accomplish anything in

A well-organized tool basket or trug can reduce the number of trips between house and garden, but some wandering must be accepted as part of the process. Let it be a reminder to slow down and look at the emerging garden as well as the chores.

the garden. I tried so hard to stick with one chore at a time, and not start anything new until that task was finished. To prove my determination, I would carry only the hedge clippers. After six or eight trips trotting back and forth to the house for other tools necessary to the little jobs which cropped up, I decided to face facts. Gardening is not a hard science. It's done incrementally, each piece related to the next, because the garden is made that way. The Scottish naturalist, John Muir, once said, "Pick up anything in nature and you find it attached to the rest of the world." In the garden, too, everything is intimately connected to everything else. Arbitrarily dividing tasks works best in simple, large-scale gardens, where there is plenty of help. Harry trims the hedge, George manures the border, Joe thins the seedlings. Terrific! However, where garden boys are few, we amateurs are stuck doing everything ourselves. In my garden, I mow the lawn, weed and mulch, water, haul manure, and groom the beds. (My husband, Mark, does the heaviest pruning and lifting and will move any new tree twice. After that, I'm on my own.) To accomplish all this, I muddle along, doing bits of six or eight jobs at once. It would drive an efficiency expert crazy, but it works, because for me, this mishmash has a logical flow. If I work at just one task, I must ignore all those other details which need attention. Unfortunately, unless coped with right when I notice them, they may not get done at all.

Working without a firm plan may not be especially businesslike, but it certainly isn't boring, and sooner or later, everything does get done (usually). Some years ago, as a sop to efficiency, I borrowed an old trick from my Young Mom days when I traded in my purse for a voluminous diaper bag that held literally everything. At first, this simply meant organizing a carrier for my hand tools. A heavy duty plastic drawer organizer for kitchenware used to serve nicely, but as my tool collection grew, something larger and stronger was required. Eventually I settled on a generously sized trug or garden basket woven of ash and willow, which has held up under constant abuse for years and is still going strong. The trug holds all my trowels, knives, pruners, and clippers, as well as a folding saw, plastic plant tags and marker pens, several grades of twine, scissors, seed envelopes, small resealable plastic bags, and a reel of paper-coated wire twists for securing light vines to their supports.

This arsenal is usually sufficient for short garden forays, but when time allows for longer working sessions, the laden tool basket goes into the garden cart, along with buckets of water, manure, and mulch and an empty one for weeds and clippings. Add a shovel, a rake, and a saw, and you will have all the tools you want right at hand next time you get sidetracked. Thus equipped, you can party on for hours, stopping only to smell the primroses, enjoying present pleasures as well as anticipating those to come.

Feminizing Pesticides

Rethinking Pest and Problem Prevention

In most households of my acquaintance, poisoning pests and weeds seems to be a male job, right up there with taking out the garbage or changing the oil in the car. So, too, is fertilizing the lawn, so when a recent article in *Science News* (a weekly newsletter long published under the aegis of the American Academy for the Advancement of the Sciences) caught my eye, I thought immediately, Somebody Must Tell The Guys! Though we prefer not to think about it, we all know that the water we drink and even the air we breathe is loaded with pollutants; that is not news. What is news is

that when we eat or drink or breathe them, many common pollutants, notably garden fertilizers, pesticides, and herbicides, mimic human hormones. To be specific, female hormones. Starting to feel nervous? We should, because excellent as they are in their proper place, estrogens in food and water may mean serious trouble, initially for males, but sooner or later for everybody.

The first effects of pollution's pervasive feminizing influences showed up in birds, fish, and aquatic mammals. Certain populations show marked declines of viable sperm and various kinds of sexual dysfunction. Now, you probably aren't reading a gardening book to learn about dropping bird sperm counts, but stay with me a minute; this does pertain to you and me, because over the past several decades, human males have displayed similar effects. In view of the population crisis, our decreasing fertility (close to 50 percent down since the 1950s) may seem like a fine idea, but that is far from the only side effect of our daily estrogen intake. Several nasty testicular cancers are becoming increasingly common, and the rising incidence of cryptorchidism.... Well, here's the point: ordinary backyard chemicals—fertilizers, herbicides, and pesticides—are definitely not good for men, young or old. They aren't great for women and kids, either, so if you're getting ready to weed-'n'-feed the lawn or holster up the old spray gun for the annual attack on black spot or aphids, stop a minute. This might be the year to rethink your position on organic gardening.

For many people, the term organic gardening conjures up a mental image of a wide-eyed, terminally earnest person who constantly lectures (boringly) about how bad everything you happen to be doing is for the earth. I admit that organic gardening is a dumb term (how would you go about making an inorganic garden?), but the idea is far from dumb. Organic gardeners use homemade fertilizers that replenish the soil without polluting water systems. They dig out dandelions and pour boiling water on persistent weeds growing where a weeding knife can't fit. They control slugs with ammonia sprays ($1/3$ ammonia to $2/3$ water), fight black spot on roses with baking soda (1 tablespoon baking soda to 1 gallon water), and buy little Chinese take-out boxes of live ladybugs to attack aphids. If the kids play hideout in the garden shed, nobody has to worry, because their shelves are full of bags of kelp meal and granite dust, not bottles and boxes marked with skulls and crossbones.

If organic gardeners must give up the convenience of using one-size-fits-all fertilizers and pesticides, they consider it a fair trade, not a sacrifice. They feel that the benefits of organic gardening are worth a little extra work. What's more, most of us consider garden work more pleasurable than health club workouts; the music, provided by the birds, is much nicer and you don't need to look like Lycra Lass or Lad to fit in. Garden work is worthy, healthy work, and on a personal level, organic gardeners want to be healthy people. They want the peace of mind that comes from knowing the food they eat and the water they drink are as clean and healthful as possible. As a group, they take community stewardship seriously; their creed is to heal and improve the land they use. On a global level, they make a small but positive contribution toward restoring everybody's environment to health.

That's a pretty terrific dividend, but the price—learning a whole new way of managing pests and problems—may still seem too high, especially if you really don't see what's wrong with using rose spray or scattering a few sacks of fertilizer on the lawn a couple times a year. It's comfortable to assume that the other guy is the prob-

lem. It's not the home gardener who is causing all this mess, it's the farmer and the fruit grower, right? Well, no. Home gardeners create significantly more pollution than commercial agriculture. For one thing, farmers are not getting rich out there. They are scrupulously careful with expensive chemicals, using (therefore wasting) as little herbicide or fertilizer as possible. Increasingly, as the hideous results of skin and lung contact with them are becoming recognized, farmers are also respectful of these powerful poisons, suiting up in contamination-resistant clothing, face mask, and respirator before spraying. Joe Homeowner wakes up on a sunny Saturday, grabs a can of whatever is on the shelf, and starts spreading death dust around the garden, usually without even donning a pair of disposable gloves. Too often, he is using a nonspecific, broad-spectrum spray that doesn't even work on whatever the problem might be. (If there even is a problem— patience is not our byword, and too many of us react rather than analyze the situation.) After the dust settles, Joe waters the lawn; the poison runs down the sewer, gets recycled into the water supply, and the next thing you know, the morning coffee tastes a little funny all over town because Joe isn't alone. There are tens of thousands of Joes in every city and suburb and town.

The point isn't how dumb we are, but how stubborn. Whether we like it or not, the world is changing and we are changing it. The good news is that we can change things for the better, starting right in our own backyard. The better news is that, once you get used to it, organic gardening is powerfully, sensually rewarding. It feels great to loll in grass that holds no insidious residues, grass that a baby can crawl through without fearing for his future manhood. It feels wonderful to listen to a full-throated chorus of birds which are thriving on the worms and bugs your clean garden pro-

Tempting as it is to wage full-scale war against slimy brutes like this imported European field slug, gardeners need to think twice before resorting to powerful poisons. Indiscriminate pesticide use can do far more damage to the entire ecosystem than the slugs do in our gardens.

vides. It's delightful to watch butterflies flock to feed on nectar from your own wildflowers, including natives that are squeezed out of their natural ecological niches by suburban sprawl. It feels terrific to set young plants in dirt that has become soil, rich and sweet-smelling, crumbling cleanly in your hands. It feels magical to perform garden alchemy, turning household garbage into black vegetable gold. It is enchanting to see the garden evolve, to watch companionable planting schemes born on paper, now performing in the border in living color. It's heady to find snowdrops in late winter and to pick the last fragrant violets as the first snow falls. Most of all, it feels deeply satisfying to know that you are making a positive con-

tribution toward healing our battered, beleaguered earth.

Some of the benefits of this peaceable way of gardening are long-term and almost abstract, but others are concrete and immediate. Since the Alar scare, we all rinse our apples, but until somebody spells it out, we prefer not to extrapolate. When, therefore, a front-page newspaper article shows researchers demonstrating that an ordinary peach from the grocery store contains traces of six different pesticides and herbicides, we feel like T. S. Eliot; "Do I dare to eat a peach?" Well, that's exactly why organic produce is a booming market. That's also why so many people are taking a second look at woo-woo practices like organic gardening. If you grew that peach yourself, without poisons, you'd feel a lot better about eating it.

This year, when pests or diseases threaten, think before you spray. A few bugs or a handful of chewed leaves is not a crisis and may not need any more attention from you than a thorough spraying with the water hose. If the problem continues or increases, call your Master Gardener hot line (check with your local county extension agent) and ask for an environmentally benign remedy for the trouble. If they can't help, stop by the library and look for books on I.P.M. (Integrated Pest Management), a newly evolving way of dealing with pests by using natural, biological controls. Even older copies of *Rodale's Encyclopedia of Organic Gardening*, or *Garden Pests*, will prove highly helpful. (See the appendix for a book list.)

All of us have simply got to learn to look at the garden, the neighborhood, and the world environment as connected and whole. On the smallest scale, if I poison my roses, the spray drift may well kill your honey bees (not to mention make your cat—or my kid—ill as well). Instead of stocking up on a multitude of poisons, we can arrange plantings that encourage birds to live in our gardens, welcoming them as natural predators, along with a host of beneficial insects that can help keep the destructive ones in balance. Balance is an important concept, one long forgotten or ignored. Now, however, we are having to accept that we are just not in a position to demand that the garden meet our artificial and highly unnatural standards of perfection. Just as we accept a few blemishes in an organic apple, we need to accept a few nibbles in the hosta leaves. We certainly don't have to sit by and watch our gardens disappear, but we do have to rethink what goes into them.

To me, gardening is a lot like bringing up kids; they have the same basic rules of conduct. Choose your ground carefully before you take a stand. Avoid unnecessary battles and compromise whenever possible, always looking for Pareto transactions (win-win, in bankers' terms). Try to help each plant (or person) to take its natural shape and develop its potential fully. Gardening differs in that we can edit out the plants that just don't do well in the conditions we can offer them. We can also actively seek out plants that will enjoy our garden, whether natives and their hybrids, related plant cousins, or imports from similar climate zones all around the world. We can also seek out the healthiest, most adaptable plants to replace our duds. If your yellow roses are always battling black spot, choose the indefatigable and glossy-leaved 'Golden Showers' or the primrose pale, sweet-scented rugosa, 'Agnes', rather than the gorgeous but always sickly 'Sombreil'. If you have too much shade for roses, grow clematis and hostas. If your soil is too sandy for certain plants, fill a couple of tubs with clay-based soil for your pets and fill the rest of the garden with plants that thrive in well-drained soils. By making intelligent plant choices, we choose health for our plants. By making healthy gardens, we can choose health for ourselves.

Once you decide to take the plunge and embrace organic gardening, you'll find there is a lot to like about it. Perhaps the very best part is that a lot of the more active organic gardening practices, like composting and mulch making, make great guy chores. What's more, none of them require face masks or lengthy decontamination procedures. Check it out.

Spittle bugs look disgusting but do relatively little harm to plants. Rather than spraying this lavender with insecticide, I simply rinse the foam off with the hose each time I notice it.

APRIL

Up the Garden Path
Getting Places in the Garden

Most of us make our gardens by eye, shaping our beds and borders according to what we find visually pleasing rather than by strictly logical rules. Paths, however, are apt to be made by feet, which have their own logic: feet seek the line of least resistance. In a young garden, paths are chiefly practical. Rough and unfinished, their course and character are determined by the immediate needs of the garden maker for the work in progress.

As the garden matures, its paths diverge; some remain practical, others become pleasurable. Those that are utilitarian in nature must be wide enough to accept a cart or a wheelbarrow, smooth enough to minimize the stress of a full load. Their surfaces must be usable in all weathers, thus made not of slippery brick but of rough-textured concrete or macadam rather than bone-jarring cobbles. However driven by necessity in form and material, such a path can be starkly beautiful, its elegance of form dictated by its obvious function.

Paths for pleasure emphasize different qualities. Meandering lines imply leisure, while those that hide their destination lend the garden a vital sense of

In April, new foliage in all its first freshness has as much visual impact as most flowers. (Northwest Perennial Alliance Border at the Bellevue Botanic Garden in Bellevue, Washington.)

The surface of this gently sloping path is lightly textured for surer footing in inclement weather. Though the side plantings soften its lines, the path remains wide enough for two. (Garden of Obi Manteufel, Bainbridge Island, Washington.)

as they direct the flow of movement. As we walk them, the paths themselves may entertain our senses. Gravel crunches underfoot, while wood shavings feel as luxuriously yielding as a featherbed. Shredded bark releases the scent of the forest floor, while cocoa bean hulls and coffee chaff evoke more domestic images. Whatever the ambiance, scale, or function, the best paths make a positive contribution to the garden as a whole.

How, then, do we decide which kinds of paths are for us? Should a given path wander or run ruler straight? Should it be soft underfoot, or scrunchy, or slick? How wide is wide enough? The answers lie in our own habits and inclinations. The beginning of the planning process, as always, is a series of questions. What are the practical issues in each part of the garden? Will certain areas be visited by lots of people? How do we want visitors to move through the garden? Do we want to evoke a single ambiance or multiple moods? Do we prefer designs that emphasize variety or uniformity? Is there room to arrange for small visual surprises? Such points are well worth pondering at length, for with a bit of ingenuity, a surprising number of functions can be filled, even within very few, very small spaces.

Once we know more or less where we want the paths to run, we need to contemplate how they might look and feel. Again, there are a number of factors to consider. Which will be working paths, which seasonal, which ornamental, or public? When we have decided all these things to our satisfaction, the actual making of the paths can begin. Actually, the making of some paths begins the minute we enter the garden. The main or entry path is almost always a straight shot from gate or entry to the front door. This is how it should be, for there is no point in gussying up a natural path with useless curves or wiggles that will only annoy you when you are in a hurry.

mystery and depth. Narrow paths feel intimate and direct our attention to the plants. Wide paths invite us to walk with companions, so the garden becomes convivial, the beds and border backdrop to conversation rather than the main event.

During the garden's quiet season, its paths are revealed as important design elements, their surface patterns functioning as garden art. Their materials, textures, and shapes reinforce the garden's ambiance and set the mood in various parts

Another kind of path also makes itself; this is the working path, the one that links the supply area to a work in progress (in this case, the garden). Here, too, a direct and untrammeled route is both more practical and less annoying than a picturesque one. Because working paths lead to the compost heap, the vegetable garden, or the storage shed, they should be wider than whatever you plan to trundle down it. A minimum width of three or four feet allows some slack for the wobbling of a cart under load. Working path surfaces should be smooth but not slippery when wet. Plain old cement can make an ideal surface if lightly brushed (when half set) for a textured rather than slick finish.

Seasonal paths are only in use during certain times of year. They might provide access into the backs of deep borders, or run between beds in the vegetable garden, or thread between a hedge and a garden bed. Access paths can be as simple as a narrow strip of no-plant's-land that lets you enter wide-bodied beds to weed, tidy, and mulch in spring and fall. By summer, these tiny paths are invisible. Discreetly placed stepping-stones work nicely too, especially if you are small, graceful, and well-balanced. If not, then well-defined paths, even if they are a mere foot in width, will prove less damaging to plants and pride than tentative teetering on mid-border bricks.

Public paths are those used by guests as well as temporary visitors like the mail carrier, the U.P.S. delivery person, or the water meter reader. Generally, public paths will feel cramped if they are less than four or five feet wide. In bigger gardens, main paths might be six or eight feet wide without looking out of scale. Paths, like beds, look better when generously proportioned. If they are flanked by plants that flop forward, like catmints (*Nepeta* species), or spread outward, like border bluebeards (*Caryopteris* species), that five-foot

stretch suddenly shrinks to three, room enough for one adult at a time.

If the garden is very small, it is a good idea to have the paths all alike, in the interest of visual unity. If room allows, path surfaces can be varied,

Irregular paving can be tightly pieced together like a crazy quilt, as the English prefer it, or laid out more spaciously, allowing mosses and mat-creepers to fill in the interstices. (Garden of T. R. Welch, Woodinville, Washington.)

the better to facilitate movement in some areas and please the eye in others. Initially, it may be easiest to make grass paths, which feel lovely on

Finely shredded bark feels firm yet giving underfoot. Many similar mulches make excellent path surfaces, offering secure footing even when wet and draining quickly after rain. The decorative hoops of spring-pruned apple twigs help to direct wandering feet. (Northwest Perennial Alliance Border at the Bellevue Botanic Garden in Bellevue, Washington.)

bare feet. However, grass paths quickly become worn if they get much foot traffic, especially in shaded areas, where moss is apt to take over. Grass path edges will also need regular hand trimming to look neat (weed whackers also whack the garden plants). When beds and borders meet hard-surfaced paths, plants can tumble over to soften the edges, giving the garden the relaxed look favored by English designers. (This is one big difference between their gardens and ours: our plants often look regimented, controlled within an inch of their lives. English gardeners strive to make their plants look at home, and the result is relaxed and delightful.)

Gravel paths crunch nicely underfoot when you are wearing shoes, but gravel bits feel horrid if you are wearing sandals and outright painful if you are barefoot. Gravel also has a nasty habit of wandering away from where you want it, whether washed by rain or scattered by feet. Concrete bumpers or curbs serve both to keep grasses and sneaky weeds like creeping buttercups out of beds and to keep gravel in the paths.

To be truly ornamental, qualifying as garden art, paths must be harmonious with the garden in style and scale. There are dozens of ways to combine even ordinary paving materials into intriguing patterns, whether elegantly simple or magnificently baroque. If you live where native rock is lovely and cheap, you can indulge in running ribbons of pewtery slate or smooth granite flagstones. In the Pacific Northwest, paths made with cross-cut rounds of tree trunks are both common and very beautiful. Anywhere, brick can be laid in herringbone stripes or woven like basketwork. Whatever you fancy is fine, but it should be as easy on the feet as on the eye; many a gorgeous path is treacherous when wet or slicked with autumn leaves.

Some of the nicest walkways and paths I have

ever seen have been made from cement, not poured in sleek, boring slabs, but sculpted into rocklike steps, or poured flat and cobbled with smooth pebbles, beachstones, even bits of sea glass and old crockery. The famous paths and steps at Hestercombe (an English garden designed by Edward Lutyens and planted by Gertrude Jekyll) are decorated with running bands of slim flints and rounded cobblestones. Though such work is time-consuming, it is very beautiful, and similar effect can be had by decorating the edges of a path, texturing just enough to be interesting, not a tedious job at all.

Crazy paving paths are also popular in England. These combine oddly shaped flat stones (or chunks of broken-up concrete) into patchwork quilts for the garden. The pieces are cemented together, leaving holes for a few plants. It's always tempting to overplant such paving, but this is both distracting and unsafe. Visiting the garden is much more enjoyable when you don't have to think about your feet all the time. Crevice plants are bound to get stepped on sooner or later, so don't plant anything you value highly in crazy paving. Doormat plants like creeping thymes, oregano, campanulas, and woolly lamb's ear, are to be preferred, for all rebound with insouciance.

Since paths influence the way we approach and use every part of the garden, it's worth doing a bit of research before making any final decisions. Visit public and private gardens and pay particular attention to the paths in each (it's especially useful to do this both during the off-season and in high summer). Take notes about surfaces you find attractive as well as those which feel comfortable or untrustworthy underfoot. Gordon Hayward's wonderful book, *Garden Paths: Inspiring Designs and Practical Projects*, will prove very helpful both when you are planning and installing your paths. Choose well, and your paths will give you a life-

time of loyal service. Make a few mistakes and you will learn an invaluable lesson: absolutely everything is subject to change. Paths, like plants, must periodically undergo the editing process. If they don't suit your needs, or no longer please your eye, it's not a problem, just a great opportunity to explore yet another portion of your own lifelong garden path.

Trailing Clouds of Glory
Spring-Blooming Clematis

In spring, even the newest garden can provide an abundant outpouring of blossom thanks to the triad of flowering trees, shrubs, and bulbs which perform effortlessly in the early months of the year. Adding another element to this exuberant mixture might seem to be gilding the lily, yet when we introduce spring-flowering clematis into our gardens, the spring trio becomes a quartet with which we can create even more satisfying floral compositions. These vines—which occupy very little ground space—are a rewarding group of species and their hybrids, some delicate, some rumbustious, all offer billows of fragrant spring bloom in return for modest care. Better still, their flowers are followed by lovely, feathery seed heads and curtains of handsome foliage that make a textured backdrop for the summer border.

The height clematis offer is especially welcome in small gardens where ground space is precious and every plant must earn its place through multiseasonal virtues. Scaling trellis or post, early clematis will quickly fill the upper level of the garden with a triumphant froth of flowers. Take them off the trellis and weave them through a shaggy informal hedge or drape them over a plain fence, and the result is like hanging a picture on a bare wall. Hoist rosy *Clematis montana* 'Elizabeth' into a towering fir tree and enjoy sheets of vanilla-scented bloom. Rope a ruffly blue *C. macropetala* into a shrubby golden privet, lace a creamy pink alpine clematis through a post-bloom purpleleaf plum tree and let garden synergy more than double the effect of both plants.

Since species clematis don't need hard pruning (just remove the dead and the duds—weak or spindly stems), it's best to pair them within formal partners. This looks pleasingly natural and saves the bother of trying to clip the host without massacring the vine. Remember too that the host must be sturdy enough for the chosen vine: a strapping *Clematis montana* will climb 20 feet up a blue spruce or cover an arbor in short order, and is better placed on a chain-link fence than a young or brittle tree. If no suitable plant host presents itself, smaller species will happily scramble up a tepee or tripod made by fastening strong, straight sticks together with wire or twine.

In a tiny urban garden, the vine of choice is probably *Clematis alpina* (Zone 5), a dainty vine that blooms abundantly in filtered shade or on a north wall. It produces its nodding, frilly bells on old wood, and reaches a mere 6 or 8 feet at maturity, making it a fine decoration for a slim 'Skyrocket' juniper or a leathery rhododendron. The plain species is rare, but there are several good forms, notably 'Ruby', a warm, mauvy rose which glows against red or purple foliage. 'Pamela Jackman' has ocean-blue sepals (the outer "petals") and ivory underskirts lightly brushed with purple, while 'White Moth' is a fluttery, creamy double which looks splendid lacing through variegated euonymous or ivy.

The downy clematis, *Clematis macropetala* (Zone 5), has finely divided petals like blue feathers, reminiscent of tattered double columbines such as 'Nora Barlow' or 'Nora's Sister'. Downy clematis is relatively delicate in scale, seldom exceeding 7 or 8 feet tall, though slightly larger in foliage and bulk than *C. alpina*. I grow 'Bluebird', a bitoned blue (deep and deeper), among the dusky leaves of purple hazel, while 'Rosy O'Grady', a sassy pink with long, pointy sepals, clambers through a twisted old plum tree to mingle with its frosty flowers. The clean white, golden-eyed form called 'Snowbird' needs a dark background, perhaps a glossy camellia or holly, in order to be fully appreciated, for it tends to get lost in a paler setting.

Lustiest of all is *Clematis montana* (Zone 5), a strapping vine which will scramble 20 or 30 feet up a blue spruce, cascade through a sturdy oak, or cover an arbor in creamy, scented sheets. Clearly, a weak or brittle-branched host is not a good idea for such a determined plant, and an immature host could quite possibly be killed by the weight. However, where a suitably stout host or wall position presents itself, do give this vine a home, for the garden holds few sights as stirring as a well-grown *C. montana* in full, triumphant flower. Its blossoms are small, shaped rather like those of dogwood in cream or chalky pink, but exceptionally abundant. 'Alexander' is a vigorous form with especially big, ivory flowers and a strong, carrying fragrance, a good candidate for screening an unwanted view. 'Elizabeth' is also an enthusiast, offering wine-stained foliage as well as clean pink

Fluttery little *Clematis macropetala* 'Rosy O'Grady' is delicate enough not to swamp a young host tree or shrub. Let Rosy trail through a murky purple smoke bush for a delightful effect.

flowers that smell of vanilla and honey. A recent tetraploid form, 'Tetrarose', has coppery foliage and large, dark pink flowers with the scent of nutmeg. Any of these will completely cover a chain-link fence or disguise an ugly garage wall with panache.

Since vines take up so little ground space, it is tempting to crowd their roots with lush, ground-level companions. One always hears that clematis like shade on their roots and sun on their faces, yet they don't enjoy smothering beneath neighboring foliage. Since crowding reduces their health, vigor, and floral output, keep their root zones clear of competition, using a ring of stones or twigs to serve as a permanent reminder. To start off right, give each vine a large hole and plant it rather deeper than usual, burying a few inches of stem as well as the crown. This will not bother the crown at all; indeed, it stimulates dormant buds along the lower stems to wake up, providing extra stems as insurance should the main stem become damaged. Remember to position the clematis at least three or four feet away from its intended support if that, too, is alive—clematis look wonderful in trees and shrubs, but when young they simply can't compete with thirsty tree roots. Once the vine is well established, you can coax its long strands to climb in any direction you like. The young shoots bruise easily, so be gentle but firm. If necessary, it's better to cut a side shoot or two off a tight-hugging stray, rather than try to force those clinging arms to loosen up. Any strands that persist in wandering can be lightly tied into place with twine or twist-ties until they get the message. Once established in their proper position, these vines are nearly always self-supporting, so you can remove any ties that mar the look of the plant.

Clematis have the reputation of preferring alkaline soils, but most perform very nicely in neutral soils and will thrive even in frankly acid clay, so long as their planting hole is well amended with pH-buffering compost and humus-rich amendments like aged manure. Acid soils can be neutralized by adding a handful of dolomite or agricultural lime to the planting mixture, blending it in well. Heavy soils must be lightened with grit or coarse builder's sand to promote quick drainage, while light, sandy ones benefit from a handful of hydrated hydrophilic polymer such as Broadleaf P4 to keep them evenly moist. Where snails or slugs prevail, use a bran-and-metaldehyde bait (the least environmentally objectionable) to protect emerging shoots for the first year or two; after that, the lower stems are woody enough to resist damage. Where pets or other animals share garden turf, a cage of chicken wire or a stiff tube of plastic gutter-guard netting will help to protect those fragile first shoots from damage while guiding them skyward. The fungal wilts that occasionally plague the big, summer-blooming clematis are often traceable to bruising and breakage of new shoots. Species clematis rarely suffer from these wilts—indeed, they are remarkably free of pests and disease problems in general—but they, too, will perform better when undamaged.

Summer-blooming hybrids are rather gross feeders, but most clematis species will remain healthy and productive on a leaner diet. An annual feeding mulch of compost, aged manure, and alfalfa pellets (see page 80) should be applied around their root zone in late winter or early spring, just as active growth recommences. Like any long-lived plant, clematis may take several full years before they begin to dazzle you, but so long as their modest requirements are met, dazzle you they will. Those who have been disappointed in clematis may try these hardy species with an excellent chance of success. Give these generous plants

Vigorous, fragrant *Clematis montana* will twine its searching tendrils around anything that gets in its way. Big vines like this need ample and very secure support. (Garden of Lindsay Smith, Bainbridge Island, Washington.)

a proper start, attend to their simple needs, and they will brighten spring with billows of blossom for many years to come.

Handsome Herbs

Culinary and Craft Plants for Garden Containers

Herbs, plants used for their flavor, scent, or medicinal attributes, are among the oldest of garden inhabitants. The first recorded pleasure gardens, from the hanging gardens of Babylon on, contained herbs as well as ornamentals. Indeed, for millennia, that distinction was rarely made, for nearly every plant grown had medicinal or culinary uses, and practical ones were held in the same esteem as the merely pretty. Eventually, however, herbs and vegetables were set apart in herb or kitchen gardens, strictly segregated from the ornamental areas. Herbs can look very attractive grown this way, but if you haven't room for a separate herb garden, don't feel bound by convention. These days, herbs are grown many ways for many reasons. Some gardeners use herbs in edible landscapes, combined with fruiting trees and shrubs as well as vegetables and flowers. Other gardeners specialize in plants that dry well, mingling silvery herbs with immortelles and everlastings. In some gardens, herbs are grown for their beauty alone. In my own garden, the ornamental borders hold generous quantities of admirable herbs, most of which are used for both culinary and craft purposes as well as garden art.

If you aren't sure how to bring herbs into the garden, let their mature shape and size be your guide. Woody rosemary and lavender make excellent little border shrubs where they are hardy. Big, bold angelica and true valerian are dramatic mid-border accent plants. Diminutive subshrubs like golden lemon thyme and wiry gray beach wormwood (*Artemisia* 'Silver Mound') can edge border or pathway. Herbs with scented foliage like lemon balm, fruit sage, and scented geraniums belong where they can be brushed in passing to release their fragrances to the air. Tall, airy fennels form cloudy pillars at the border back. Tender perennials like lemon verbena can be grown in pots to decorate patio or doorstep in summer, retreating to a sunny indoor window for the winter.

Quite a few woody herbs take kindly to life in pots, which extends their effective range into cold winter regions. Moreover, many tolerate tight shearing as well, so can be clipped into dapper herbal topiary. Glossy *Laurus nobilis* (Zone 7), source of bay leaves, makes agreeably plump balls or charming mock Christmas trees. Sturdy cuttings may also be trained into standards, single-trunked, lollipop-headed trees a few feet high. In the ground, bay laurel becomes a large shrub or small, often multi-trunked tree, slowly reaching 12 to 20 feet. It hates wet feet and is very drought tolerant when established, but plants in containers need more moisture. In winter, they require shelter from frost, but appreciate whatever natural light is available. A sun porch where temperatures don't drop below the high twenties all winter makes an ideal shelter for potted laurels.

Rosemary (*Rosmarinus officinalis*, Zone 6) is similarly adaptable to the indoor-outdoor gypsy life and several selections will thrive in large containers. A flowing ground-cover form, *R.* 'Prostratus' (Zone 8) will pour over the lip of a large stone tub like living water, while the upright 'Tuscan Blue' (Zone 7) will stand sentinal duty in doorway or garden. In the ground, ordinary rosemary becomes a sprawling, informal shrub as much as 6 feet high and 10 feet across in favored spots. Several fine garden forms remain shapelier, including 'Benenden Blue', a tidy clumper some 2 feet high and perhaps 4 feet across, and the more compact 'Huntingdon Blue'. Like many Mediterraneans, rosemary needs full sun and does best in lean soil with good drainage. Richer diets promote lush growth that ages poorly, so overfed plants will need regular replacement.

Lavenders, too, make good pot plants, especially *Lavandula angustifolia* 'Hidcote' (Zone 5), a gray-leaved dwarf form 1 foot tall, with dark purple flowers, and the slightly larger 'Munstead', with green foliage and periwinkle blue flowers. Taller (to 2 feet) garden forms include pink-flowered 'Jean Davis' and rotund, floriferous 'Twickle Purple'. A recent introduction, 'Fred Boutin', offers sea-blue flowers on very long stems, ideal for making lavender bunches and braids. Lavenders do best with plenty of sun and good but well-drained garden soils. Older plants can be clipped to encourage bushiness, but cutting back to old wood will result in bare patches that will not resprout.

English broadleaf cooking sage (*Salvia officinalis*, Zone 3, to 2 feet) is an excellent mixer, for its elegant, gray-green foliage and smooth, mounded form complement every perennial in the garden. It doesn't bloom, but 'Berggarten', a robust, very gray-leaved form, sports stubby, deep-blue flower spikes in early summer. Several culinary forms are splendidly colored, particularly 'Purpurascens', with matte purple leaves and purple flowers set in dark red bracts. 'Tricolor' sage is streaked with cream and pink and soft green, while 'Icterina' is a cheerful lemon and lime blend. All are under 2 feet tall but may spread as much as 3 feet across. They tend to get leggy after a few years, so take a few cuttings in late spring or early summer to ensure a steady supply of plants.

Border oreganos include sunny *Origanum vulgare* 'Aureum' (Zone 3, to 2 feet) as well as cream-splashed 'Variegatum', both of which form soft, cascading mounds crowned with airy purple florets clustered at the tips of arching stems. These stone-shaped plants contrast pleasingly with sharp bladed iris or crocosmias, and their long-lasting leaves contribute color for months on end. Ornamental hybrids like 'Hopley's Purple' and 'Kent Beauty' (both probably Zone 7) are modest-looking plants, low growing and dark leaved, but offer rather showier flowers or bracts in shades of lavender or rose and purple. These flower heads dry very nicely, holding both herby scent and color well, and make a nice adjunct to kitchen herb wreaths. These relatively tender oreganos are happy to grow in large pots, perhaps decorating the feet of a laurel or lavender. They, too, like sun and good, open soils, growing well at the border's edge or placed where they can dangle their long arms over a wall.

Mints offer a multitude of pretty and flavorful forms, with scents ranging from apple to pineapple. Variegated apple mint (*Mentha* x *rotundifolia* 'Variegata', Zone 4, to 1½ feet) is among the handsomest in manners as well as looks. It spreads moderately fast, small clumps melting into thick carpets of fresh green, each leaf iced

Bushy and well-rooted, this young rosemary plant will fill out rapidly as the season warms up. The gray, round-leaved immortelle beside it is *Helichrysum petiolare*, which will spill in silvery cascades by midsummer. (Withy/Price garden, Seattle, Washington.)

with a sugary white rim, each stalk tipped with pink-and-white flower heads. It is one of the few mints I grow in the open ground, for it can be kept firmly in check through annual thinning and resetting. Most others, however beautiful, are confined to pots which are in turn set into solid saucers to prevent their persistent, seeking roots

Ornamental oreganos like this dusky beauty (*Origanum laevigatum* 'Herrenhausen') can do double duty, moving easily between the border and the kitchen or cutting garden.

divided every year or it will exhaust its soil. It will continue to grow—you can't keep a good mint down—but its plumy stalks will be dwarfed and its flowers less generous.

These and dozens of other gardenworthy herbs await our notice. We might weave fragrant thyme carpets of creeping sprawlers and little sub-shrubs, plain and variegated, their living shag alive with bees. Catmints and yarrows, borage and burnet might all earn their way into our ornamental gardens. Common myth suggests that all herbs are wild plants which will grow in the worst conditions without care. In truth, though herbs are indeed adaptable and tough, they will be healthier and handsomer if given decent conditions. Treat herbs like dirt and they will look like weeds. Treat them as if they were garden perennials, recognizing and serving their simple needs, and these ornamental herbs will repay your care many times over.

The Art of Eating

Feeding for Floral Frenzy

April borders are still full of bare spots, for though the garden race is well begun, it isn't until May that the soil disappears completely beneath a billow of greenery. Plants waking up from their long winter nap are hungry, eager to feed shoots and roots, and fast unfurling new leaves. Now, while ground is still visible between plants, we can apply spring feeding mulches to get our ardent plants off to a great start. Gross feeders like roses, bearded iris, and delphiniums appreciate an autumnal meal as well, but for most plants, from border trees and shrubs to perennials and bulbs, a single spring feeding will satisfy their supplemental nutritional needs for the whole year.

Though commercial feeds abound, home-made ones are preferable for several reasons. For one thing, commercial foods tend to be like plant steroids, promoting quick bulk and spectacular

from sneaking through the drainage holes. Suckered by its long, fluffy mauve flower heads, I mistakenly allowed the silver-frosted buddleia mint (*M. longifolia*, Zone 6) to roam through a large-scale border. After a year, I removed a full garden cart (nearly 6 square feet) full of thick, white roots from a scant square yard of ground. Now, buddleia mint is sequestered along the driveway where the U.P.S. truck keeps it at bay. It will grow very nicely in a large container, but must be

bloom rather than steady, sensible growth and production. Too much fertilizer can burn or kill young or stressed plants, including new transplants, fresh divisions, or mail-order acquisitions. Mature plants are better equipped to take up stronger nutritional doses, yet in mixed borders or small gardens, less is usually better than more. Even when well staked, overfed plants produce excessively lush foliage which collapses under heavy summer rains, leaving smothered neighbors and unsightly gaps in their wake. Overfed plants also require more water and more grooming, and those which continue active growth well into autumn are prone to winterkill.

In contrast, custom feeding blends can promote steady, appropriate plant growth while conditioning and enriching the soil. By doctoring the mix a bit, we can offer plants both quick-release and slower, long-lasting foods, or design specific mulches for a few pampered pets with special needs. Besides, mixing a batch of plant food is a pleasant operation, reminiscent of making bread for the family.

Feeding mulches are indeed a bit like bread, for they are the staff of garden life, made from simple and wholesome ingredients. All plants, but especially young ones, need good soil and good growing conditions, which means enough space

Where favorite herbs are too tender to winter safely out of doors, they can be persuaded to thrive in pots and containers, which can shelter in basement or garage over the winter. (Garden of Lindsay Smith, Bainbridge Island, Washington.)

and water, light and air, and the right food, easily digested and readily available. Unlike a chemically induced high, these factors ensure long-term health and success in the garden.

So what makes a good feeding mulch? Since few of us start out with perfect—or even reasonably good—garden dirt, soil amendments are the main component. Here in the maritime Northwest, soils tend to be high in potassium, but low in phosphorus. Bonemeal and rock phosphate will boost phosphorus levels, the former immediately, the latter over time, so they are generally used in combination. Our soils are often low in nitrogen as well, so we add aged manure and alfalfa pellets, both of which improve the tilth, or texture, of the soil as well. To reduce the natural acidity, we can use dolomite or agricultural lime. Kelp meal, like a soil vitamin pill, adds trace minerals and elements. Some or all of these ingredients can be used, depending on what kind of gardening you want to do.

East of the mountains, my mother gardens on hardpan, alkaline soil, so her amendments look a bit different. She, too, uses a lot of naturally neutral ingredients like compost and aged manures, but instead of lime, she might add gypsum to encourage her heavy soil to develop a finer grain and to boost the naturally low levels of calcium and sulfur. A mere mile or two away from my garden, an elderly friend keeps her delightful garden jam-packed all year round despite its base of pure sand. She, too, adds large amounts of mulch and compost to her soil every year, enough so that her garden stays fresh all summer though she waters less often than any of her neighbors. Further up the island, a woman whose sloping land runs

down to Puget Sound gardens on silty soil that locks up tight in summer, becoming impervious to water. To keep her soil open, she adds large quantities of coarse grit or builder's sand to let in air and water, as well as humus to help retain moisture. To learn which amendments will be most helpful in your particular situation, contact your local county extension agent. Local nurseries and experienced gardeners will also prove better resources than any generic guide can be.

My favorite all-purpose spring feeding mulch is one of the simplest. Try this one on lawns, established borders, and mature gardens where most of the plants have settled in nicely, or use it to perk up a tired hedge or shrubbery. Neutral in pH, it couples long-term soil conditioners with a quick but moderate dose of nitrogen (manure and alfalfa are synergistic, releasing more nitrogen when used together than alone).

It's much easier to measure parts by volume, using the same scoop or bucket for each ingredient, than to try and weigh everything out. Mix things up in the wheelbarrow, then transfer any leftovers to a watertight container (small, heavy plastic garbage cans are ideal).

Basic Broadcast Feeding Mulch

2 parts large, untreated alfalfa pellets

1 part aged manure (bagged is fine)

1 part compost

Check hay and feed stores for good prices on bulk alfalfa pellets; 50 pounds of untreated dairy feed alfalfa should run you about $7.50 and will cover about 200 square feet of border. Toss it around in generous double handfuls, directing them toward bushes and border plants, or aiming

Hybrid tea roses like the fabulous, fragrant 'Just Joey' are garden hogs, demanding deep, luscious soil, plenty of water, and a constant supply of nourishment. In borders, roses nearly always require more food than their neighbors.

for a generally even scattering on lawns or in heavily planted areas. (With big pellets over an inch long, you should see roughly four pellets per 3-inch square of soil.) You can blend the ingredients in a wheelbarrow before spreading or broadcast them separately by the scoop.

A terrific general-purpose spring feeding mixture comes from The Territorial Seed Company, famous for selling regionally appropriate vegetables only to gardeners west of the Cascades. Their spring tonic mixture is suitable for vegetable gardens or mixed plantings in new gardens, or where soil is unimproved or exhausted of nutrients. Strong mixtures like this are not broadcast, but placed around each plant individually and scratched into the soil or covered with additional mulch. This individual treatment not only reduces waste of costly fertilizers, but encourages us to pay attention to our plants, admiring their individual progress and spotting potential problems before they escalate. It is also ecologically smart, since excess fertilizer is a significant water pollutant and nearly all of it comes not from agriculture but from homeowners. (Fertilizers are much too expensive for farmers to misuse.)

Spring Tonic Mixture

4 parts cottonseed or soy meal

1 part dolomite or agricultural lime

1 part rock phosphate or $1/2$ part bonemeal

$1/2$ part kelp meal

Scatter a thin layer of feed around each plant, from the crown or trunk out to what will be the dripline in midsummer, then lightly scratch it into the soil. (Fertilizers left exposed to air and rain will quickly turn rank, so they must be integrated into the top inch or two of soil.) After two weeks, blanket the bed or border with Basic Broadcast Feeding Mulch.

Whether your soil is naturally acid, base, or neutral, there are plenty of plants that will like it just fine. If you grow a lot of native plants, or have spent time learning what grows well in your soils, the last thing you want to do is alter its pH. Here is a good neutral soil booster for established ornamental borders. Neutral compost replaces the lime, and rock phosphate gives way to a combination of steamed bonemeal, which is immediately available to the plants, and raw bonemeal, which breaks down slowly. This feeding mulch is not broadcast, but scattered around each plant and lightly scratched into the soil. After two weeks, blanket the bed or border with Basic Broadcast Feeding Mulch.

Neutral Spring Border Booster

5 parts compost

4 parts cottonseed or soy meal

$1/3$ part raw bonemeal

$1/3$ part steamed bonemeal

$1/2$ part kelp meal

Unless you are blessed with deep, near neutral loam, soil building is as much a constant as feeding and will prove at least as helpful to your plants. The easiest way to introduce soil amendments is by blending them deeply into the borders before you plant them. However, there is no need to disturb an established garden, for they can also be worked into feeding mulches. Scatter them thickly on top of the soil and let the worms do the mixing for you.

This stunning border is shown in its very first year, a convincing testament to what the designers call "the power of poop"—lavish mulches of aged manure. (Northwest Perennial Alliance Border at the Bellevue Botanic Garden in Bellevue, Washington.)

MAY

Building Garden Communities
Matching Cultural Needs

Much is said about the differences of climate and plant behavior that separate gardeners in various countries and regions. Indeed, though English garden books continue to be enormously popular on this side of the water, even their most ardent appreciators hasten to qualify their enjoyment as fantasy. "Of course, we can't possibly make such gorgeous gardens over here," they often say, or, "Obviously those plants won't grow for us as they do in England." It is very true that gardening in England is quite a different experience from gardening in North Dakota, or Florida, or even California, let alone upstate New York. However, any of us can make the kind of garden we admire, planting in a particular style, anywhere we happen to live. Which plants we use will vary, but the effects we achieve with them can be amazingly similar, so long as we use plants that are well adapted to our locale. This is true because the basics of gardening remain virtually the same all over the world. Wherever we live, no matter which plants our garden holds, those plants still need the nourishment of sun and soil, air and water. In every region, in every climate, all gardeners must

The glowing golden hood and unfurling foliage of western skunk cabbage, *Lysichitum americanum*. Like its eastern counterpart, this magnificent native wildflower adapts well to life in the border.

do the same two things. We must learn which plants will grow happily under the conditions we can offer, and we must discover precisely what those conditions are.

For most of us, seeking out practical plants is too much fun to feel like work. We begin by touring local nurseries and gardens, seeing what is readily available and growing well for others. Next, we consult books such as Nicola Ferguson's *Right Plant, Right Place* (see the appendix), an extremely useful handbook which lists plants of all sorts that thrive in shade or drought or despite pollution. Let's not neglect specialty nursery catalogs either, particularly those which serve our corner of the world. We might contact the local county extension agent or master gardener program as well. As our skills and curiosity grow, we look farther afield, to regional botanic gardens, native plant societies, or educational institutions with active horticultural programs. By the time we have done all this, our list of possible garden plants will be considerable, even if we live in Willow, Alaska, or Brownsville, Texas.

If we want to stretch the envelope a little further, we try to find places and ways to coax less reliable plants to grow for us. All over the country, there are dedicated (possibly even fanatical) gardeners who consistently grow things they aren't supposed to be able to. Grow rosemary in Ontario? The fabled blue Himalayan poppy in Vermont? Impossible, right? Well, no. Not impossible, just not according to the rules. When you read garden books and nursery catalogs, you will notice that there are often widely diverging opinions about a given plant's hardiness. One source will assert firmly that a certain shrub is only hardy to Zone 6, while another cheerfully recommends it for Zone 4 and a third puts it more conservatively into Zone 5. These differences of opinion reflect each author's experience and probably that of their friends and connections within the horticultural community. It also reflects their temperaments; some people like to play it very safe while others prefer to encourage the spirit of hopeful experimentation which prompts gardeners to keep trying to grow the "wrong" things. Less sanguine authorities think this a silly waste of time and money. The risk takers see it as a thrilling challenge in which they may, however unexpectedly, succeed. If not, well, no harm done—another good plant gone west, but that can happen to the best of us under the best of circumstances. If our gamble pays off, then we have enriched not just our own gardens, but the whole gardening community. This doesn't mean that the person who assigned that shrub to Zone 4 is wrong or foolhardy, but it may mean that the shrub in question will indeed grow nicely in Zone 4 so long as all its cultural needs are met. In Zone 5, it may only need careful placement, while in Zone 6, it may survive rough or callous treatment.

This business of cultural needs is a key concept, and those who get away with horticultural outrages like growing rosemary in Ontario often succeed because they pay wholehearted attention to each plant's requirements. Sometimes such plants survive in unlikely places because gardeners are willing to go to great lengths to make them comfortable. Perhaps they build special winterizing containers for their plants, or bring them indoors to winter over in the basement or sun porch. In other cases, the magic is worked more simply; if the plant prefers good drainage, the gardener plants it in sandy soil, or adds copious amounts of fine grit or coarse sand to open up a heavier, clay-based soil. A winter-blooming plant may be coddled in a sheltered corner, protected from battering winds by evergreens or house walls, its root zone carpeted with a thick, evergreen ground cover. Borderline tender plants or those that often lose buds to late frosts are placed away from early morning sun, for branches or buds frozen after a cold night expand too quickly in that sudden warmth, so their stems split or their cells burst. If they thaw more slowly, as they do in north- or west-facing corners, they will be ready to receive the benison of afternoon sun.

Of all the techniques and guiding theories we can learn from great gardeners around the world, the most universally useful are those which govern plant placement. Our primary goal is to choose and use plants so that their natural qualities are exactly what we want from them. Our next goal is to treat them so well that they need very little care. In order to do this, we must discover and try to meet each plant's cultural needs, then develop groups or communities of plants with similar requirements. Doing this serves both the gardener and the plants. Such like-minded communities simplify care, since all members appreciate the same sort of soil and amendments, the same kind of feeding, and the same amount of water. Proper care improves the health of the whole group; very often plants fail because we want them to live where they cannot thrive. Proper placement reduces the stresses that arise when we try to impose our will by asking plants to behave inappropriately, against their natural proclivities. By turning things around and finding out instead what each plant needs and what it does best, we greatly increase the likelihood that our plants will grow well and that we will be pleased with the results of our efforts.

We can more effectively expand our plant palette after we have identified all the microclimates and varying conditions we can offer them. Though a small yard may not seem to offer much variety, observe it closely over the seasons. Plots with uniform conditions are very unusual, and virtually none remain unchanged through the

The fabulous Himalayan blue poppy is the stuff garden dreams are made of. Inspired by plant love, a surprising number of gardeners have managed to please this proud beauty in some highly improbable places.

year. One side may be shadier or moister than the other. A sloping hillside may be hot and dry if south facing, cool and shaded if north facing. Quick-draining, sandy soil may give way quite suddenly to stodgy clay or rocky loam. The entryway may be sunny and exposed, hot with reflected heat off sidewalks and neighboring buildings. The inner yard may receive blocked or broken light thanks to those same buildings. The back

Putting our plants in places they enjoy or can adapt to readily makes good horticultural sense. Grouping those plants into like-minded communities greatly increases our chances for successful garden making. (Garden of Bobbie Garthwaite and Joe Sullivan, Bainbridge Island, Washington.)

ter bloomers like hellebores, and to persuade borderline hardy plants to settle in. Once you have located and identified the particular nature of as many special condition areas as possible, mark them on your garden map. (If you don't have a garden map yet, this is a great time to make one. Even a very simple sketch, with blobs for each area, will be a helpful reminder during the planning process.) Now, armed with plant list and site map, you have enough information to begin to figure out what to put where.

The typical suburban lot is planted with appalling lack of imagination, let alone any appreciation of its possibilities. This is sad, because however simple, such lots hold many—or at least several—areas, each with a distinct character just waiting to be recognized. Once your investigative garden tours turn them up, you can begin to develop their potential. The more you know about each part of your garden, the more you can emphasize its qualities, increasing the range and variety of both plants and ambiance that even a small garden can encompass. Let us suppose that your front yard holds a flowering cherry tree, all alone in a dull sea of grass. Surround it with a small community of shade-loving plants, and that lonely, rather meaningless tree becomes the focal point of the yard. Beneath its canopy might spread an intermingled colony of dwarf rhododendrons, ferns, and wildflowers that tolerate dry shade. Luckily, there are scads of them, from lungworts (pulmonarias) to big, balloon-flowered evergreen spurges, *Euphorbia robbiae*.

Next, we turn our hand to the barren sidewalk strip and the sloping, south-facing hillside. You might plant these with mounding Mediterranean herbs like rosemary and lavender or carpet them with creeping thymes laced with hundreds of small bulbs. You can fill the hot, gritty driveway strip with desert, prairie, or beach plants—spiky

may seem empty yet be overhung with large shade trees, its soil compacted and full of roots. The more we know about the site, the better we can assess which plants will succeed in each of its areas.

Look, too, for protected places that are sheltered from wind and early morning sun in winter yet are open in summer. Such hot spots make attractive seating areas even during the colder months. Their mild microclimate makes them good places to coax extra performances from win-

yuccas, golden perennial sunflowers, and ruffled, blue-leaved sea kale (*Crambe maritima*). The damp, shadowy walkway between the garage and the house becomes enchanting when paved with flagstones and thick moss. Its bare walls might be decked with summer-blooming clematis or gold-splashed ivy, while a little wall-hung recirculating fountain makes the endless music of falling water echo through the warm months.

Sometimes you will have to make changes before your communities will grow well. The cherry tree, for instance, has probably infiltrated the ground beneath it with questing roots. Before you give it neighbors, you need to make a hospitable place for them. Take up the sod that surrounds it and lay down a circle—or oval or irregular sweep—of horticultural barrier cloth to keep those hungry tree roots from robbing your new bed. (Leave a 12- to 18-inch ring of free space around the tree's crown, however, to keep it from smothering.) Cover your cloth with fresh topsoil or compost; a depth of 8 to 12 inches is sufficient to grow practically anything. Slope the soil down at the edges of the bed, and in toward the tree's crown, knitting these little hillsides in place with small, fine-textured ground covers like *Vinca minor* 'Miss Jekyll's White' (Zone 4) or our native Allegheny spurge, *Pachysandra procumbens* (Zone 5). Now you can fill the new garden space with kindred spirits like hostas and Solomon's seal, knowing they will relish both the conditions and the company.

Plants, like people, thrive in supportive community. When different conditions and microclimates are emphasized, it is possible to create plant communities with very different needs, even where ground space is strictly limited. When plants are placed where they want to be, surrounded with appropriate companions, in return those plants offer the very best performance.

The Stuff of Romance
Peonies for Small Gardens

In my garden, May brings a favorite though fleeting partnership. Early on, a compact peony called 'Audrey' opens in the dappled shade beneath an ancient apple tree, her plump buds unfurling into creamy pink blossoms with a mild, innocent fragrance. 'Audrey' is not a beruffled double peony but rather has delicate single flowers, their petals cupped into bowls. These are delightful in themselves, but the soft spring breezes transform them

When plants of many kinds are grouped according to their cultural needs, they form naturalistic communities. Here, sun-loving plants appreciate the extra heat reflected off the graveled path. (Garden of Steven Antonow, Seattle, Washington.)

into the stuff of magic. From the apple tree above, pale flowers sift down like fragrant pink snow, filling the rosy cups with petal fall.

This is Audrey's moment of glory, long awaited and soon over. Some gardeners grudge ground space to herbaceous peonies, feeling that their flo-

The tight, glossy buds of the double fernleaf peony, *Paeonia tenuifolia* 'Rubra Plena', expand almost overnight into big, ruffled, ruby red blossoms. The plant's shrubby form and thready foliage make it a valuable addition to the border in or out of flower.

ral contribution is too evanescent. Were it their only strength, the point would be well taken, yet they are no briefer in bloom than lilacs, tulips, and many another beloved plant, few of which are as decorative out of bloom as a happy peony. Hardy, (most hybrids to Zone 3), healthy, easy to please, and amazingly long-lived, peonies would seem a natural choice for busy gardeners, and it is curious that they no longer enjoy the popularity they have always merited. Once a staple of garden and border, peonies fell out of fashion during the middle decades of the century as longer-blooming perennials reached the nursery market. These traditional favorites deserve a revival, for peonies have virtues beyond mere blossom.

Like rhododendrons, peonies are best chosen as whole plants. While it is fine to fall for a flower, we can ask—and receive—a lot more from a peony than pretty blooms. In late winter, their new shoots emerge splendidly lacquered in ruby or burgundy or black, the color especially rich when Japanese species figure into their bloodlines. Young peony foliage is deeply quilted and veined, its top sides glossed with a metallic sheen of bronze or copper. Thanks to complex ancestry, peony foliage is diverse in texture and form, varying from feathery and finely divided to bold, big lobed, and leathery. When mature, it develops a distinctly exotic quality, for few common perennials have so large or shapely a leaf. Exciting in spring, dependable in summer, peony foliage often takes on handsome autumn color as glossy greens deepen to orange and copper, gold and bronze. Showy seed-pods, lined with screaming pink silk and packed with jet black seeds, may further extend fall interest. Though old-fashioned estate peonies may be too big for tiny modern gardens, lovely dwarf peonies abound. Where space permits, the largest peonies should be welcomed as excellent foliage plants which bring the sculptural solidity of shrubs to the border, anchoring lesser creatures with their majestic bulk.

Perhaps peonies would be more popular if the densely doubled blossoms known as bombs weren't the most common flower form. For one thing, their blowsy heads often draggle in the mud, for the sturdiest stems will bend beneath their considerable weight. For another, their flamboyant artificiality makes them look ill at ease in naturalistic settings, like a duchess at a real picnic, trying to eat soggy chips with a plastic fork and finding the experience far from quaint. Up-facing single peonies and the delicate Japanese, or anemone-flowered, varieties perform nicely in wet weather and have a grace of line which makes them better mixers in informal or woodsy gardens. Singles have one or two rows of broad petals, usually cupped or chalice shaped, with a central boss of flossy yellow stamens. Japanese peonies are similar but slightly fuller, their hearts filled with tufted, ribbony petaloides. Semi-doubles are looser than bombs but more ruffled and fluttery than singles, with shaggy hearts of gold. Peonies are also classified for bloom time, ranging from the very early, which open in late April or early May, to the very late, which bloom at the tail end of June, so although each individual peony may flower for no more than a few weeks, careful selection will deliver a steady stream of peonies over several months.

Among the first to bloom for me is 'Sanctus', diminutive in stature but large of leaf and covered in April with glowing white single flowers. Under 2 feet in height, it could grace the tiniest garden, though mine is placed halfway into a large border. It nestles beneath an arching, white Spanish broom, *Cytisus multiflorus*, the pair encircled with green and white viridiflora tulips called 'Spring Green' in a truly breathtaking combination. It is followed shortly by 'Coral Charm', a stunning

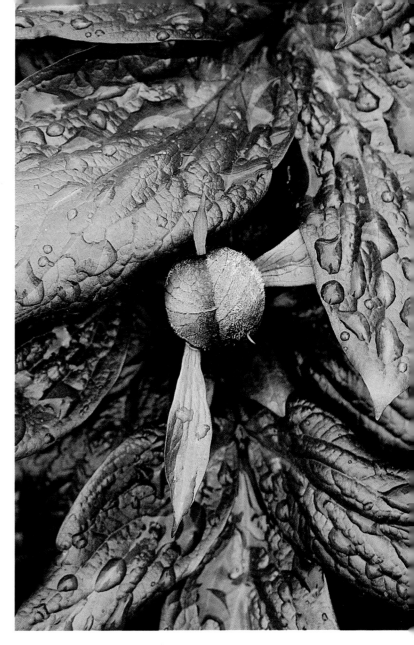

Peony foliage is often remarkably beautiful in its own right. The leaves of many hybrids are excitingly bronzed and lacquered in spring, then color marvelously again in autumn.

semi-double which may be memorably partnered with 'Apricot Beauty' tulips against dusky purple hazel (*Corylus maxima* 'Purpurea') or ruddy sand cherry, *Prunus* x *cistena*. 'Coral Charm' is a good-sized plant, reaching 3 feet in height and girth, but in a smaller garden, the dwarfer 'Coral Sunset' would fill the same color niche. Those who like the feathery foliage of the fernleaf peony, *Paeonia tenuifolia*, but find its high price tag prohibitive will be delighted by the early single

'Laddie', a diminutive border peony with delicate foliage and glossy, single blossoms the color of ripe cherries. Pair this one with the regal red early tulip 'Couleur Cardinal' and the midnight red dwarf border quince called *Chaenomales* 'Fuji' for a heart-warming garden valentine.

A few weeks later, peonies are opening thick and fast. 'Monseigneur Martin Cahuzac', an older

Species peonies have their own graces and virtues, among them an elegant simplicity of form. *Paeonia veitchii* var. *woodwardii* grows happily in my mixed borders, never plagued by pests or problems.

hybrid still considered to be the darkest of all peonies, holds up midnight red blossoms against a cascade of dark red barberry, while hot red oriental poppies just beginning to pop are sandwiched between the two. Down the border a bit, tall stalks of pearly, green-eyed 'White Innocence' (to 6 feet) tower above a froth of white Jupiter's beard, *Centranthus ruber* 'Album', and the creamy, luminous double 'Prairie Moon' peeps through a cloud of white *Clematis recta*. By mid-June, the shell-pink single 'Seashell' opens in concert with billows of white sea kale, *Crambe cordifolia*. As July approaches, lava red blossoms of 'Mt. St. Helens' open like fragrant fireworks. Last of all comes the midsized double 'Chinook', a frilly fantasy in pastel salmon fading to peach ice which finds sympathetic echoes in the glorious, gingery tea rose, 'Just Joey'.

Though peonies are most often grown in full sun, shade gardeners need not deny themselves the pleasure of their company. Most species and hybrids bloom abundantly in light or filtered shade, and their ephemeral flowers last considerably longer out of the sun. Wherever you choose to plant them, prepare their future dwelling place with especial care, since the peony you plant this year may still be hale and hearty when Halley's Comet returns. Peonies prefer humusy, neutral to slightly acid soils, but their strictest requirement is for good drainage. Their roots dislike constant wet; indeed, well-established peonies are highly tolerant of drought. Open heavy soils by adding plenty of coarse builder's sand, and enrich light, sandy ones with generous helpings of humus. Make the hole several feet deep, then fill the bottom with compost and aged manure. Add a layer of good soil to keep the manure a discreet distance from the roots, making a high-centered mound. Place the crown so that the "eyes" (buds) will be an inch or two below the soil surface, with the roots dangling down the sides. Deeper planting can cause peonies to be "blind," or flowerless, so lightly mark the stems with tape to give yourself an accurate depth indicator. Fill in the hole, water it well, and double check your planting depth. If in doubt, plant shallowly rather than deep, making up the difference with mulch.

Properly planted peonies need very little care. A light mulch of compost and bonemeal in spring and fall will keep them fit year round. Trimming off all foliage at year's end will largely eliminate diseases: It's that simple. Problems usually arise when plants are overfed, especially where springs are cool and wet. Though plants on leaner diets are rarely troubled, excess nitrogen can encourage disfiguring botrytis blight which burns new shoots and blasts buds. If peony foliage or buds turn black, carefully cut away all affected stems at ground level and burn them (sterilize your clippers with rubbing alcohol to avoid spreading the problem). After the foliage collapses in autumn, trim away all peony leaves and stems and burn them too, for tossing them on the compost could spread the pathogen through the garden. Observe these precautions scrupulously and the problem should resolve itself.

It's best to shop for peonies when the plants are blooming so you can judge their relative merits for yourself, rather than being swayed by catalog prose (or mine, either). Garden center peonies grown in pots may be transplanted any time, but if you select your peonies from a specialty nursery (which is an excellent way to see a wide variety of mature plants), expect to pick up or receive your division in autumn. Give new plants an extra thick blanket of mulch to bring them safely through their first winter. After that, they will require only a few minutes of care a few times a year, surely a modest demand from plants that may offer a century's worth of garden glory.

Wild Things
Native Shade Flowers with Willing Ways

Here in the maritime Northwest, many gardens are dominated by towering trees, our borders displayed against the lush understory of native salal (*Gaultheria shallon*), evergreen huckleberry (*Vaccinium ovatum*), and feathery young cedars. Maturing gardens throughout the country are similarly blessed with large trees, their sunny patches shrinking over the years. Though we may initially fret about the prevalence of shade, a bit of catalog browsing will convince us to see it as an asset. Not only will many border perennials flower quite well in light shade, but there exists a great and varied host of native American wildflowers which will bloom cheerfully beneath sheltering trees. Most are healthy, hardy creatures which adapt well to woodsy garden or mixed border settings while requiring (indeed, preferring) a minimum of human intervention.

To find such cooperative plants, we need only to step out our own back doors. Shady lanes and woods and even some city alleys are full of flowers in May. Our Seattle alley held such escaped Europeans as ruddy Jupiter's beard (*Centranthus ruber*) and silver-podded money seed (*Lunaria annua*), as well as true natives like bleeding heart (*Dicentra formosa*). (I am often asked whether this is really a Chinese plant hailing from Formosa; the Latin for that would be *formosana*, while *formosa* means "shapely.") Their flowers dance down curving stems like rosy hearts above lacy foliage that has the look of flat Italian parsley. It is something of a thug, spreading faster than is really considered polite, and its flowers are usually very dull shades of pink. However, it has numerous gardenworthy cousins, notably the prettier and less aggressive southern form found in the Oregon woods (*D. f.* ssp. *oregona*, Zone 3, to 15 inches), with lavender-tipped ivory flowers and feathery, intensely blue foliage that persists all summer and turns gentle gold in fall. A finer-textured version, delicate as fennel, is called 'Boothman's Variety' or 'Stuart Boothman' (they are one and the same, hardy to Zone 3, to 12 inches), with dark, rosy flowers. Runners rather than clumpers, they make exciting ground covers in shrubby borders. Their moderate spread is easily controlled, and extra bits can always be swapped for friends' treasures.

In my neighborhood, ditch banks and road verges are softened by masses of foamflower, *Tiarella trifoliata* (Zone 4, to 20 inches), a charming low carpeter with rounded leaves, often as boldly lobed as those of maples, and sheaves of greeny white bells on slender stalks. Given shade and good garden soil, a colony of foamflower will bloom from late spring through summer. Once they begin to self-sow, select plants with bigger or more deeply lobed foliage for propagation to develop your own strain. The eastern version, *T. cordifolia* (Zone 3, to 14 inches), has starry little flowers in soft shades of pink or ivory. It, too, shows quite a variety of leaf forms. Several catalog nurseries offer fine selected forms such as *T. c.* var. *collina*, the oakleaf tiarella.

Though its flowers, little bells striped in cream and chocolate, are curious rather than pretty, the similar-looking western piggy-back plant, *Tolmiea menziesii* (Zone 6, to 18 inches), is always fun to grow. In its native woods and meadows, its fuzzy round foliage, lobed and scalloped, is often evergreen. Elsewhere, it is a favorite children's houseplant, prized for carrying its babies atop the leaves. A cheerful, variegated form called 'Taff's Golden' might better be called 'Taff's Butter and

Cream', for true gold it is not, yet it does brighten its corner with the look of soft sunshine. Brightest in spring, it dims to an attractive, dappled chartreuse in summer.

False Solomon's seal, *Smilacina racemosa* (Zone 4, 3 to 5 feet), is a widespread native found in many parts of the country. It has several distinct regional forms, so plants bought as southeastern natives will be compact and usually under 3 feet in height, while western plants run considerably taller. Both boast graceful, arching stems hung with narrow leaves, each wand tipped with a long, creamy panicle of fluffy, fragrant florets. (Real Solomon's seal, *Polygonatum biflorum*, looks very similar, but dangles little ivory bells down its stems.) By summer's end, the flowers have been replaced by fat little red berries which become speckled with purple and black as they ripen. Elegant rather than showy, false Solomon's seal makes a handsome, upright companion for mounded foliage plants like lady's mantle (*Alchemilla mollis*) and dwarf hydrangeas, which also bloom nicely in light shade.

Where boldness is wanted, our native skunk cabbages make splendid and dramatic border plants. The English find them irresistible and are always puzzled that we don't use these strapping beauties in our gardens. Perhaps people are put off by the common name, but unless the foliage is wantonly crushed, these plants don't stink at all. Indeed, floral designer Barry Ferguson uses skunk cabbage in stunning large-scale flower arrangements. "Stand the flower stems outdoors in a pail of warm water for a few hours before using them, and the unpleasant scent will be completely gone," he reassures the timid, with perfect truth. Looked

West coast native *Trillium chloropetalum* boasts dramatic, dappled foliage as well as fascinating flowers. The East coast native, *T. sessile*, is quite similar; both grow happily in garden settings where their simple needs are met.

Our magnificent native skunk cabbages are highly prized in England, where they are considered splendid architectural border plants. Don't let the common name put you off; unless they are damaged, there's absolutely nothing skunky about these gorgeous creatures.

emerging through the chilly ground in late winter. By spring, the spathes are vivid yellow and quite showy. The big spathes of western skunk cabbage, *Lysichiton americanum* (Zone 7, to 4 feet) emerge frog green and gentle to citrus yellow, while those of *L. camtschatcense* (Zone 6, to 3 feet) are glowing white. All are readily grown from fresh seed, available in most bogs and wetlands, or can be bought from wetland plant nurseries.

The East Coast woods offer several picturesque natives with striking foliage to contrast with broad hostas and airy ferns. Plants grown from seed are available from many specialty nurseries, and though transplanted wildlings rarely survive, nursery plants can do well in the garden. Their greatest needs are to be given the conditions they crave—humus-rich soil, consistently moist but never soggy, and partial or filtered shade—and to be left undisturbed while dormant. Dapper Jack-in-the-pulpit, *Arisaema triphyllum* (Zone 4, to 3 feet), sends up flaring, tubular green flowers striped in subfusc tints of brown or purple between large three-fingered leaves. A striking pale form, *A. t.* var. *stewardsonii*, has clean white markings, while *A. t.* 'Zebrinus' wears stripes of ministerial black and white. Southern dragonroot, *Arisaema dracontium* (Zone 3, to 3 feet), would be worth growing just for the name, but the long-tailed green flower is weirdly wonderful, arriving alone and leafless in mid-spring, and followed by big, divided leaves and chunky little tomato-colored berries in summer. Mayapples, *Podophyllum peltatum* (Zone 3, to 18 inches), are impressive all season long. The stalks erupt like little white knobs in early spring, then leap up into tightly furled umbrellas. By April, these snap open into fringed parasols a foot or so high, and by May each stem sports two leaves above a fat white flower, soon followed by plump yellow fruit. As a child, I read that the fruits were used by the local

at closely, skunk cabbages are indeed glorious plants. In early spring, their great candles arise, loosely wrapped in sunny yellow spathes. Later, their huge rosettes make beautiful and imposing accents in shady borders, their rich summer green fading to soft autumn gold. The East Coast version, *Symplocarpus foetidus* (Zone 3, to 3 feet), is the hardiest, its mottled purple and green spathes

Indians and ate some before learning that the use was medicinal, not dietary. My guess is that they were an emetic of some kind. The tart, almost lemony flavor was quite pleasant, though the aftermath was less so.

Only slugs—and perhaps angels—climb the stiff green rungs of Jacob's ladder, but its combination of dissected foliage and abundant flowers earn it a place in any shady garden. Creeping Jacob's ladder (*Polemonium reptans*, Zone 3, to 14 inches), native to the eastern woods, is a rather floppy plant with pallid blue flowers, but it has a number of better forms, among them 'Sapphire', a soft, warm blue, and the luminous 'Blue Pearl'. Its western counterpart, *P. foliosissimum* (Zone 4, to 28 inches), is larger and more upright, producing large clusters of deep lavender-blue, cup-shaped flowers over a long period. Whichever form you grow, its narrow, finely dissected leaves will assort pleasingly with dwarf shrubs and broad-leaved perennials. Though tolerant of many soil types and a fair amount of sun, both eastern and western Jacob's ladders perform most generously when given decent garden soil and a shady situation. Another westerner, *P. carneum* (Zone 5, to 18 inches), blooms briefly in various shades of apricot or peachy pink, all pretty but fleeting. This one is harder to please, showing a decided preference for light shade and open soils with quick drainage.

Invaluable as natives are in the garden, they are even more so in the wild. It's important that we buy such plants from reputable sources, rather than dig them from the woods.

Lovely as a well-grown wildflower may be, an unhappy one can quickly become unsightly, its leaves browned and curling or disfigured with powdery mildew. To prevent spring beauties from lapsing into midsummer liabilities, shade lovers must be given the conditions they crave right from the start. In general, they prefer moist or retentive soils and shady sites, though many can tolerate drier soils if well mulched. Since garden shade is usually cast by trees and large shrubs, the shaded sites wild things prefer are often infiltrated with woody roots that compete successfully against young, newly planted, or shallow-rooted perennials for available moisture. To give perennial woodlanders a proper start, their planting site

This Chinese Jack-in-the-pulpit, *Arisaema candidissimum*, is a strong grower that can multiply quickly in shady gardens. It rises late in spring and blooms rather later than our eastern native.

should be amended with compost and other humus-based soil conditioners as well as a water-storing polymer or hydrogel. (Choose gels that are a minimum of 94 percent copolymer for the best and most lasting benefits.) Many spring bloomers would just as soon go dormant as desiccate, but a thick, moisture-conserving mulch, monthly deep watering, and a high summer dose of manure tea (brewed from one part aged manure to twenty parts water), should keep them awake and in good looks. An annual spring feeding mulch of compost mixed with alfalfa pellets (see page 80) will keep soil and plants alike in good heart.

Staking One's All

Encouraging Upright Behavior in Plants

Those persistent April showers did their proverbial trick and May flowers are appearing with alacrity. April's winning combination of soft rains and relatively warm days encourages exuberant growth which can be both satisfying and scary. As garden plants reach for the sky, their soaring spires are lovely to see, yet many will need support to keep wind and rain (not to mention spring cat fights) from dragging them back to earth. There are many ways to stake a plant, and since the gardener's goal is to encourage upright behavior without cramping any plant's natural style, we must develop a full range of staking techniques, matching each to specific plants.

To be good matchmakers, we must be observant, aware of each plant's tendencies, and well equipped, armed with a full arsenal of devices that control or direct plant growth. We must be sensitive as well, able to coax cooperation from each plant rather than force compliance upon an unwilling victim. We must be flexible, for what works one year—or four years out of five—might easily fail when a very wet or hot season produces unusu-

al growth patterns. When we first begin gardening, the concept of staking seems simple indeed; if something starts to flop, whack a thick stick into the ground, wrap some twine around the tilting limbs, and string the poor creature up. This rough-and-ready method may be perfectly acceptable in the vegetable garden, but in ornamental gardens, it looks both undecorative and unkind. The best plant–stake matchups are all but invisible and create an impression of great naturalness. This is good for our horticultural reputation and equally good for our plants.

The first step to good staking is to recognize the nature of each plant's need for assistance. Spiky things like delphiniums want to rise straight up, but many forces—gravity, weather, dogs, slugs—conspire to bring them down. When heavy with flower, those stretching stalks snap quite easily, so each stem needs a separate support. To be effective, the stakes must be almost as tall as the main stems themselves. Place these well out from the crowns and sink the ends deeply into the ground, positioned to support potential flower heads. Ideally, these sticks would be invisible, and many advancing gardeners decide against staking because the bare sticks are so blatant early in the season. However, if shorter stakes are used, the flower stalks will snap off at exactly the height of the stake during the next wind or rain storm, so bite the bullet and use really big ones. Thick bamboo wands are strong and relatively inconspicuous, particularly those colored dark green or black. Skinny steel rebar also works well, and its dull silver coat soon discolors to a rusty brown that looks convincingly sticklike. Secure the enlarging stems to the stakes, tying the new growth every 12 to 18 inches as it grows—you may have to add new ties each week or so—and the sticks will soon be covered.

Swoopy, sinuous verbascums look like sacrificial victims when tightly bound to tall stakes, yet without restraint these generous creatures spill huge lower leaves over their neighbors. Since such affectionate proximity can be fatal, early training (tying each main stem to a sturdy, 3-foot stake) will improve community relations greatly. By early summer, the side shoots will be long and tall, seeming to be sturdily independent. Don't be fooled, however, for as soon as the flowers begin to open, those ramrods become sway-backed and wayward. Give each a slim bamboo cane and bind it lightly with a couple of stretch ties to keep it on the straight and narrow.

There are many tying materials on the market and they, too, must match the needs of the job. Whatever you use, it should have some give to it—you don't want to strangle anything—and be unobtrusive in color. The traditional favorite is garden twine, not tightly wound cord but coarse, hairy string. Climbing plants can get a good grip on this rough stuff, yet it is soft enough in texture that it doesn't cut through tender stalks when wind tumbles them about. Pale, straw-colored string will gleam out betrayingly between the leaves, so choose the darkest possible brown, which will blend into the background nicely. If light-colored string is all you can find, soak it overnight in tea or old coffee to darken it up. Thin wire ties coated with paper or plastic are useful for lightweight stems. This stuff comes in precut measures (always too short or too long) or on hundred-foot reels, and is generally a good, subfusc green that disappears obligingly into the foliage. Stretchy plastic tie-tape would be great for many occasions except for its color, a glaring green that looks like nothing in nature.

Tall trumpet lilies droop under the weight of their great, heavy buds, yet their whorling foliage can't adequately mask stakes and string. These are best kept vertical with single-stem hoop stakes. These consist of metal wands of varying heights,

The sturdy, wire-bound stakes in this rose tripod are set firmly into the soil. This extra measure of support is necessary by midsummer, when well-grown plants may become amazingly heavy.

each with an adjustable hoop that can be moved up and down the stick. For trumpet lilies, which can exceed 7 feet if happy, use the tallest hoop stakes you can find; they should project 3 to 4 feet above the ground. Use as many stakes as you have lilies in a given clump, placing the wands as soon as the fat shoots appear and positioning each hoop above an elongating stem. Check back each week or so and move the hoops steadily upward as the stems grow taller. You can also use several hoops on a single wand to support bearded iris or a cluster of top-heavy freesias. Hide the wands behind the fans of foliage and use the smallest size of hoop to make the propping less blatant.

Peonies have a terrible tendency to droop, and the entire plant may splay open at the heart when

Strong, flexible, long-lasting, and inexpensive, the steel rebar sold in hardware stores is an invaluable staking material. Its rusty patina makes it visually unobtrusive in just a few weeks. (Garden of Steven Antonow, Seattle.)

weather stressed. To rectify this, you can cut a large circle of chicken wire (tuck in the edges or cover them with strapping tape to protect fingers and foliage from cuts) and set it on the ground where the peony will emerge. As the plump shoots rise up, their unfolding leaves will lift the wire along with them. Soon it is firmly enmeshed in the stems, yet hidden by foliage, and no amount of wind or rain will knock it down. You can also use peony cages, much like squattier versions of tomato cages, with two or three tiers of wire wrapped around four or five outward-slanted support legs. These are inexpensive enough (under two dollars) to buy in quantity and will also work nicely with big, sprawling hardy geraniums. If the legs are cut down a bit, they also serve for low, long-armed veronicas like 'Crater Lake' which otherwise grovel about ineffectually at ground level. The flash of metal can distract your eye early in the season. Soon it will be obscured by foliage, but in the meantime, you can wrap wire hoops and cages in strands of weeping willow or last year's rough-textured hops vines to give them a pleasingly rustic look.

In mid-May, I set three-tiered tomato cages over several plants which start life upright, then experience a midseason slump. Feathery, 4- to 5-foot purple fennel is a big offender, for its early season promises of good behavior are always broken by midsummer unless steps are taken. Several of the taller bellflowers (*Campanula* species) also benefit from such restraint, as do hollyhocks. Taller, four-tiered tomato cages are set over big meadow rues like the yellow-flowered *Thalictrum glaucum* and the vivid pastel purple *T. dipterocarpum* 'Hewitt's Double', which often slouch in part shade. The cages also improve the look of shrubby (rather than climbing) *Clematis recta*, turning its slumping stems into a controlled cascade of white stars. Cut in half lengthwise, these same cages make half-hoops to support slower risers. Inserted in place in late July, they will hold up tumbling asters unobtrusively during September and October. Really tall asters and the strapping magenta *Geranium psilostemon* demand English border hoops. These are metal rings crisscrossed with gridwork and supported on trios of metal legs (they are available in several heights and sizes). Hoops are also good for restraining monk's hoods (*Aconitum* species), and sunflowers (*Helenium* species).

Simplest of all supports are what the English refer to as "pea-sticks," stout, twiggy branches, usually of hazel or alder, which are firmly set into the ground around floppy plants. Often the sticks are doubled over for extra reinforcement and stuffed very firmly indeed about the plants' underskirts, rather like the "rats" with which ladies plumped out their hair at the turn of the century. Properly executed twigging looks like the remnants of Hurricane Andrew for a few weeks, but amazingly soon, all traces are lost beneath an effulgence of leaf and flower. Homemade cedar-slat fence sections (2 by 2 feet) have three sharp legs which I jam in front of late-season floppers like crocosmia and chrysanthemums once they begin to sag. A store-bought wire system in various sizes works similarly, with linking L-shaped sections that can be arranged in rows or rings or whatever configuration is necessary.

However you decide to stake, act soon, for timing is crucial to success. To be effective, staking must be done before the need is obvious; by the time the plant is in trouble, it's really too late to do a good job. Limbs broken by wind and rain or kinked from stretching for the sun will never straighten out again. Often there's nothing for it but to cut the sorry mess to the ground. However, if you use the kind of garden journal with space for several years' notes on each page, you can pre-

This lovely melange would soon dissolve into chaos were the decidedly non-erect *Clematis recta* left unsupported. Instead it is restrained by a tall, four-tiered tomato cage. The other plants are *Spiraea japonica* 'Goldflame' and *Nepeta* 'Six Hills Giant'.

vent the tragedy from recurring. This year, for instance, the entry for early April began with last year's belated notation to support the fennel early, a task which takes one person a moment in May, but takes two people an unpleasant half hour in August. Another emphatic note reminds me to shear back the catmints and oriental poppies before they fall apart of their own weight. (I used to blame the cats for these disasters, till I realized that it was rain and the lankiness born of cool, wet springs that caused them to flop open.) This spring, I obey the voice of my own experience with pleasure, knowing that a little thoughtful staking now will result in a whole summer of enjoyment.

JUNE

Putting Plants in Place
Balancing Shape and Form

If garden making is an art form, garden design is a craft, governed by rules of proportion and scale. Most books on the subject address shaping the garden itself, directing the paths, forming the beds, placing key plants such as trees and shrubs which will become architectural features in their own right. Important as such macro-planning is, there is another, less obvious side to the designing of beds and borders. Plant placement, the arrangement and relationship of garden plants, is a subtle skill which nonetheless has as much impact on the ambiance of a garden as the placement of its gates and walls. While much has been written about creating plant combinations and even about building more complex vignettes with several plants, specific guidelines about more general plant relationships are rare. This is probably because there are few definite rules that govern such relationships. While it isn't very helpful to tell an aspiring garden maker, "Just push the plants around until they look right," that is exactly what many experienced gardeners do when planting beds and borders. The problem with this advice is that you must have a pretty clear idea

June brings roses in its entourage, among them the sugary pink 'New Dawn', an American classic that was the very first plant to be patented.

Harmonic balance is never static, especially in a living, changing garden. By combining evergreen plants with contrasting shapes and textures, we create flowing foliar tapestries that give the garden form and definition all year round. (Beasley garden near Portland, Oregon, designed by Michael Schultz.)

about what each member of the plant community you are building will look like next year, let alone in five years, or ten. If you don't, then odds are good you will be rearranging most of that bed or border in the near future. This is not necessarily a bad thing—I personally enjoy active (as in shovel-wielding) garden making far more than the ongoing maintenance a supposedly finished garden requires to keep it from changing too much. However, it's one thing to replant sections of the garden because you are struck with inspiration or because your taste is changing, and quite another

to be forced to rework the whole thing because the plantings are out of balance.

Balance, long-term and short, is the real key to good planting. Balance is what informs all powerful and pleasing compositions, in the garden or elsewhere. It doesn't have to mean the static balance of formal design, in which each plant or object is matched by a partnering shape, or carefully equipoised between perfect pairs. Japanese Zen gardens, employing a planting style that could be called formal naturalism, are based on balance and tension, with both plants and objects having equal value. In England, geometrically flat lawns and sheared hedges are balanced by ebullient, billowing borders. North American garden designs are often influenced by organic, rather than geometric models, the bold colors and naturalistic plantings displaying the lively balance found in Impressionist landscapes.

When it comes to creating a satisfying, artful garden in your own backyard, all this can be a bit bewildering. Do we copy the English, emulate the Japanese, or try to figure out something of our own? The point, always, is to make a garden that pleases you personally, in as many ways as possible. In an earlier chapter, we looked at the considerations that can shape the garden itself. Once the shape of the garden has been decided, we can turn our attention to filling the beds and borders. Every gardener develops a personal palette of favorite plants, and it only makes sense to include as many of your own cherished ones as possible. Before you begin to play around with their placement, it is very helpful to categorize them in terms of their shapes, both in youth and maturity. Lady's mantle, for instance, is a rounded mound, delphiniums are spires, and copper fennel a wide column, while maiden grass is a fan and dwarf sitka spruce a pyramid. To simplify visualizing all this information, try cutting plant shapes out of colored paper (choose a simple scale, perhaps 1 inch = 1 foot, for these models), writing the name of the plant on each. Take a plain piece of paper and sketch out the bed or border to the same scale. You can then layer and transpose the cut shapes in various combinations until you hit on the most pleasing.

Some people find paper designs frustrating, because what looks great in two dimensions may not work so well in three. They may prefer to use the clear plastic architectural blueprint kits for garden designing, several of which are on the mar-

ket. These have a gridded ground sheet which can be altered to match your own piece of ground, and several sheets full of printed, 3-D symbols for plants and hardscape, which stick on the ground sheet. Others are hampered by the unfamiliarity of the design process, and feel that they can't possibly design a garden by themselves. If you feel this way, look for other places in your life where you express your artistic sensibilities freely. Most of us are more experienced with pulling together terrific clothing outfits, making lovely and comfortable living spaces, or producing knockout meals than in building wonderful gardens. Fortunately, the same skills are at work in each case, and with practice, they can be applied in any arena. In every instance, it is balance which makes or breaks the result, and balance which turns a good idea into a work of art.

In the garden, the designer's goal is to create balanced plantings with just enough tension to please the eye (too much will merely tease it). In gardening, as in art, tension refers to the visual balance between objects. In a formal planting, for instance, every element is balanced exactly by something of equal weight, size or importance. In more casual or naturalistic plantings, the balance is often less obvious, though just as important. Rather than planting in strict pairs or symmetrical patterns, each vignette, partnership, and combination must work (be visually pleasing) independently as well as in relationship to the border as a whole. If they aren't, the result is fragmented and restless rather than harmonious.

To discover how to create such balanced plantings, play with plant shapes, balancing rods and cones, hemispheres and ovals. Push them around until they form pleasing juxtapositions and relationships. Think of the skyline as well as the body of each bed. Rather than arranging plants rigidly by size, so the garden in profile

resembles a loaf of bread, sketch their placement in tiers and triangles. In the garden, those triangles will be three-dimensional pyramids, each group rising to a peak and sloping gently back to ground level. This produces both interior topography and a gently stimulating skyline. Nothing leaps violently out of place or is left unlinked to its neighbors, yet there are plenty of changes of height and shape. The eye is led up, then down, led in, then back out, gracefully coaxed along to discover each new vignette. In moderation, such movement is invigorating, but too much of it creates a restless feeling. Again, the goal is to build a harmonious balance between movement and restful peace.

Arranging plants in tiers produces similar effects. By echoing the relationships plants have in nature, we can weave a multitextured tapestry of form and foliage which rises and falls in soft vegetable waves. Small trees and big shrubs form the top tier, followed by medium-sized shrubs and large perennials. Next come the compact, intermediate plants, and finally the ground covers, which can be low-growing shrubs or perennials. By keeping their natural relationships in mind, you can create groupings of plants that look comfortable and convincing right away. Large or small, primary or secondary, each group has a fundamental plant surrounded by attendant companions. The key plant need not always be placed dead center in its group, but should be central in visual importance.

When it comes time to put the plan into action, you may find it helpful to borrow a trick from the English, who grid off their beds with agricultural lime to make clear guidelines for planting. Such gridwork can also be done with bamboo canes and string, but these powerfully suggest an archeological dig and are quite awkward for large people to work around. Give yourself 2- or 3-foot squares to plant, and your paper garden will appear in real life surprisingly quickly. It is important to give each plant enough room to develop properly, but if you are using small plants, it can take a few years for the garden to catch up to the plan. Should the garden look a bit thin and uncertain in its youth, don't hesitate to fill in the gaps with good-mannered annuals. These come in a huge range of sizes and colors and will entertain the eye nicely while you wait for your perennials and shrubs to mature. These temporary place holders won't hurt a thing and they will help your garden maintain its balance, which, after all, is the point of the exercise.

Ardent Annuals

Fast Workers for Gaps in Bed and Border

As garden centers and nurseries spill over with colorful annuals, eager gardeners snap them up by the cartload. Cheerful, hard-working, and easy to please, annuals are asked to perform a multiplicity of tasks in our gardens. We plug them into window boxes, tubs, and hanging baskets, line them along the driveway, arrange them in shaped beds, and row them out in the cutting garden. Despite their popularity, annuals don't enjoy much respect; sold as "color spots," they are usually valued for their flower power alone. Indeed, we tend to buy annuals the way we buy groceries, relying on an automatic list of staples. Instead of milk, eggs, and bread, we stock up on petunias, marigolds, and geraniums, without questioning

To develop our eye for border design, we need to look at plants in terms of shape and form as well as color. These spiky *Eremurus* 'Shelford Hybrids' pull the eye insistently upward, yet they are balanced by the encircling mound of ox-eye daisies.

Mixed borders include plants of many kinds, arranged in the tiers we see in nature. Trees support vines and shelter shrubs, which in turn anchor perennials, bulbs, and ground covers. Planting in these tiers produces restful, natural-looking gardens.

the process. Now, there is absolutely nothing wrong with growing any of these plants, but just as we have learned to alter our daily diets in the name of nutrition and health, we might expand our garden palettes in the name of change and excitement.

This year, before you load up on familiar choices from the front racks, stroll past the back shelves where choicer plants are often lurking. Some offer unusual foliage, like the dramatic *Amaranthus* 'Illumination', its long, heart-shaped leaves splashed with lava reds and ember oranges. Others are uncommonly colored, like green and white snow-on-the-mountain, *Euphorbia marginata* 'Summer Icicle', or interestingly textured, like airy, netted baby's breath, *Gypsophila elegans* 'Covent Garden'. Annuals fragrant enough to perfume the whole garden include flowering tobacco, *Nicotiana alata* 'Sensation Mixed' and the 'Domino' series, as well as mignonette (*Reseda odorata*), its green flowers homely but potent.

Despite the preponderance of screaming colors on those front racks, one can find annuals to suit every color scheme, classic or wild. Charming but ordinary baby blue eyes (*Nemophila menziesii*) is now joined by dapper cousins, black and white 'Pennie Black' and the white and navy '5 Spot'. Pastel lovers will enjoy sugar pink 'Imperial Princess' pansies and sky-blue morning glories peeking through silvery tangles of lotus vine in basket or window box. (For more drama, replace the lotus vine with a tumble of 'Kniola's Purple-Black' morning glories.)

If you are a confirmed marigold fan, consider adding plants with different foliage and forms to get more textural interest in the beds. Warm oranges and yellows can look a bit insistent alone, but echoing them with softer shades will create subtler color runs. African daisies offer both feathery white foliage and striking black-eyed flowers. The *Venidium fastuosum* species produces masses of hand-sized daisies in sherbet orange and black on 18- to 24-inch stems, while *V. f.* 'Zulu Prince' is a knockout in cream and black. Both like a warm position with good drainage, and either will spill delightfully from container or window box. Transvaal daisies (*Gerbera* species) are equally long blooming, and come in both the Mardi Gras series of hot sunset colors and the distinctive Blackheart mixture, running from cream through burnt orange, all with a dusky black eye. Dwarf treasure flower, *Gazania* 'Talent Mixed', can edge the marigold bed with tufts of silvery, fine-textured foliage and wide, whiskery daisies in dozens of colors, from butter through bronze and copper and red to dark chocolate. If these murky colors start to feel too hot, cool things off with an infusion of bright blue daisies (*Felicia dubia*) and add more creamy flowers to balance the blend. If you really don't want anything but marigolds, try something very old instead of something new. A tall (24-inch) antique marigold, *Tagetes* 'Striped

Marble', once a choice florist's flower, is now a collector's treasure. Its big, tawny red flowers are striped with buttery yellow, a rich and showy effect which carries well across the garden. This splendid bedder lasts very well as a cut flower and is a favorite with flower arrangers.

A few annual giants toward the back of the bed will add height and depth to any planting composition. Red castor beans, *Ricinus communis* 'Carmencita', are great candidates, offering both sculptural, ruddy brown foliage and vivid red, spiny seedpods on stalks some 4 to 6 feet high. These are exciting plants, as potent in shape as many a shrub. Robust sunflowers also provide an uprising note, and they come in all sorts of sunny colors, from dawn gold to burnished sunset reds. The mixture sold as either *Helianthus annuus* 'Autumn Beauty' or 'Autumn Giant' runs from cream and old gold through mahogany, rust, and velvety browns, with huge flowers held high on 5- to 6-foot stems. If your bed edges into a shaded area where sunflowers won't thrive, a tall flowering tobacco, *Nicotiana sylvestris* (sylvestris meaning "sylvan" or "woodland") will bring both height and scent. This bold-leaved species carries great, drooping hanks of white, night-fragrant flowers on 4- to 6-foot stems.

Annual vines can cover a fence or trellis in no time, making a colorful backdrop for border or bed. Sweet peas are always favorites, especially

This confectionary blend includes fragrant annual 'Salmon Madness' petunias and honey-scented 'Apricot Shades' alyssum as well as a perennial twinspur, *Diascia* 'Salmon Supreme'. The sweet alyssum is a reliable self-sower that colonizes readily in sunny gardens.

strongly perfumed blends like 'Antique Fantasy' and 'Summer Breeze'. More delicate annual vines can be allowed to twine through rose bushes or bring a second bloom to spring shrubs. Try threading a big shrub rose like 'Graham Thomas' with a moderate morning glory such as *Ipomoea* 'Kniola's Purple-Black', its deep purple trumpets streaked with black. A variegated form, 'Roman Candy', has big, rosy flowers with a clean white picotee

Bold in form and color, annual castor beans can exceed 10 feet where summers are warm. Compact forms like ruddy 'Carmencita' are better bets for small borders where space is at a premium.

edge above white-splashed leaves, a charmer alone or running through a dark yew hedge. If you don't have much for climbers to climb, diminutive bedding morning glories look charming in pots and boxes or lined along the border's edge. *Convolvulus tricolor* 'Rose Ensign' makes tidy 15-inch mounds smothered in trumpets that shade from rose through pink to lemon and white. The slightly larger 'Blue Ensign' has sea-blue trumpets with yellow and white centers. The Dwarf Rainbow Flash series comes in a dozen shades of pinks and blues, all with dark eye zones lined with white and gold.

Sold as an annual foxglove, *Digitalis purpurea* 'Foxy Mixed' must be sown in late fall or early winter if it is really to bloom the first year, but furry rosettes bought from the nursery are reliable bloomers, producing relatively short (30- to 40-inch) bloom spikes in a range of pinks and purples, with a few creams and whites as well. Ordinary foxgloves are biennials—plants with a life cycle of two or three years—but their year-old rosettes are often sold with the annuals, ready to bloom. Among the prettiest border strains is 'Apricot' or 'Sutton's Apricot', yielding tall spires of dreamy gilded pink, the very color of a ripe apricot. The color is surprisingly complex, holding a variety of tints and tones, and working equally well with gentle pastels and deeper hues. Set a flock of 'Apricot' foxgloves behind dwarf, buffy pink quince *Chaenomeles* 'Cameo', with pink and white iris, or range them against purple smoke bush or copper beech foliage to awaken subtle color echoes.

Another biennial, silver-podded moon weed (*Lunaria annua*), is too coarse for the border in its plain, purple-flowered form, but any of its several variegated forms deserve placement. White-splashed, white-flowered 'Stella' will light up a shady corner before and after it flowers, while the cream-streaked leaves of purple-flowered 'Variegata' develop sumptuous, wine-red coloration when grown in full sun. Both moon weeds rise into tiered towers of glowing foliage, each layer trimmed with tufts of flowers followed by the round, silvery seedpods. Both forms self-sow generously, and young seedlings show their variegation strongly. Thin them early, discarding any plain ones and leaving the best to stand a good two feet apart. Seedlings and young plants often appear to lose their variegation in summer, but it will reappear in full fig next spring.

A pair of astonishing bellflower (*Campanula*) cousins are starting to appear in nurseries as bloom-sized biennials. These giant bellflowers have daunting names, especially *Michauxia tchihatcheffii*, which noted English authority Graham Thomas says sounds "rather like a sneeze" when properly pronounced. It helps to know the name commemorates the French botanist Michaux. Thus you can say *Mee-show-sha* for the first bit, and *chat-cheff-ee-eye* for the next part, which refers to a Russian botanist. *Michauxia campanuloides* (the specific name meaning "like a campanula") is rather easier on the brain. If you can't quite get your tongue around them, order them from a seed or nursery catalog and avoid the issue entirely. (If people ask their names, just show them the plant tags.) Both skyrocket 5 or 6 feet up from rough, rather hairy basal rosettes into wiry turrets, their dark leaves and stems flushed with mahogany red. Plump, lanternlike buds hanging off stiff, angular arms proclaim their relationship to the bellflowers. These buds open into improbable, hand-sized white swirls, like a passion flower or a clematis on steroids. These amazing creations—they look more like constructs than a "natural" flower—belong at the back of the border, for dazzling as they are at their peak, they are homely before and after they bloom.

A wealth of annual flowers is available to any who seek them out, and most are as easily raised

White-splashed, white-flowered 'Stella' is the most refined form of the biennial, silver-podded moon weed (*Lunaria annua*). It self-sows abundantly, with a high percentage of seedlings running true to form.

as mustard and cress. Browse through the pages of a good seed catalog such as Stokes' or Thompson and Morgan and ponder the possibilities before making your final choices. Though you may end up deciding to stick with Martha Washington geraniums, blow a buck or two and give Martha a new bedmate, perhaps pairing red hot 'Vulcan' geraniums with red 'Talent' gazanias, or matching gentle pink 'Virginia' geraniums with *Alyssum*

'Apricot Shades'. There's no need to scrap your old annual palette all at once in favor of these newcomers, but add a few to your usual mix, just as you might try out a new sauce or spice in a familiar dish.

A Rose in Bloom

Well-Bred Roses with Company Manners

To most people, the word "flower" suggests a rose. These most beloved of blossoms are popular everywhere, grown from Alaska to Florida, yet roses are generally not good mixers in the garden. Many are prima donnas, reliant on chemicals, demanding attention, and throwing tantrums if forced to share ground—or food and water—with neighbors. While such tempestuous beauties have their share of admirers (or, as is often the case, far more than their fair share), there are other roses with more comfortable ways and prettier manners. Such well-bred beauties are to be found among both very old and very new roses. Many species and the ancient hybrids known collectively as "old roses" are remarkably robust and resistant to diseases. Though rosarians accepted their darlings' chemical dependence for years, these days the majority of gardeners prefer to garden without poisons. Happily, a new breed of hardy, healthy roses has entered the market. An English nurseryman, David Austin, began crossing species and old roses with generous floribundas and fragrant tea roses. After some forty years, he has developed a line of roses that are spectacularly varied in form and coloring and voluptuously fragrant—a quality many modern roses lack. Moreover, these new roses are long-blooming and disease resistant and they are attractive in habit and plant form. Best of all, many of these English, or Austin, roses grow well in mixed border settings without special treatment.

Roses are traditionally grown in splendid isolation for several reasons. Many are gross feeders that hate competition. Many are highly prone to diseases like mildew and black spot. Grouping them makes it easier to treat their woes, but it also underlines their ugliness as an overall plant. Not only are rose ghettos unattractive, massing roses is like spreading forth a salad bar for their pests. Like many species roses, English roses can be tucked into border and bed where they are less obvious targets. Though their disease resistance doesn't guarantee perfect health, it does mean that these roses are slow to become infected and quick to recover once problems have been corrected. A hard spray of water from the hose is enough to knock back aphids, for instance, and mildew may be averted by avoiding dry soil (especially when roses are grown close to walls). Once black spot is in a garden, it is very hard to avoid, yet certain roses are amazingly unsusceptible, while in others it can nearly always be controlled through a program of frequent grooming. (Remove yellowing or spotted leaves as they occur, bagging them for burning rather than adding them to the compost pile, where they will further spread the problem.)

The list of English border roses is large indeed, and more of them appear in nurseries and catalogs each year. As with any family of plants, certain of them perform better where summers are hot, while others adapt well to cool nights and gray days. As the English roses become better known, regional favorites will emerge. At this point, however, we know that though the yolk-yellow double 'Graham Thomas' seems to adapt well from Ontario to Texas, in New England it makes a shrub some 4 feet tall, while in the Midwest it may be a 6-footer. The small climber 'Constance Spry' reaches perhaps 8 feet in height and blooms only once in cool northwestern gardens, yet in California she may be nearly 20 feet tall and bloom repeatedly. Other Austins show similar regional variations, but if you can't find a reliable local source of specific suggestions, all are worth experimenting with.

For starters, consider dainty, green-eyed 'Fair Bianca', compact enough for the smallest of gardens. Her shining foliage sets off masses of ivory flowers, their inner petals "quartered," or drawn into four circlets within a rounded cup of guard petals. Encircle her with the dwarf *Campanula lactiflora* 'White Pouffe' and white Jupiter's beard, *Centranthus ruber* 'Album', to achieve a delicate, moonlit effect. For exquisite bud and flower form, few roses rival the velvet red, tightly doubled 'Prospero', another small (3 by 4 feet) shrub which combines well with the dark-leaved, red-flowered *Lobelia* x 'Queen Victoria' and fleshy red stalks of *Sedum maximum* 'Atropurpureum'. Equally compact in stature, plump little 'Wife of Bath' is smothered all season in cheery, pink-cheeked roses with a heady, complex scent. Give her long-lasting companions such as 'Blue Beauty' catmint (*Nepeta*) and the pink and gold feathers of annual squirrel tail grass, *Hordeum jubatum*.

In a deep border, midsized English roses can anchor groups of perennials all summer long. 'Windrush', a rounded shrub some 4 feet high and across, opens acid yellow buds into cupped, semidouble confections of lemon and cream. It blooms in flushes from May until hard frost, combining equally well with tall blue *Campanula lactiflora* 'Pritchard's Variety' in early summer and floods of periwinkle blue *Aster* x *frikartii* later on. The coppery pink shrub rose 'English Elegance' looks smashing against red or purple foliage, while the Chinese lacquer red blossoms of 'The Squire' glow against a backdrop of old gold or deep green. The instant classic shrub rose 'Graham Thomas' is perhaps the best of the bunch, glorious in color and form. Its perfect buds, long and elegant as those of any hybrid tea, are deep apricot, unfolding into perfectly doubled blossoms of imperial yellow that fade to biscuit. Their fascinating fragrance travels on warm air, perfuming the garden around them. It looks remarkable rising above a swirl of *Spiraea* x *bumalda* 'Goldflame', with copper and gold foliage, perhaps partnered with the striking black spires of *Cimicifuga racemosa* 'Atropurpurea'.

Best known of the English roses is the yolk-yellow 'Graham Thomas'. Named for the famous English plantsman, it is appropriately long blooming and deliciously scented.

The largest of the English roses need plenty of room, but make magnificent border centerpieces in good-sized gardens. A splendid 6-footer,

Tall, shrubby 'Charles Austin' is a splendid color blender, for its toasty pink buds fade to champagne as the flowers mature. Pair it with spires of buff-colored English 'Chater's Double Chamois' hollyhocks for a subtly sumptuous effect.

'Charles Austin' arches showers of roses—toast-colored in the bud and cinnamon pink in flower—over sheaves of rustling maiden grass (*Miscanthus sinensis*) and bold-leaved hydrangeas. The soaring 'Swan' looks terrific near the border back, its buttery white flowers spilling over slate-blue wands of arctic willow (*Salix glauca*) and spires of white fireweed (*Epilobium angustifolium* 'Album'). Where space is limited, these larger shrubs can be trained into smallish (6- to 10-foot) climbers. Fastened against wall or trellis, the thickest canes become a permanent woody framework. Each spring, tie new shoots out lengthwise, or curve them into the border. (Hold them down with wire hoop pins or tent stakes.) This encourages flower buds to break from every leaf node, rather than clustering only at the tops of the stems. Long-armed 'Abraham Darby', with salmony buds and ginger-peachy pink flowers, works nicely as a small climber, either propped into an elderly fruit tree or given a sturdy mid-border post for support. The lusty, peony-pink cabbage rose 'Constance Spry' will cover a fence or garage wall, spreading in a wider fan each year with encouragement.

In my garden, several dozen English and species roses thrive in companionable proximity with trees, shrubs, vines and perennials. All receive a nutritious feeding mulch of compost, aged manure, and alfalfa pellets in spring and fall (see page 80 for the recipe). They also get an occasional booster of water-soluble fertilizer (I favor Peters 20–20–20) if summer heat causes them to flag. However, in cold winter areas, it's best not to feed English roses after midsummer (late July or early August), since late-forming new growth is highly susceptible to frost damage.

Thanks to heavy clay soil and deep mulches, my borders only need a single deep watering each month in summer. However, in lighter, less retentive soils, you might well need to water more despite deep mulch, since excessively dry soils often lead to powdery mildews. Although many English roses are considered drought tolerant once established, all need adequate moisture if they are to settle in well, and most repeat bloom more reliably if kept reasonably moist through the growing season.

Pruning of English roses is less brutal than that of tea roses, for they were bred to have an attractive natural habit or form. English roses should not be pruned at all for a year or two after planting, except to remove dead, crossed, or injured stems. As a woody framework begins to develop, judicious thinning will accentuate and balance their natural shape. As plants mature, a few of the oldest canes are removed each year and the remaining canes are cut back by half or a third. This promotes the steady production of new wood while preserving a full, rounded form. At season's end (or early in September in cold winter areas), allow hips to form instead of trimming off the fading flowers; this triggers the hardening-off process that prepares plants for winter.

Once the cold comes, remove any foliage and mulch the rose crowns with at least 10 or 12 inches of chopped straw, heaping compost or soil over the top of the mulch for extra insulation. Where winter frosts and winds are fierce, add a sheltering layer of pine boughs as well to protect the upper woody growth. In early spring (usually March or April), trim off any winterkill, loosen and spread the mulch and add several handfuls of alfalfa pellets. (Alfalfa is an excellent soil conditioner and a good source of nitrogen.) With this simple routine, you can enjoy all-but-effortless roses all through the growing season.

The Gardener's Guiding Hand
Garden Grooming for Ongoing Beauty

Summer is upon us at last. The garden spills over with roses and peonies, poppies and delphiniums. Warm breezes carry the soft scent of locust trees and the lilting music of a song sparrow. Bright blossom and swelling bud promise waves of color and fragrance all through the summer. The garden is gorgeous in June, fresh and unspoiled, but if it is to stay that way for months on end, we need to give it a hand.

Quite literally, nothing is so good for the health and looks of the garden as the gardener's hand. When we are touching our plants every day, grooming them for success, we are necessarily in touch with them. We can't help but notice plants that look peaked or need a bit more room and we can deal with small problems before they turn into big ones. Best of all, we become more aware of the progress of summer through the borders. When we groom our gardens every day, we actively watch flowers bud and bloom and fade. When at last we trim away the spent stems, it is with a sense of fulfillment, not sorrow for a blossom that we never even noticed. Some chores, like weeding and pruning, seem to direct our attention so narrowly that we can't see past them, but garden grooming opens our eyes to the beauty of the day. Grooming is an ongoing, indeed a never-ending activity, yet it is a restorative one which enriches both garden and gardener.

Garden grooming is minor maintenance, the horticultural equivalent of brushing teeth and combing hair. It consists of small-scale adjustments—removing dead flowers and aging foliage, snipping off an errant twig here, redirecting a stray shoot there. None take much time, yet they have a surprisingly powerful visual impact, for well-groomed gardens look loved. Done daily, grooming takes just minutes and the decorative detritus will fit in the kind of handsome baskets English ladies carry in glossy picture books. Done on a semi-weekly basis, the job may require an hour and fill a bushel basket. If you can only manage weekend work, be ready to spend a couple of hours and fill a wheelbarrow. However pleasant and interactive, garden grooming is not a romantic chore but a very practical one. The aim is to clean up the past so the present is unmarred and the future develops properly.

Perhaps the most vital part of garden grooming is deadheading. This doesn't mean rock gardening with Jerry Garcia, but refers to the practice of removing wilted flowers to stimulate the production of fresh ones. With many annuals and short-stemmed perennials, deadheading can be done by pinching off the old flower head with your thumb and first finger, a slightly messy but efficient process. With longer-stemmed plants like shasta daisies, *Achillea* 'Goldplate', or Canterbury bells, where the flowers are clustered on spikes or stalks, the whole stem should be cut off at the base using sharp garden clippers. This is important, because dull clippers, especially anvil pruners, tend to mash the stems rather than cut them cleanly. Since stem damage is a primary gateway for disease, good pruners may even improve plant health. Serious gardeners usually prefer scissor-action blades such as the Swiss-made Felco secateurs. These are expensive but durable (all parts are replaceable) and highly satisfying to work with.

Some people shy from cutting back a whole stem for fear of weakening or hurting the plant, yet the technique has several clear benefits. First off, hard cutting (to or near the crown) avoids the hedgehog syndrome of bristling, bare sticks that occurs when only the flower heads are removed from long-stemmed plants. Secondly, hard cuts stimulate healthy new growth from the crown, which renews plant vitality. Thirdly, such fresh growth may provide another flush of bloom without harm to the plant. To encourage this, mulch cut-back plants with compost and aged manure, water well, then offer a moderate dose of fertilizer, either manure tea (made by soaking 1 part manure in 20 parts water) or a dilute solution of a commercial product such as Peters 20–20–20.

Discolored foliage may be a symptom of disease, but most often it is just part of the aging process. Though very natural, browning foliage can give the garden a tired look. Removing aging leaves rejuvenates the border much as color-rinsing refreshes prematurely graying hair. If you find yourself picking up more and more foliage and leaving bare stems behind, take a closer look; you may have an unhappy plant (or it may be autumn, in which case you just relax and let things go gloriously gray). Yellowing foliage on a single plant may signal root damage. If caused by rodents or moles, remove the plant, flood the tunnel, then replace the plant. Root rots caused by too much water and not enough air may be rectified by lifting the plant and adding coarse grit or builder's sand to the soil, or by moving the plant to a drier place and substituting a bog lover.

While you primp, keep your eyes open for signs of trouble or imbalance. Here, an overeager catmint might be swamping a delicate coral bell. There, aphids might be attacking the nasturtiums. Not every problem calls for reaction—a few spit bugs are no big deal—but when every stem of your favorite phlox is covered with their soapy-looking spittle, it's time for action. A hard squirt from the hose will wash the gunk off before any harm is done. Indeed, frequent rinsing with plain water discourages many pests, from aphids to leaf rollers.

After each grooming session, jot down any observations in your garden journal. This enables you to schedule an effective and productive activity day each month, when you can take care of more time-consuming problems. Journal notes can also remind you to change annoying situations, perhaps moving daylilies to border or path edges so the sodden remains of yesterday's blossoms can be reached without damaging neighbors. Write down the names of self-cleaning roses and clematis you notice, varieties that shed their petals cleanly, rather than clinging to those unsightly, browning tatters. When you notice them at a nursery, buy them to replace sloppy offenders with less tidy ways. Record names or tape in plant tags from annuals which go on blooming even if you don't deadhead every day.

Large gardens like mine love attention, and I could cheerfully—and profitably—spend most of every day tinkering in the borders. However, I don't have hours to spare, so I have to make do with minutes. Happily, there are several very effective ways to keep any garden looking good all summer, regardless of its size and our schedule. Over the years, I have learned that no garden investment pays off better than soil improvement and that mulch is the busy gardener's best friend. Good soils make for healthy plants, and deep mulches suppress weeds while keeping soils cool and moist. The third trick is to choose plants with independent natures; not rebels that sulk or terrorize their companions, but happy, self-sufficient plants that love being in your garden but don't really need you very much. To find them, you need to know what kind of conditions various parts of your garden

Garden grooming is a perpetual chore, yet it is far from boring drudgery. Carried out in a spirit of renewal and connection, the grooming process refreshes both garden and gardener.

have to offer. Next, choose plants that like those conditions and put them where their needs can be met without much effort. All these things can greatly reduce the amount of work your garden requires of you, so that moderate but frequent grooming may be enough to keep the garden in good looks all summer long.

Dazzling new daylily hybrids are true American beauties, yet they are also major offenders in terms of grooming. Yesterday's drooping blossoms are decidedly unsightly, so position these plants within an easy arm's reach of the border edge or path.

Perennial Pleasures

Long-Lasting Combinations

Fun as it is to simply grow and enjoy flowers, it is even more satisfying to paint with them. Plants can of course be coupled in beautiful combinations, but they can also be grouped in larger-scale compositions, blending shade and hue with leaf and petal instead of paint. Gardeners who whole-heartedly enjoy creating the infamous riot of color, filling their flower beds with carefree abandon, may not want to bother with refining that time-honored technique. Those, however, whose interest is piqued by subtle washes of pastels or smashing successions of tightly interwoven hot colors will be drawn to experiment with floral garden art.

Traditional bedding-out arranges bright annuals in simple patterns that are showy but usually rather crude in effect. The sumptuous color combinations we admire in English borders are more carefully orchestrated, moving from tint to tone in closely graded increments. On this side of the water, artful gardeners often prefer to work more boldly, splashing color about freely and permitting less cautious juxtapositions. When we develop color combinations in our own gardens, any approach will be more effective when we take into account not only flower color but texture, form, and timing as well. This—looking at the whole plant, not just its flower—is the heart of the art of creating perennial combinations. There is no better way to create garden art, no surefire method, no hard-and-fast rules. In truth, the experience of color is highly personal and your own appreciation outweighs any arbitrary rules of "good taste." In color work, the best guide is your own pleasure in what you see.

Monochrome borders, in which all the flowers are white, or red, or blue, might seem the easiest place to start. In fact, they are challenging exercises in uniting the many shades and intensities of a particular color. Though useful for opening our eyes to color subtleties, monochrome combinations usually provide more intellectual fun than beauty. Simple and satisfying color borders can most easily be created using two or three colors. Instead of making a blue or yellow or white garden, mingle the three and lovely things will happen quite naturally. If we rely on spectrum colors, the effect is cheerful but relentless. Clean pastel shades of buttery yellows and chalky blues will clarify the color mixture, while grayed pastels—French and ocean blues, ivory and pearly whites—bring depth. Soft off-whites add sparkle and brilliance to the tapestry. Stretching any color theme to its fullest provides a rich and fascinating palette to work with.

Most people begin by combining certifiably tasteful colors—gentle pinks with lavender, blue, and silver. This is a great place to start, especially if you genuinely adore hazy pastels. However, if your taste runs to the exotic, consider making a gloriously brash Mexican fiesta border, or a smoldering sunset garden full of oranges and reds. It's important to remember that the garden exists to give us pleasure. This isn't something we have to do "right" by anybody else's rules. The idea is to have fun with color. If we are to become garden artists, we must experiment freely, without fear of doing something "wrong." We need to use color playfully, inventively, even provocatively, enjoying our successes and learning from our inevitable failures.

That said, certain factors do make combinations easier to assemble. Though we speak of partnerships and pairs, most good combinations involve not two plants but several. Pairing plants with contrasting form, leaf shape, and texture creates visual interest which persists through all seasons. A few strong, spiky plants will break up a boring stretch of rounded mounds while large, simple leaves set off delicate, lacy foliage. Such contrasts remain effective both before and after the flowers appear, so they bring lasting strengths to combinations. When floral pairings are involved, timing is crucial, because flowers must overlap reliably to work in combination. Since weather patterns and plant health affect flower timing, journal notes recording when flowers typically begin and end blooming are a big help, especially when they record your direct experience over a number of years. (Journals that offer room for several years' notes on the same page are particularly useful for this.) The most dependable floral partners are usually those with extended bloom periods, since they are bound to overlap sooner or later, even in an off year.

In my garden, a favorite combination illustrates all these principles. It begins with a Greek yarrow, *Achillea taygetea* (Zone 5, to 2 feet), a vase-shaped, upright plant with gray, much-dissected foliage. Its tiered plates of flowers open sulfur yellow and fade to butter, and it reflowers generously if kept deadheaded. Behind the achillea rises a big hybrid catmint, *Nepeta* 'Six Hills Giant' (Zone 4, to 3 by 3 feet), with long spikes of deep blue blossoms on softly arching stems. This one needs plenty of room, but if its lanky stems are sheared back by half each time the flowers fade, it reblooms faithfully all summer. Next comes a peachy, reblooming daylily called 'Three Bars' (Zone 4, to 3 feet). This trio is backed by a tall column of copper fennel (*Foeniculum vulgare*, Zone 4, to 6 feet), a garden form of the kitchen variety that looks smoky black in full sun. In late summer, its flowers look like Queen Anne's lace in old gold, but I value it most for the texture of its foliage, thready and glittering. These four plants work well together for months, acting as the sturdy cornerstone of a large border. Their muted colors are compatible in value—they have the same strength, or intensity, of tone. There are contrasting plant forms and leaf shapes; both upright and mounded plants, broad, strappy leaves and little lacy ones. Moreover, the fennel acts as a backdrop, framing the trio of flowering plants into a complete picture. It also acts as a transition plant, linking the smaller perennials to the more substantial shrubs massed behind them at the back of the border.

ABOVE: The easiest kind of color scheme to develop is not a monochrome one but a simple combination of two or three harmonious colors. This blue, yellow, and pink border section illustrates the principle delightfully. (Northwest Perennial Alliance Border at the Bellevue Botanic Garden in Bellevue, Washington.)

OPPOSITE: Repeated elements make important visual links that guide the eye through complex garden plantings. The cascading Chinese grass, *Hakonechloa macra* 'Aureola', is an excellent plant to use repeatedly, because it combines supportively with practically anything.

Equally important, this combination is linked to others around it through repeated elements. The garden holds many other fennels and catmints, yarrows and daylilies. Garden artists repeat and vary such cornerstone combinations just as a musician unites a symphony through theme and variations. To make visual connections, repeat some portion of the cornerstone combination each time a key element is used. If a catmint appears further down the border, it will be accompanied by a dark fennel or a pale daylily. A more strongly colored yarrow will be partnered with a vivid daylily or a deeper blue catmint. The entire group may be repeated as well, but not too often, especially if the garden is small. If too much variety leads to visual chaos, repetition without variety leads to boredom. Dullness can be eliminated by repeating the pattern while using different forms of the same key plants. This way, one creates serial combinations that are united by the similarities of plant form and habit, yet very different in color effect. To deepen the color run, use a pastel yarrow like *Achillea* 'Lavender Beauty' (Zone 4, to 2 feet) and blue rue, *Ruta graveolens* 'Jackman's Blue' (Zone 5, to 2 feet), instead of catmint, backing the whole with a grassy-leaved daylily like blue-purple 'Russian Rhapsody' (Zone 4, to 3 feet). To brighten it, try 'Salmon Beauty' yarrow (also Zone 4), a darker catmint, *Nepeta* 'Blue Wonder' (Zone 4, to 1½ feet), and the apricot and salmon reblooming daylily, 'Sing Again' (Zone 4, to 40 inches). To soften the effect, use dusty rose 'Heidi' yarrow

Great combinations like this deserve careful study. The graceful fountain-shaped maiden grass, *Miscanthus sinensis* 'Variegata', both frames and sets off the mounded form and reflexed flowers of *Echinacea purpurea* 'White Swan', while the hot little firecrackers of red and green *Alstroemeria psittacina* add warmth and snap to the otherwise cool combination. (Northwest Perennial Alliance Border at the Bellevue Botanic Garden in Bellevue, Washington.)

(Zone 4, to 2 feet), the little daylily 'Lilac Greetings' (Zone 4, to 1½ feet), lavender with a rose eye-zone, and pale blue catmint, 'Dropmore Hybrid' (Zone 4, to 20 inches) with compact

habit and grayer foliage. The fennel might be repeated in copper or plain green, or replaced by almost anything that stops the eye, whether tall, bushy perennials or compact border shrubs.

In another happy combination, *Gaillardia* x *grandiflora* 'Burgundy' (Zone 3, to 2½ feet), a wine-red blanket flower, is fronted down with tall, red-stemmed *Sedum maximum* 'Atropurpureum' (Zone 3, to 1½ feet), which looks like a mahogany-stained version of the famous 'Autumn Joy'. This same pair is repeated three times down a 30-foot stretch of border. Each time, it is flanked by dusky daylilies: dainty crimson 'Little Business' (Zone 4, to 1½ feet), cranberry-red 'Cape Cod' (Zone 4, to 20 inches), and plum-colored, long-blooming 'Little Grapette' (Zone 4, to 1½ feet), with running red ribbons of blood grass, *Imperata cylindrica* 'Red Baron' (Zone 5, to 20 inches), to fill in the gaps at ground level. Each group has a lustrous clump of annual squirrel tail grass, *Hordeum jubatum*, nearby, tucked behind the smaller daylilies or banked in front of taller ones. These groups are good-looking from late spring straight through autumn. By summer's end, the blanketflower becomes rather sprawling, but the big, fleshy sedum gives it firm support. Squirrel tail grass opens its feathery brushes from midsummer into winter. They shade from green-gold to pink and dark red accentuating the tints of neighboring plants in every season, and lightening the solid-looking sedum and big red daisies with their delicate texture. The wider, ribbonlike blood grass foliage starts out a fresh and sparkling green just touched with maroon in spring, but deepens dramatically through the summer, brightening to clear flame red as autumn approaches. These similar groups anchor a sunny kitchen border full of low, shrubby herbs like lavender, rosemary, and santolina, making bright sparks of color amongst the softer grays and blues of their backdrop.

An excellent way to develop your own combinations is to look long and hard at plant groups you admire both in photographs and in other gardens. Analyze the role of each plant in each combination. Why is it there? What is its primary function? What is it doing for its companions? Its contribution should always be more than pretty flower color; every plant should be earning its place with graceful form, strength of line, handsome leaves, or splendid berries. It is often said that those luscious English color borders can't be duplicated here in North America, and it is very true that in many regions our plant palettes are restricted by harsh winters and torrid summers. However, in every North American zone, we can grow a great galaxy of wonderful plants. When we analyze those glorious groupings, therefore, our next job is to figure out which plants might effectively fulfill those same roles in our own gardens. Once we have our list of possible candidates, we can begin to paint. The secret of success is to mix and mingle our garden plants with the same deliberation we apply to assembling an outfit, matching hanky to tie, earrings to handbag. Look carefully at each plant, recognize its strengths, admire its details. Start simply, then build up as you gain confidence. Before long, you'll be creating your own garden art, painting seasonal pictures with living pigments.

JULY

Layering Plants

Creating a Green Haven

As summer waxes and June's perennials fade, there often comes a lull between the exuberance of early summer and the renewed fireworks of fall. In cool summers, when flowers fail and gray skies leave us longing for warmth and color, or when dog day heat crisps the blossoms and leaves us panting for respite, nothing is more soothing to the spirit than a leafy summer haven. Wind ruffled into a thousand shades of green, a tightly tiered planting of trees and shrubs creates an illusion of spaciousness and depth in the smallest gardens. Woven on a larger scale, alive with birds, such a tapestry evokes the charming wildwood of song and story. There are swags and flourishes of flowers to decorate these leafy walls, yet the leaves themselves are the vital element. Leaves, like flowers, come in many shapes and colors. Intermingle those green leaves with leaves of gold and blue and red, and the tapestry is enriched all season long, flowers or no flowers. Add lacy leaves and bold ones, frilly leaves and strappy ones, and its texture becomes as important as the colors. Dark, shadowy corners can be lit up by leaves that are liberally variegated in moonlight silver or sunny gold.

Ruffled and diamond-dusted, modern hybrid daylilies fill the borders with ebullient bloom. This one is 'Candlestick', surrounded by foamy pink *Alstroemeria* 'Dr. Salter's Mix'.

The layering theme can be applied to understory plantings as well as shrubs and trees. By contrasting and varying leaf size and shape, a foliar tapestry is developed that is rich in pattern and texture, no matter what the scale.

Leaves alone rarely make a garden, yet if we arrange leafy plants cleverly, they will form communities so natural as to convince even the birds of their inevitability. How is this managed? The answer lies in a first principle of garden making: layering, or planting in the tiers we find in natural settings. In woods all over the world, trees shelter shrubs, which themselves form transitions between the large (nearby buildings or mature trees) and the intimate (the flowering plants of the garden). Shrubs in turn offer protection to colonies of perennials, annuals, and bulbs, while under them all run the ground covers, spreading in quiet carpets of greenery.

When we apply these layering principles in our own backyards, we accomplish a small roster of achievements in one fair swoop. First, by encircling the garden space with tall plants, we define the garden space, instantly clarifying its identity. Next, by planting middle-sized shrubs, we make visual steps that lead the eye both up to the tree tops and down to the borders. The trees—which can be very small ones—link the little garden to the larger landscape. The shrubs provide a backdrop for the flowering things at their feet. If half our shrubs are evergreen, the garden will remain attractive through the winter and our early bulbs will be showcased against their greenery instead of blooming lonely in a sea of mulch.

The scale of such plantings will be dictated by the size of the garden, yet even in tiny gardens, the principle holds true. In very small gardens, the tree role might be filled by 8- to 10-foot shrubs, with each corresponding tier similarly scaled down. However, those who love larger plants can successfully recreate entire plant communities in very limited spaces simply by making careful plant choices. When choosing a tree for such a spot, pick one that won't outgrow its welcome. Happily, there are many such, but unfortunately, the plant label at the nursery may not be your best guide to them. It is fast becoming common practice to label trees not with their true mature height but with their height at five or ten years. This is not done to deliberately trick anybody, but rather reflects the fact that the current expected life span of a garden tree is less than ten years. Before you buy trees (or larger shrubs), consult a good regional reference guide, talk to experienced nursery folk and local gardeners, and try to visit parks or botanic gardens where you can look at older specimens of the plants under consideration.

Once you have made an informed choice, place the plant with care so that its demise doesn't bolster that sad statistic. Remember not to plant any tree near a house wall; even the smallest tree belongs a minimum of 5 feet away, and 10 is better. Know where your sewer and water lines run, too, and avoid plants with wandering roots (willows and poplars are infamous offenders) or plan on getting to know your Roto-rooter rep very well indeed. Even a small tree with a moderate growth rate can cause problems if not placed with the future firmly in mind.

To illustrate the layering principles, let's turn an urban dooryard, say 12 by 12 feet, into a green haven. We'll begin by choosing a diminutive, slow-growing tree to act as guardian over its lesser companions. A graceful dogwood such as *Cornus florida* 'Cherokee Sunset' (Zone 5, slowly to perhaps 20 feet) offers beauties for every season. In winter, its upraised arms are clothed in silky, lavender-gray bark. In spring, its golden leaves are crowned with deep red flowers, followed in summer by fat red berries. In autumn, the brightly variegated leaves deepen from lemon and lime to copper and bronze. All in all, this is a most attractive choice, except where anthracnose runs rampant. Though newer hybrids like 'Cherokee Sunset' are more disease resistant than older ones, if dogwoods all around you are dying, a cutleaf Japanese maple might be a wiser choice. There are literally hundreds from which to choose, and it's worth taking the time to find one with all the qualities you want. *Acer palmatum* 'Orido Nishiki' (Zone 5, slowly to perhaps 18 feet) is an outstanding candidate. Its tightly fitted gray bark is striped with green and streaked with red, and its brilliant fuchsia young twigs rise in delicate tracery against the winter sky. It slowly builds from a

ruffle-skirted shrub into a slim, rounded tree some 15 feet tall in as many years. In spring, its little flowers and fruits and fresh foliage are all a glowing shrimp pink. The palmate, deeply lobed leaves mature variously; some are pure pink, others are cream or green, while the majority are flecked and stippled with a mixture of all three. (Any branches that develop only solid green leaves must be carefully removed lest the variegation be lost, but 'Orido Nishiki' is less prone to such reversion than many of its relatives.) As summer ages, the frilly leaves darken until autumn fires them into fingers of flame.

Transition shrubs must also suit their setting through their life span. Judicious selection can eliminate the need for hard pruning or remedial shaping, and again the choices are myriad. Where shrubs are to screen away the street and neighboring buildings, bypass space-hogging old faithfuls like laurels in favor of slender, columnar Irish junipers (*Juniperus communis* 'Stricta', Zone 2, slowly to 12 to 20 feet) or skinny hillspires like *J. virginiana* 'Skyrocket' (Zone 2, slowly to 10 to 15 feet). We can mix in some deciduous shrubs that flower and fruit for contrast. Plain privet is dull, but golden *Ligustrum* 'Vicaryi' (Zone 5, to 12 feet) has lemon-colored leaves, brightest and best when unsheared plants are allowed to develop their natural, upright shape, and panicles of fragrant white flowers in midsummer. Elderberries often have unusual foliage; *Sambucus canadensis* 'Laciniata' (Zone 3, to 12 feet) has lacy green leaves, while those of *S. racemosa* 'Plumosa Aurea' (Zone 4, to 12 feet) are like golden feathers. (*Plumosa* means "feathery," while *aurea* means "golden.") Both American and European elders come in gold or silver variegated forms, and there are several purple-leaved varieties as well.

Instead of ordinary weigela with its bubble-gum pink flowers, try apple blossom 'Dame

Blanche', dashing 'Java Red', with dark red leaves and rosy flowers, or 'Variegata', with reddish flowers, its leaves brightly striped in ivory and green (all Zone 5, to 8 feet). Bold hydrangeas may have gold- or silver-variegated leaves, as do numerous euonymus forms. Round-leaved smoke bushes like *Cotinus coggygria* 'Royal Purple' or 'Nordine's Red' (both Zone 5, slowly to 12 to 15 feet) have colorful foliage all season (the "smoke" occurs when their tiny flowers form a cloudy mass above the leaves).

There are so many wonderful border shrubs, we can afford to be choosy about foliage form and coloring. Little barberries like *Berberis thunbergii* 'Crimson Pygmy' (Zone 4, to 2 feet) can edge the border front, while taller *B. koreana* (Zone 5, to 6 feet) with showy yellow flowers, fat red fruits, and big, rounded leaves that color splendidly in autumn, can double as short hedging. A colorist's delight, *Spiraea* x *bumalda* 'Goldflame' (Zone 4, to 3 feet) turns from coppery red in spring to old gold in summer, heating again to bronze and ember red in fall. An antique kitchen herb, blue rue (*Ruta graveolens* 'Jackman's Blue', Zone 5, to 2 feet) offers teardrop-shaped leaves of lustrous, steely blue and mingles exceptionally well with shapely perennials.

Hardy broadleaf evergreen border shrubs are invaluable garden elements, providing good company for winter-blooming perennials such as

Layered garden plantings evoke the feeling of being in a natural environment. When transitional plants (usually shrubs) are gracefully handled, larger elements link effortlessly to smaller ones. (Garden of Lindsay Smith, Bainbridge Island, Washington.)

hellebores, as well as spring bulbs. Among my favorites are a dwarf honeysuckle, *Lonicera pileata* (Zone 5, to 3 feet), which rises in flat, architectural tiers but can be kept lower by annual clipping if desired. Native *Leucothoe fontanesiana* (Zone 4, slowly to 6 feet) arches in elegant little curves, its new growth a vivid red that contrasts pleasantly with its clustered ivory bells. The leaves take on autumnal tints of coppery red and bronze, and often hold their color through the winter. Dainty rhododendrons (zones and heights various) with frosty or felted foliage relate equally well to taller shrubs and smaller perennial companions. Sweet box, glossy little *Sarcococca hookerana* var. *humilis* (Zone 5, 2 to 3 feet), offers up its bakery fragrance of honey and vanilla on the chilly winter air. It grows well in shade, and makes a supportive companion for evergreen ferns.

We can plant an interesting selection of these structural, leafy plants in our little dooryard, according to the layering principles seen in nature. Our little tree takes pride of place, companionably encircled with smaller shrubs and their attendant perennials. Larger shrubs line the sidewalk and the property line, their height stepped down with smaller shrubs. The street view is screened, yet plenty of light enters the small garden. The height of the trees and shrubs, coupled with their interlayered planting, creates an impression of depth and abundance which suggests that the space is far larger than it really is.

When trees and shrubs are interwoven in this manner, they create both framework for the garden and backdrop for the summer bloomers gathered about their feet. This is their usual *raison d'être*, but the best effects of all are achieved when a shrubby tapestry is woven with an eye to the special attributes of each living component. Just as perennials are partnered and paired, so, too may

Compact border shrubs combine readily with perennials, offering solid structural support to a changing flow of ephemera. Here, the colorist's delight, *Spiraea japonica* 'Goldflame', is paired with a black bugbane, *Cimicifuga racemosa* 'Atropurpurea'.

leafy plants be mixed into a mutually supportive community, each plant complementing its companions. Thus, when flowers fade in the summer heat, the lovely leaves carry on, their soft susurration and shifting shadows creating green havens of soothing peace.

Garden Workhorses
Long-Blooming Plants that Just Won't Quit

As summer settles in, even those of us who love working in our gardens like to take a break now and then. When the weeks fill up with visitors and excursions, we appreciate anew our garden workhorses. These old faithfuls aren't glamour plants, just reliable, hard workers that earn garden room with long bloom and independent ways. Workhorse plants respond to good treatment with alacrity, but will also perform well when conditions are less than ideal. In or out of bloom, they remain tidy and attractive with a minimum of grooming. Most will flower for several solid months and the few that don't will produce repeated bursts of bloom throughout the summer. Though none will ever stop traffic or attract flocks of admiring friends to the garden, all are plants you can count on, year after year.

Most workhorses are highly adaptable, and many will thrive in gardens around the country. Outstanding among these are the yarrows (*Achillea* species), with ferny foliage and flat, platelike flower heads. Hardy to Zone 2, yarrows prefer plenty of sun, but aren't particular about soil so long as drainage is good. They do best when not overfed, and those with silvery foliage may turn green and produce lush foliage at the expense of flowers if given too rich a diet. Many species and older garden forms are unruly, flopsy creatures, a fault that has given the family a name of dubious repute. These have largely been replaced by top-notch German hybrids (of *A. millefolium*) with upright carriage and an extraordinarily long bloom season. Jewel-bright 'Paprika' (to 18 inches) opens ruby red, then fades to wonderful shades of rust and mahogany that blend beautifully with dusky red and copper chrysanthemums and slate-blue asters. 'Sulphur Beauty' softens from chalky deep yellow to butter and cream, while 'White Beauty' maintains its crisp, clean color for well over a month. Others in the Beauty series flower in shades of pink and salmon, rose and lavender. Plants like these represent a significant breakthrough and they are indeed a bevy of beauties. However, the best of the oldies will always be worth growing as well. Among the tidiest and most cooperative are *A. decolorans* 'W. B. Child', a short, green-leaved form with frothy white flowers, and a gorgeous Greek, *A. taygetea*, with its silver lace foliage and chalky lemon-yellow flowers.

Any yarrow can be encouraged to produce more blossoms by frequent deadheading, removing the flower heads as they fade. Trim the stems down to the next pair of leaves; the next batch of flowers will begin to form from the lower leaf nodes, a process that may continue all summer. If you prefer to dry the flowers for arrangements, cut the stalks hard (to a few inches above the ground) when the first flowers are at their peak. The crown will refurbish itself nicely and reward you in late summer with another set of flowers.

Common *Crocosmia masoniorum*, too aggressive for most gardens, has a number of better-mannered cousins. These late bloomers open long racemes of narrow, tubular flowers from high summer into fall. Their sheaves of broad-bladed foliage are striking from early spring on, standing up proudly without staking when given sufficient sun. This swordlike foliage contrasts strongly with rounded or lacy leaves, and looks splendid with a bib of woolly gray lamb's ears (*Stachys byzantina*). If gigantic, demon-red 'Lucifer' (4 to 5 feet) is too bold for your borders, try shorter forms like warm yellow 'Citronella' (to 2 feet), the softer 'Norwich Canary' (to 28 inches), or the burnt orange and wine colored 'Emily MacKenzie' (to 24 inches). Colorists and flower arrangers adore golden-

Tall *Crocosmia* 'Firebird' has flame-colored flowers, fat, knobbly seedheads, and magnificent foliage that spread in fans like gigantic peacock's tails above smaller perennials.

belled 'Solfaterre' for its deeply bronzed leaves. In the garden, these combine dramatically with billows of shimmering blue rue (*Ruta graveolens* 'Jackman's Blue'). Most crocosmia hybrids are hardy to Zone 5, but even in Zone 8, very cold winters deplete their ranks. Throughout their range, deep planting and an autumn mulch of shredded bark or straw will usually see them through nicely. (Even established colonies may need resetting every few years, for the bulbs have a tendency to rise to the surface of the soil.) In colder regions, crocosmias should be lifted and stored in a frost-free area over the winter. If this seems like too much trouble, try planting them in pots which may be sunk into the garden for the summer and lifted easily when winter rolls around. You will probably need to thin these fast-increasing bulbs each year, refilling their pots with fresh soil as you do so.

No flower in the world has been more improved than the tawny daylily. These days, some are long-petaled and spidery, many are round as a cookie, while others are ruffled like a prom gown, their stiff petals glittering with diamond dust. There are thousands to choose from, in nearly every color but spectrum blue, including white and near black, and ranging in size from diminutive window-box plants to statuesque border beauties. Though certain modern hybrids perform best where summers are long and hot and winters are warm, others do well wherever they go. Gardeners who must contend with unusual or harsh conditions should consult Barbara Barton's classic, *Gardening by Mail* (see the appendix) to find local daylily nurseries where folks can steer them toward regional best bets. Most of us, however, will be able to grow most daylilies very well indeed. Part of the key to using daylilies well in the garden is to give them supportive companions. Grown *en masse*, daylilies lose their architectural qualities, but when spaced throughout the border, intermingled with plants of various form and habit, their strength and elegance of line become apparent. They also contrast pleasingly with structural perennials such as *Heuchera* 'Palace Purple' and lady's mantle, *Alchemilla mollis*. Their strappy foliage, either broad or grassy, makes them good companions for dwarf border shrubs, whether glossy broad-leaved evergreens or mounded herbs.

Great performers among the small fry include 'Little Grapette', a dwarf (to 12 inches) variety as dark as Concord grapes and a good rebloomer that makes excellent company for purple sage or woolly gray horehound. So, too, does the taller (18 inches) 'Pandora's Box', which produces a nearly constant stream of creamy flowers with wine dark eyes. Shrimp-pink 'Louise Manulis' (18 inches) blooms from mid-June into September, outdone only by the indefatigable little 'Stella de Oro' (12 inches), a gold star plant if there ever was one. Particularly productive taller daylilies include citrus-yellow 'California Sunshine' (32 inches) a showboat that matches *Spiraea* x *bumalda* 'Goldflame' for intensity. Flounced white 'Crinoline Petticoat' (30 inches) stands out crisply against fine-needled rosemary, while velvet-red 'Chicago Brave' (28 inches) is a knockout against a backdrop of dwarf arctic-blue willow (*Salix glauca* 'Nana'). Delicate-looking 'Ming Porcelain' (28 inches), ivory tinted with pink and peach, proves as robust as its humble ancestor, and reblooms generously, as will 'Olive Bailey Langdon', an older lady decked in rich, matronly purple. Both look lovely in front of red sand cherry (*Prunus* x *cistena*) foliage or a red-leaved *Weigela* 'Java Red'.

Daylilies do best in humus-rich garden soils and they respond very well to mulching, particularly with materials like compost and rotted manure that improve soil tilth. Their greatest need is for water, both before and during their flowering period. Indeed, plants in overly dry situations are apt to be shy bloomers and slow to increase. Adding a handful of hydrated polymer such as Broadleaf P4 to the planting hole will greatly improve daylily performance in light, sandy soils, as will a water-conserving mulch of shredded bark or chopped straw. Though daylilies are sun lovers, many modern daylilies will bud well so long as they receive at least four hours of direct sun each day. Indeed, the deeper reds and purples may fade when they receive too much sun, especially in hot summer regions, so a few hours of midday shade can be a distinct advantage.

The sunflower clan offers a number of workhorse plants, among them the blanketflowers. Many of these bloom in brash shades of gold and orange that make them most at home in sizzling hot borders. Among the tallest of the bunch are *Gaillardia* 'Tokajer', warm yellow with a rosy-red central cone, and the sunny 'Yellow Queen' (both 20 inches, Zone 3), somewhat sprawling plants that look best in informal plantings, associating with brilliant reds and coppery oranges. Ruddy 'Burgundy' is quite a different proposition, enriching soft blends of silvers and mauves and lavenders as well as deep-toned reds and blues and purples. Like many of its relatives, it blooms nonstop from late June until hard frost, as prolific as any annual. Try 'Burgundy' among misty pastel paper sage, *Salvia viridis*, and sapphire-blue *Lobelia vedraiensis*, or set it between blue catmints and the red-black foliage of cardinal flowers like *L. fulgens* 'Queen Victoria' or 'Illumination', both of which produce vivid red flowers from June through August.

In light, open soils, blanketflowers will spread modestly over the years, often moving about in fits and starts as the original plants die out and new

The delicate eye zone markings on this modern hybrid daylily, 'Chinese Watercolor', look as if they were hand painted. This one blooms for a full month, and may have twenty blossoms open each day.

offshoots take their place. In heavy clay soils, however, most increase slowly and tend to die from winter rots. Improving soil drainage with builder's sand or coarse grit will add years to their life, as will a lean diet.

Border geraniums are not tender annuals like Martha Washingtons (which are actually pelargoniums) but adaptable and hardy perennials. Some are far too easily pleased to let loose in small gardens; avoid those with tags that say "spreads readily" or "very easy," or you may be weeding them out for years to come. However, the family also includes steady bloomers that increase moderately and deserve placement anywhere. Many perform as well in shade as in sun, including *Geranium sanguineum* (Zone 4, to 15 inches). If its vivid, pur-

ple-pink flowers with their snapping black eyes are too potently colored for you, try its clean white form, 'Album'. Both make compact, well-furnished mounds, and will bloom from mid-June into September, as will another low clumper, the gentle pink *G. endressii* 'Wargrave Pink' (Zone 4, to 12 inches). A taller Tibetan, *G. himalayense* 'Gravetye' (Zone 5, to 18 inches), named for the famous garden of English garden writer William Robinson, offers loose clusters of large, deep-blue flowers from June into August, while *G. h.* 'Johnson's Blue' has slightly smaller, sky-blue flowers over the same period. The large leaves, fuzzy, gray and scalloped, of little *G. renardii* (Zone 6, to 10 inches) are as handsome as the pale flowers, mauve streaked with wine, that appear in flushes

through the summer. This plant works wonderfully in subtle color schemes, where its low mounds make a lasting contribution. European meadow geraniums, *G. pratense* (*pratense* meaning "meadow-dweller"), are tall (Zone 4, to 28 inches), fountain-shaped plants with lacy, snowflake foliage and abundant flowers of white or ocean blue from late spring to high summer. These hold their own mid-border, bringing a pretty contrast of form and texture to broader-leaved plants. There are dozens more geraniums to choose from, with likes and requirements to suit them to any garden situation.

If your garden lets you down after the spring rush is over, invite a few of these garden workhorses to show their paces. Given half a chance, any or all of them will give you a summer full of flowers in exchange for simple kindness and a place to stay.

Children of the Sun

Dealing with the Dog Days

Summer heat always comes as a shock to some plants, but when unusual weather patterns make the onslaught sudden, as has occurred all across the country in recent years, even sun worshipers may be taken aback. Anytime overcast skies and modest temperatures give way overnight to torrid sun, some plants will have trouble making the transition. Whenever hospital emergency rooms fill up with sunburned humans, gardens throughout the region are likewise full of vegetative sufferers that don't even enjoy the option of sunblock. We can help out extreme cases of sun shock by providing first aid—a daily dose of water, delivered directly to the root zone, can work restorative

wonders. Plants with severely wilting foliage often perk up if given some shade as well. This can be arranged by draping the entire plant (or a few supportive sticks) with cheesecloth, or by propping an old window screen nearby to temper hot afternoon sun. With a day or two of such intensive care, most heat weenies will bounce back and be ready to move on. They may have a little moving to do, though, for this is when flowers that like it hot come into their own.

Where summers are warm, these children of the sun are apt to be very well represented, their consistent successes earning them placement in every garden. In cooler mountain regions or foggy, coastal ones, such sun-loving plants may seem less obvious choices, yet even where summers are brief and temperate, it's a good idea to stock the garden with a fair percentage of these stalwarts. Most perform pluckily in cooler conditions, but when the heat is on, so are they. It isn't hard to identify these plants; simply stroll through any garden or nursery on a scalding August afternoon. The plants that are blissfully basking in the light are the ones for the job. Many of the most enthusiastic are native Americans that hail from our deserts and mountains, prairies and plains. Sages and penstemons, red flax or blue, golden poppies and desert globemallows, prairie and evening primroses can all be found growing happily in sunny, arid sites across the country. Not all species adapt readily to garden life, but many of their hybrid offspring are hard-working, long-blooming garden plants. A number of plants that make the transition from prairie to hot spots in the garden have *hel* in their names, not so surprising when we realize that *helios* is the Greek word for sun. Annual sunflow-

Hardy geraniums bloom for months on end, thriving in ordinary garden soil with a modicum of care. Here, *Geranium riversleaianum* x 'Mavis Simpson' scrambles into a patch of the tall sedum, 'Autumn Joy'. (Garden of Steven Antonow, Seattle, Washington.)

ers, *Helianthus annuus*, come in all sorts of wonderful colors these days, from the creamy 'Italian White' to the claret, mahogany, and rust reds of the 'Autumn Beauty' strain. These southwestern natives have loads of perennial relatives, among them the willow-leaved sunflower, *H. salicifolius* (Zone 3, 5 to 10 feet), a strapping creature with hundreds of branching arms, laden from August

Coarse in form and earthy in tone, the lovely *Rudbeckia* hybrids of the 'Nutmeg' seed strain produce floods of chocolate-centered blossoms from late summer well into fall.

into October with 2-inch lemony flowers with hot brown eyes. Its attractive, slim foliage and upright character make it an excellent garden plant. So is the bold swamp sunflower, *H. angustifolius* (Zone 6, 5 to 7 feet), similar yet larger in leaf, flower, and stature, with architectural good looks. The showy sunflower, *H. decapetalus* (Zone 4, 4 to 6 feet), is another late bloomer, offering its brassy, semi-double flowers with big burgundy buttons from high summer into autumn. An English form, 'Miss Mellish', has old gold flowers, while those of 'Loddon Gold' are a brighter, warmer yellow.

All sunflowers want from us is decent, well-drained soil in full sun and enough elbowroom to develop their tremendous potential. It is fascinating to watch them turning their shaggy heads through the day to follow the path of their name-sake above, but don't make the mistake I once did and plant them in an open border that will be viewed from the north, or all you will see is the backs of their heads! This doesn't mean you can't grow sunflowers unless you have a south-facing border; plants that face east or west will provide you with plenty of color.

False sunflowers, their eastern counterparts, are equally long and late bloomers. *Heliopsis scabra* (Zone 3, 3 to 4 feet) is a handsome species with ruffly, yellow-orange flowers and emphatic foliage. A selected form, 'Summer Sun' (36 to 40 inches), is a versatile bloomer that may produce single, double, or semi-double flowers, all golden-quilled and centered with a brassy button. 'Summer Sun' is widely available here, but many worthy named varieties await us once we convince our nurseries that we would buy these lovely plants. (Ask for things you want by name, again and again.) A fine English selection, 'Morning Star' (4 to 5 feet), decks its crisp, dark foliage with hand-sized sunflowers, their petals crayon yellow, their green-eyed hearts fluffy with orange-peel chenille. 'Light of Loddon' has paler yellow flowers, while 'Gold Greenheart' looks just as it sounds. False sunflowers were quite popular in England earlier in the century, but the best (and newest) hybrids come from Germany. Recent imports like the double-flowered 'Goldgefieder' ("golden plume") and the curving, coppery 'Sonnenschild' ("sun shield") are winning instant converts wherever they appear. A distinctive new strain of German hybrids features large and long-stemmed flowers that work equally well in arrangements or in the border. 'Jupiter' (3 to 4 feet) has enormous tawny heads, while 'Karat' is a glowing gold, and 'Mars' a deep, smoldering orange.

Helen's flower (*Helenium autumnale*, Zone 3) is a common and modestly attractive native with a host of stunning offspring, nearly all products of English nurseries. Most bloom for two or three months, and it is easy to arrange sequences of similarly colored heleniums to carry us from June to October. 'Moerheim Beauty' (3 to 5 feet) is indeed a beauty, its well-clothed stems topped with toothed, fat-petaled flowers of deep, bronzed red. By August, its flowers are nearly spent, but 'Copper Fountain' carries on the good work in July and August, while 'Riverton Gem' and 'Bruno' continue from late summer into autumn. 'Butterpat' and 'Canary' are late summer bloomers in soft yellows that blend with everything in the garden, while midseason 'Crimson Beauty' is a wonderful, murky root beer color rather than true red, equally splendid with rich blues and purples or salmony oranges.

The great American coneflower clan is a varied and generous one which includes lots of heat lovers. In Mexican hat (*Ratibida columnifera*, Zone 3, 1 to 3 feet), the familial cone- or thimble-shaped center is exaggerated until the flower really does resemble a drooping sombrero. This copper and claret colored coneflower thrives in any decent well-drained soil, blooming almost nonstop all summer long. A variant form, *R. c.* var. *pulcherrima* (the name means "especially beautiful," and it is), is a stunner with sharply reflexed, blood-red petals and long, nearly black central cones. Its elegant lines and subtle coloration make it welcome in the most sophisticated garden schemes.

The cutleaf coneflower, *Rudbeckia laciniata* (Zone 3, 5 to 12 feet), is grown more often in Europe than here, where it still tends to be considered an attractive local weed. Its reflexed yellow petals pour back off tall green cones, giving the plant a windblown look that makes it most suited to natural or wild gardens. The species is quite invasive in a lush border setting, as is its old-fashioned form, *R. l.* var. *hortensia*, which our grandmothers called 'Golden Glow'. A newer, more compact form called 'Golden Globe' (or 'Goldkugel') has wandering ways as well, but the lemony, densely doubled 'Goldquelle' (also called 'Golden Fountain') is more restrained in manners. Though the black-eyed Susan (*R. hirta*, Zone 4, to 3 feet) of the eastern countryside is short-lived, it is a charming wild garden plant, while its offspring, the pretty, painted Gloriosa daisies, fit comfortably into cottage gardens and borders. Overexposure has lessened our appreciation of the showy coneflower, *R. fulgida* 'Goldsturm' (Zone 4, 2 to 3 feet), a sturdy and long-blooming brown-eyed Susan. Nicely as it partners arching grasses, this diehard perennial looks even better sandwiched between mounds of catmint or golden oregano and sheaves of midnight blue asters or hybrid lobelias. Connoisseurs consider the great coneflower, *R. maxima* (Zone 6, 6 to 10 feet), to be the queen of the crop. Tall as it is, it deserves a front-row position, for its chief beauty lies in its foliage. Wide basal rosettes of foot-long leaves, rounded and steely blue, pro-

duce slender stalks topped with long-petaled yellow flowers with dark brown cones. This outstanding creature is unlike anything else in the garden and always receives a good deal of attention from visitors, yet it is oddly difficult to track down. Nurseries that specialize in native or prairie plants (see the appendix) are the most likely sources for this one.

Gaily striped Indian blanketflower, *Gaillardia pulchella* (Zone 3, 1½ to 2 feet), has sharp-rayed, golden-tipped petals of rich, bronzed red surrounding bright red and gold buttons. This hard-blooming, short-lived perennial has been crossed with its cousin, *G. aristata* (Zone 3, 2 to 3 feet) to produce a host of hybrids. One of the smallest, 'Baby Cole', makes dwarf tussocks under a foot in height and smothered in red and yellow blossoms. Taller 'Burgundy' (2 to 2½ feet), solidly wine red in petal and central boss, is an excellent mixer, compatible with any and every color and indefatigable in flower production without being coarse or crowded in bloom. Pure yellow 'Golden Queen' (1½ to 2 feet) is similarly hardworking, as is the taller 'Monarch Strain' (2 to 3 feet) in various combinations of reds and golds. All prefer open but decent soils, tolerating summer moisture but dying off quickly if winter drainage is poor.

The popular prairie tickseed, *Coreopsis lanceolata* (Zone 4, 1 to 2 feet), went to European finishing school to refine its manners. As a result, selected forms like the compact 'Goldfink' are welcome in the politest of borders. Low-growing (8 to 12 inches) and attractive in form, 'Goldfink' produces masses of vivid golden daisy flowers from July until hard frost. Its long neglected cousin, *C. rosea* (Zone 4, 1 to 2 feet), is gaining recognition as well. Diminutive (10 to 15 inches) in stature and dainty in foliage, *C. rosea* is another real trooper in moister soils, pouring out endless streams of small pink daisies from late June

ABOVE: This chance seedling of *Helenium* 'Wyndley' is even more coppery than its parent. Many named plants now gracing countless borders were orphans like this one, chosen by gardeners who found them appealing.

OPPOSITE: False sunflower, *Heliopsis scabra* 'Summer Sun', blooms from high summer into autumn. As the flowers mature, flocks of small birds arrive to feed on their ripening seeds.

through October. Several forms, called aptly enough 'Deep Pink' and 'Pale Pink', are available, and since the species is quite variable, you can also select the shades you like when you find nursery plants in bloom, as you will in August. *Coreopsis* 'Moonbeam', the much-heralded hybrid discov-

Brown-eyed Susan, *Rudbeckia fulgida* 'Goldsturm', is one of the longest bloomers in the coneflower family. It is best used in larger gardens, where it can spread as much as it likes. (Northwest Perennial Alliance Border at the Bellevue Botanic Garden in Bellevue, Washington.)

ered a few years ago in North Carolina, is taller (18 to 30 inches) but similarly airy in form, with rather larger flowers in pastel lemon-lime, a shade which complements nearly every other color in the border. Their greatest strength—ardent and lengthy bloom—is also their weakness, for unless they are divided and reset in replenished soil every three or four years, the tickseeds tend to exhaust both their soil and themselves, literally blooming to death.

All these natives appreciate good garden soil of almost any type. Most prefer quick drainage, but those referred to as swamp or streamside plants will tolerate moister situations. Though most will grow well in light shade if necessary, they will be most magnificent if given as much full sun as possible. These ardent late bloomers will be most effective when intermingled with

other late season performers such as asters, chrysanthemums, and tall sedums like 'Autumn Joy' or 'Meteor'. Meet their simple needs, and these sun lovers will reward the best we can offer with outstanding dog day performances, come rain or shine.

Water Wisdom

Making the Most of a Precious Resource

Changing weather patterns and community restrictions can spell real trouble for gardens that have always enjoyed unlimited quantities of water. We may be used to the luxury of watering madly when things get hot, but times are changing and our habits need to follow suit. When the need for serious change is recognized, ardently politically correct gardeners will want to try their hand at xeriscaping—landscaping without any supplemental water. Moderates may ask which water-wise changes will be most effective, while the pragmatic will want to know what can be done with the least effort. Each approach is valid, and the answers to each are quite similar. Wise gardeners looking for practical ways to reduce dependence on supplemental water can do this in part simply by being less wasteful, but several more positive steps will help even more. The first is to improve the soil wherever possible to encourage healthy, stress-resistant plants. The second is to mulch all plantings thoroughly and appropriately. The third is to give preference to plants with modest moisture requirements. Thirstier plants can be grouped so their needs can be efficiently met, perhaps by running soaker hoses under the border mulch, and by adding hydrophilic polymers to the soil. The fourth step is to water less often but more deeply, a pattern that promotes the development of deep root systems which can utilize ground water well below the soil surface.

Soil improvement is an ongoing project in most gardens, and some part or other of the process can be worked on in any season. Heavy clay soil should be lightened with humus (compost and aged manure), then opened with grit or coarse sand to keep it from locking up in dry heat. Sandy soils need all the humus they can get, on a regular and continuing basis. The easiest way to provide it is to blanket the soil twice a year, in early spring and late fall, with a 2- or 3-inch layer of compost mixed with bonemeal and other nutritional amendments. Few of us are about to dig up an established garden just to improve its soil, but much can be accomplished simply by improving the planting spot each time we add or move or divide a plant.

Mulching (which is discussed in more detail on pages 78–83) can similarly be done piecemeal, improving each site as we work on it during the summer. It is far easier to mulch the garden as a whole in spring and fall, when many plants are dormant. Mulching for water conservation involves covering the soil with a thick layer of shredded bark, chopped straw, or similar substances to minimize moisture loss (and reduce weed seedlings as well). Many native and drought-tolerant plants will do fine without mulch once

Though tough and drought-tolerant once established, daylilies flower far more abundantly when given a moderate but reliable supply of water before and during their period of bloom. They also make good temporary homes for tiny tree frogs.

they are well established, but immediately after planting, and for the first several years of their garden life, a water-conserving mulch gives them a better start.

When planning newer garden and borders, make a point of choosing plants—both natives and exotics—that have proven reliably drought tolerant in your region. Give these tough plants a great start in life by preparing their home ground well, amending it according to its type. However, rather than ripping out established gardens in the name of ecological righteousness, simply replace lost or struggling plants with sturdier creatures. Xeric gardening or Xeriscape usually employs a combination of drought-tolerant native plants with others from similar climate zones around the world. Hundreds of such plants take drought in stride, from ornamental trees and flowering shrubs down to perennials of all sorts. To learn which are likely to thrive in your area, consult your county extension service agent, or look through the excellent regional lists included in *Xeriscape Gardening* by Connie Ellefson, Tom Stephens, and Doug Welsh (see the appendix).

Though most gardeners accept the need to change our watering ways, for some, it smacks of deprivation, like giving up a favorite food. It helps to think in terms of change rather than sacrifice. Indeed, many of the plants that fill my own extensive borders are not especially drought tolerant, yet even in hot summers they thrive on a single monthly watering. Why? Because when I do water, I water deeply, until the soil is wet a good 8 to 10 inches down. Thick, moisture-conserving mulches keep the soil cool and damp despite drying sun and wind. Third, these borders are built on beautiful, homemade dirt, improved continuously with mulches and amendments.

How we water makes a big difference as well. Oscillating (back-and-forth) sprinklers are popular but inefficient and can actually promote mildews and other diseases. Impulse or impact sprinklers are rather better choices, their larger droplets reducing evaporation loss and delivering more uniform water coverage, not puddling at both ends of their range. Water-wasting soaker hoses are now illegal in some areas, since they are so often turned on and forgotten, but a good drip-line system does everything a soaker hose does, only better. Drip irrigation consists of sturdy hoses and emitters that release water at a slow but steady rate. Though extremely efficient, it offers the gardener a bewildering array of options. Happily, Robert Kourik's excellent book, *Drip Irrigation for Every Landscape and All Climates*, explains those options with clarity and humor. (If you can't find it locally, it can be ordered for $16 post-paid, from Drip Irrigation Book, P.O. Box 1841, Santa Rosa, CA 95402.) However you water, an inexpensive automatic timer that attaches at the tap outlet is a waste-reducing convenience.

Watering habits can be hard to change, but it's worth making an effort. To encourage deep roots rather than shallow ones that dry out quickly, we must water deeply and evenly. The thirsty roots will follow the water down and away, like an impatient batter chasing a good slider. Done well, it need not be done often. New transplants should be hand watered on a regular and more frequent basis, but established plants are tougher. Let the topsoil dry out to a depth of 3 to 4 inches before watering again. Pampered plants may protest a bit, but unless they really look sad, make them tough it out a little longer than usual. Once your soil is well prepped, amended, and mulched, you will find yourself watering less and getting more for your efforts.

In very dry soils and situations, garden hydrogels can make a world of difference to plant performances. These new garden gels (made from

In high summer, our small island water company asks that we restrict garden watering. If the borders are deeply prepared and well mulched, they hold up beautifully on a single monthly watering. However, daily hand watering of pots can't be neglected.

such various substances as cornstarch and petroleum by-products) are among the best soil amendments money can buy. "Hydrophilic" means water loving, and these products act like little reservoirs for our plants. They also condition soils, opening heavy ones to air and water, and making light soils more water retentive. The gels are sold as dry powders or crystals that look much like rock salt, and come in several grades from ultra-fine to coarse. Add a tablespoon of this stuff to a bucket of water, and an hour or so later, the bucket will be full of glistening, icelike chunks of gel. Each piece is essentially a little water bag, its skin easily penetrated by plant roots which can then use the water as they need it. When rain or dew falls, or when you water the garden, the "bags" refill. No matter

what their derivation, these gels are nontoxic and neutral in pH, and when they do break down, in anything from a few months to five or more years, they degrade into nitrogen, ammonia, and water.

There are many brands on the market, but they are not created equal; only those which are at least 94 percent copolymer will hold up in the garden setting. The cheaper kinds are fine for use in containers and baskets, where they only need to last one season (and where they may reduce water needs by as much as 75 percent). For garden use, however, we want long-term performance, and should invest in more permanent gels. In my own tests over the past five years, I have found Broadleaf P4 to be the longest lasting, with Viterra Aqua-gel running in second place. Where salt con-

The new Northwest Perennial Alliance Shade Border at the Bellevue Botanic Garden in Bellevue, Washington. Complex plantings like this require thoughtful planning and placement of drip irrigation lines.

centrations are high, as in seaside gardens, even the best polymers tend to degrade fairly fast, and will need replacement every few years. Otherwise, sunlight is their worst enemy, and a thick, shielding mulch proves their best friend.

Hydrogels should be plumped with water before you use them, for it is difficult to get an even distribution of dry gel and soil. I keep a 5-gallon bucket of hydrated gel at my potting station, and add it to the bottom half of every seed tray or container. I also dip cuttings and divisions into the gel before potting them up, and use it with all newly purchased plants, which nearly

always need an immediate move to the next pot size up. I also keep a smaller bucket of hydrated gel on my roving potting station, an old rusted-out wheelbarrow which carries compost, pots, and tools wherever I am working in the garden. Whenever a plant is added to the border, it gets a handful of hydrated gel at the root zone—a heaping tablespoonful for a 4-inch pot, a quarter cup for 2-gallon pots, a whole cupful for a large tree or shrub. The gel must be well incorporated, not left in lumps, or it can promote root rots instead of healthy plants. Shallow-rooted shrubs like rhododendrons and azaleas will benefit enormously from gels; to introduce gel to established plants, make a number of deep, narrow holes around the shrub, within its root zone, and fill them with a mixture of gel and compost. Water well, mulch the whole area, and watch the plants sail through the drought. Young, vigorous plants take about two weeks to find and tap into the gels, but older, slow-growing plants may need three or four weeks to show results, which, over time, become both obvious and impressive.

These polymers can be used in all ornamental situations, and are also valuable in the vegetable garden, though they should not be used with root crops (not that they are toxic, but it is not a good idea for humans to ingest polymers). Gels work water-saving wonders in lawns, though until now, it has only been practical to get them there when making a new lawn or completely renovating an existing one. However, a new gadget has been developed which injects hydrated gels directly into existing lawns. Though too expensive for most homeowners, the device may be available locally through machine rental shops, and is worth checking around to find. Whether we use polymers or not, we can effectively reduce the amount of water we spend on our lawn by watering it intelligently. In most areas, lawns should be watered only once or twice a month, but deeply, so the ground is saturated to a depth of at least 8 inches. When summer heats up, set the mower blades high, and the grass will both shade and mulch itself, further reducing thirst. In really hard

summers, the grass will go dormant early, turning a delicate shade of brown. It will renew its color with the first rains of autumn, but those who can't wait may console themselves with grass paint in several fresh shades (this stuff has been selling very well in California for years). As a longer-term solution, large expanses of grass can be replaced with drought-tolerant ground covers that hold their color through the heat, and just a small patch of lawn for sunbathing or picnicking on can be kept lush with extra water.

Ornamental gardens of all kinds can be designed and modified to be surprisingly conservative of water, without loss of beauty or complexity. My own extensive mixed borders, which hold thousands of thirsty plants, are watered only once a month during the summer. Thanks to a combination of all the steps outlined above—regular soil improvement, mulching, efficient watering techniques, and grouping plants by their needs—the garden remains full and handsome all summer despite receiving significantly less water than the average suburban lawn. (For scoffers who think the Pacific Northwest is a rain forest, I must add that we often receive less than an inch of measurable rainfall between May and October.) Applying all these changes will radically reduce the garden's dependence on supplemental water. Adopting even one of them will help to make the most of a precious resource that is not in truth at our disposal.

AUGUST

Finding Focal Points
Creating Centerpieces for Each Bed

The next time you drop by a bookstore, thumb through half a dozen handsome garden books. Chances are good that the same gardens will appear in several of them. Chances are even better that you will see variations of the same shots from each garden, over and over. If these are gardens you have visited yourself, you may wonder why your own favorite area or border never appears. The answer is probably because, though beautiful, those particular scenes are not photogenic. Even the best gardens only have so many great photo opportunities, despite being full of wonderful details.

This may seem puzzling, since, for the most part, the things that make a garden especially good are also photogenic—plenty of structure, firm lines, and abundant planting. However, a key element that often makes or breaks a composition is a focal point, a strong, emphatic shape that commands our attention and makes visual sense of each bed or planting. In small gardens, where structure is often in short supply, focal points give greater power to plantings that lack coherence on their own. In larger gardens, the borders may

Blazing 'Red Night' Asiatic lilies glow fire bright against a somber backdrop of purple redbud, *Cercis canadensis* 'Forest Pansy'. (Garden of Eleanor Carnwath, Kirkland, Washington.)

Where most of the plant elements have similar weight and value, the addition of an object like this elegant stone pot can emphasize the sculptural qualities of a garden composition. (Garden of T. R. Welch, Woodinville, Washington.)

vignette of each one and helps to emphasize its individual qualities.

In the garden, such a focal point might be a striking plant, perhaps a splendid *Rodgersia pinnata*, with gigantic, pinnate leaves, or a sculptural clump of bear's breeches, *Acanthus mollis*. In garden pictures, the focal point is often architectural, a weathered wall, an Elizabethan sundial, or a piece of actual sculpture that lends its own strength to bed or border. Such objects are nearly always more photogenic than the most structural of plants, and if well placed, are able to unite even disparate plantings through sheer domination. If your garden has areas that please you generally, yet seem to lack punch, or if certain combinations just won't come together, try adding some sort of focal point to intensify their effect.

Whether made by plants or objects, garden focal points help us to organize what we are seeing. Very often, border areas don't "read" well because nothing commands our attention. Plantings may be too similar or too sparse. At times, too, the common advice that all border plants be used in sweeps results in visual mishmash. Although stingy or timid planting is seldom effective, using too much of any single element also reduces impact and quickly becomes boring. This is especially obvious in gardens suffering from Ground Cover Syndrome, where the motto is clearly: When in doubt, smother it with ivy. Acres of ground covers are preferable to acres of weeds, but when was the last time you were irresistibly drawn to admire a mass of ivy, or pachysandra, or St. John's wort? Your eye reads the whole thing immediately and moves on, for nothing compels you to look again. The same holds true within the border, particularly when the garden is small and the beds narrow. In such situations, expanding our plant palette to increase the variety of plant forms and textures will

be dominated by their framework: an excess of hedge and hardscape—walls and paths, patios and arbors—can diminish the effect of mere flowers. The garden as a whole has plenty of definition, yet the beds and borders seem secondary in importance. Giving each bed or border a focal point or centerpiece of its own makes a finished picture or

help, but arranging the plants to lead up to a distinct focal point will strengthen the effect far more. Take that same ivy patch, add a group of glossy, cut-leaf red astilbes (perhaps 'Fire' or red-leaved 'Montgomery'), center them with a birdbath or a sculptural rock, and the dull scene becomes memorable, not to mention photogenic.

Focal points lend meaning and coherence to undefined plantings. Even in a tiny bed, a chubby cherub can soothe a flurry of little plants, while a simple stone lantern can make thin planting look spare and purposeful. To place the cherub or lantern well, think about Japanese gardens, where practically every element is a focal point from some angle. Keep moving that lantern—or cherub, or rock—until the result seems inevitable and looks right from as many viewpoints as possible. If nothing works, experiment with larger or smaller objects. Imagine the effect of a carved stone goddess carrying a swag of flowers. Too fussy? How about smooth balls of stone (or concrete), a stack of rounded beach stones, or an antique washtub planted with trailing vines?

If no object feels right, perhaps the composition needs another plant. A shrub with bold foliage such as oakleaf hydrangea or purple hazel has the potency to anchor a restless sea of too-similar perennials. A spiky red New Zealand flax (*Phormium* species) is a powerful antidote to amorphous plants. The plant placement process is the same as for objects, with one exception: Plants grow. If you can't visualize how the plant will look in maturity, make a rough model, using a flat cardboard representation of the shrub's outline for height and width, or filling a plastic bag with crumpled newspaper to approximate area and mass. Try to do these things when the neighbors are on vacation, because they can make you feel pretty silly. Do them anyway, though, for

however foolish-looking they may be, both methods are better placement guides than inexperience.

Figurative sculpture or objects like this playful astrolabe are best admired against a textured, rather than colorful, backdrop. Use them in areas where relatively plain mixtures of foliage would otherwise be the main attraction. (Garden of Lindsay Smith, Bainbridge Island, Washington.)

Many gardeners shun the fun or whimsical for fear of transgressing the implacable rules of good taste. However, not only is there nothing wrong with kitsch (if you genuinely enjoy it, indulge yourself—it's your garden!) but good taste is that which seems good to you. At Sissinghurst, Vita Sackville-West ended a long vista with a crumbling stone chair, its seat filled with fragrant thyme. This sculptural giant's seat suits its setting

This clever quartet of turf-seated chairs was made from old picket fencing recovered from a dumpster. This sort of garden art is refreshingly lively, infusing this quiet garden area with life and fun. (Garden of Geoff Beasley, designed by Michael Schultz, near Portland, Oregon.)

admirably, yet would look sadly out of place in most North American gardens. Near Portland, Oregon, the Beasley garden holds a quartet of garden chairs made from an old picket fence, with seats of turf. These, too, function like garden sculpture, giving importance to a stretch of lawn and very simple plantings. Their effect is surprisingly sophisticated, yet they would look entirely at home in many North American settings.

Gardens make natural settings for garden art of various kinds. Artful gardeners often take pleasure in using underappreciated colors as well as offbeat materials. At Wave Hill in The Bronx, New York, Marco Polo Stufano has made dynamic and internationally renowned color borders, transfusing tasteful blues and purples, pinks and silvers with vilified colors like magenta, hot orange, and screaming pink. Put in context, these colors become breathtaking rather than offensive, even to those who usually shun them. Similarly, Portland designer Michael Schultz incorporated the despised, low-brow glass gazing balls into his steel-and-glass garden Stonehenge, a witty garden sculpture that reflects sky and clouds, past and future. Another friend chose glass gazing balls in a dozen colors to hang from trees like oversized fruit. This made me think how luscious they would look if mossy and wet, provoking a woodland fantasy. Our back woods are full of rotting old tree trunks, green with thick moss. Why not pipe the crumbling end of such a log and let water trickle through the moss? How magical to cluster in its deep cleft six or seven shiny, deep-green glass balls, perhaps in several sizes. Partially covered with moss, partially shiny, they would look like exotic peas in a velvet-lined pod.

Genuine art, serious or playful, can elevate ordinary plantings and make living galleries of extraordinary ones. In my narrow boxwood border, a crocodile head (cast from lowly concrete) lurks beneath a froth of ferns, its poking snout startling more than one visitor into a closer look. In Berkeley, California, sculptor Marcia Donahue carves stone faces to drown in garden pools and stone skulls that lie unprotesting beneath one's feet. She also plays on color themes with a "silver garden" of silverware and cutlery and mingles marbled bowling balls among the ground covers. Edith Eddleman's splendid display borders at the North Carolina State University Arboretum are punctuated by aluminum dinosaurs painted in fetching pink and purple plaids to complement the neighboring perennials. When winter scours the borders bare, the tall, rustling grasses show remarkable winter color that has prompted many a visiting horticulturist to exclaim in admiration. Why should they feel foolish to learn that the color is not the work of nature but a collaboration between nature and Eddleman, who decorates them with (ecologically benign) spray paints?

There is no set formula for creating a garden focal point; they can be simple or baroque, formal or casual, serious or amusing, beautiful or severe. Experiment freely to find what kind of elements look harmonious in your own garden and what kinds of objects (if any) are compatible with your personal gardening style. Perhaps you will string an old iron bedstead with sweet peas, as my kids did, or perhaps your garden calls out for a formal quincunx of huge terra-rossa pots. Consider anything and everything, then select those which best balance the plantings they interact with. This, the final editing, is what proves hardest for many people. Remember, there's no time limitation involved. If you aren't sure about a piece or its placement, move it, change it, then give it—and yourself—time. If everything pleases you in turn, consider using a revolving series of objects. After all, even art galleries change their shows every season, so why shouldn't we? In every case, the point

remains the same: a focal point of any kind should attract our attention and make sense of its surroundings.

Plug-in Plants

Instant Replacements for Midsummer Duds

In high summer, borders rich in perennials come into their own. The muggy August heat brings them from swelling bud to triumphant maturity. Wherever we look, all is lush and full. Or is it? Ideally, midsummer gardens are supposed to look magnificent, yet in reality there are often quite a few disappointments to bear. Gardening is like any other team sport—if the whole line-up is healthy and at their peak of power, the results can be stupendous. The problem is that things seldom come together quite so neatly in real life. Garden plants are just as variable in performance and timing as people and they, too, have their slumps as well as their moments of glory.

In the best of years, the performance percentage is pretty good. Most plants are looking great, blooming at the right times and in the right combinations. However, a cold, wet, windy year or a hot, dry one will throw off the timing or influence the performance of many plants, and there's not a thing the gardener can do about it. In any year, plants die for all sorts of reasons, creating unsightly gaps. Spring bloomers may retreat into premature dormancy, leaving behind holes that need filling without harming the slumbering plant. Cat fights, dumb dogs, or errant soccer balls can wreak havoc in a flash. The gardener may simply grow tired of a timid color scheme. High summer doldrums stem from many causes, but few gardens escape them entirely.

All this could be viewed as a terrible tragedy, but who needs the extra stress? Seeking perfection or total control is a losing game anywhere, in or

Outsized tender plants like this bronze form of *Cordyline australis* make splendid accents for bed or border. This one is threaded with annual *Mina lobata*. (Author's garden.)

tions to garden difficulties are worked out. If purists grumble about horticultural cheating, just mention Gertrude Jekyll (which rhymes with "treacle"), the turn-of-the-century grande dame of the mixed border whose dictates still hold sway. She invariably refreshed her borders with potted plants, sometimes sunk into the ground, other times set on the ground in handsome containers. What was good enough for Gertrude is good enough for anybody.

Ms. Jekyll grew pots of wonderful accent plants just for this purpose. I don't bother, finding that midsummer shopping sprees are good for the soul and good for the garden as well. My forays always yield horticultural gold, giving the garden a new lease on life and me more options each autumn. As I tidy and reorganize the borders, I have plenty of choices on hand when it comes time to rearrange problem areas and replace failures. With this in mind, it makes sense to choose plants that will be welcome permanent additions to the garden whenever possible, though a splendid annual in full fig is excuse enough for purchase.

Before you shop, analyze your trouble spots so you can choose appropriate reinforcements. Are they shady or sunny areas? Would something with height and architectural lines, or something soft and cascading be more complementary to the setting? Which colors are wanted? Would a bold foliage plant be best? What kind of pot would be most suitable? (Remember that pots set on the ground will add their height to the plant's.) Once this checklist is complete, you can head for the nurseries, armed with accurate information and ripe for ideas.

Even in late summer, well-stocked nurseries should still have plenty to offer. If you need filler with height as well as character, look for outsized, buxom annuals like giant red-leaved castor beans (*Ricinus communis*), which can exceed 6 feet if

out of the garden. It's much more fun to see the midsummer slump as a chance to treat yourself to a few new plants and invigorate the garden with an infusion of fresh talent. Wise gardeners make any disaster an excuse to cruise nurseries for good-sized replacements in bud or bloom or lovely leaf. Plants of any kind—annual, shrub, bulb, or tree—are worth considering for the role of temporary placeholder until more permanent solu-

given enough sun and elbow room. Thready thimbleflower, *Gilia capitata*, rises in netted columns some 3 to 4 feet high, each delicate stem decorated with fluffy, sky-blue thimbles. Strapping, 3- to 5-foot dahlias, shaggy or sleek, could enliven the border back, as would tall sunflowers in rust and copper and tawny gold. Bigger border-back gaps can be filled by young potted trees with colorful foliage. A false acacia, *Robinia pseudoacacia* 'Frisia', is a charmer with sun-yellow, ferny foliage. Its branches are rather brittle and it needs shelter from strong winds, but it colors best when given at least half a day of full sun and in such a situation will hold its lovely gold through autumn. Purple weeping birch, red or green Japanese cutleaf maples, or variegated dogwoods all make marvelous fillers where large accidents have occurred. Any of these can sit happily at the back of the border in a huge container, waiting until fall for your final placement decision.

Moderate mid-border gaps can be disguised with big pots of trumpet lilies. Glorious Aurelian hybrids come in rose or lemon, peach or apricot, and fit nicely into narrow spaces between wider plants. The late-blooming oriental lilies are open and starry, their pale throats alight with gold. Pristine 'Casa Blanca', warm pastel 'Salmon Jewel', and hot red dwarf 'Star Gazer' all make excellent pot plants. Standard roses—the kind grown as tiny trees with fat pompon heads—or topiary rosemary with the same shape create firm anchors amid soft-textured, shapeless perennials. A multitude of young shrubs will do this as well, especially those with big, exotic foliage. Variegated *Hydrangea mariesii* has wide, toothed leaves edged with cream and flat, lacecap flower heads in rose and pink. Dapper *Daphne* x *burkwoodii* 'Carol Mackie' has trim, ivory-edged leaves. Dwarf buddleias like 'Pygmy Purple' or 'Nanho Blue' offer narrow leaves and conical flower heads alive with

butterflies. Variegated *Buddleia* 'Harlequin' blooms bright wine-red above slim leaves stippled with sage and cream. All of these are handsome temporary border members, growing well in containers or in the ground, but if you love the effect they produce and decide to give them a permanent position, remember to allow plenty of room for future expansion.

Certain houseplants double as summer boarders as well, particularly large-leaved exotics like rubber plant (*Ficus elastica*). This glossy creature boasts broad green foliage as much as 12 inches long, which strikes quite a note amid a drift of soft perennials. There are several handsome forms with red, cream-striped, or almost black leaves, all of which make the summer transition to the garden with grace. Equatorial-looking dwarf banana tree (*Musa cavendishii* 'Nana') is another splendid commuter, bringing tremendous foliage and the flavor of the tropics in its wake. Windmill palms (*Trachycarpus fortunei*) revel in the open air in warm regions, and the many-spoked wheels of their spiky foliage provide exciting contrast of form and texture in the border.

Whatever you decide to patch your holes with, all will need preventive health care before taking on the task. Where plug-ins are to replace defunct border members, remove the old plants and loosen the soil well. If near neighbors may be damaged by your border spade, gently tie or stake them back out of harm's way before you begin the operation. Thoroughly replenish the soil with compost and aged manure before replanting and check the plant itself; this late in the season, nursery plants may be root bound, their roots running round and round in tight circles, their soil exhausted. If so, soak the plant by immersing it in a bucket of water until no more air bubbles appear. Next, gently loosen the crowded roots, shaking out the old soil (there may not be much).

Now, place the plant, checking to see that it faces front (often pot-grown plants show a definite orientation, and will look "backward" if placed differently from the way they were grown in the nursery.) When it looks right, sift fresh soil between the roots and backfill the planting hole, heaping the soil around the stem, then watering it in gen-

This black-leaf rubber tree, a fancy form of the common houseplant, was a $5.98 special from the grocery store. It winters over in our sun porch or a friend's greenhouse. (Author's garden.)

erously. Add a tad of fish fertilizer (dilute to one quarter strength or even less) to the water to reduce transplant shock. Finally, mulch the entire area thickly and release the surrounding plants from their bonds.

Where plug-in plants will remain in pots, whether above the ground or sunk, they, too, should be treated for bound roots before repotting. New pots made of clay or other porous materials must also be well soaked to prevent the thirsty pot from sucking away all the moisture you are trying to offer the new plant. Pot nursery plants up at least a full size. Move gallon-sized plants into larger (2- or 5-gallon) containers, using a water-retaining soil mixture with some compost added. Blend in a handful of hydrated polymer such as Broadleaf P4 to conserve water, then mulch the pot's soil with shredded bark. If the container you have chosen is more than five times larger than the original pot, it's best to use the oversized pot as an outer shell. Line the container bottom with damp sphagnum moss—this comes in stringy bundles and holds many times its own weight in water. Don't try to substitute powdered peat moss, for it won't work well at all. Drop in the smaller, repotted plant, and fill the spaces between them with more damp sphagnum moss. (This, however, must never be allowed to dry out, for it is very hard to rewet thoroughly. If it does, pour in hot water.)

Once your new plants are comfortable, it's time to introduce them into the border. Properly positioned, they should appear thoroughly at home and long in place. If a terra-cotta pot looks glaringly new, wet it well, paint it with buttermilk, and rub on a bit of moss. (Some gardeners actually rub their pots with mud to give them an antique look.) If the pot looks too hard-edged, add a tumbling pansy or trailing lobelia to soften the lip. Now, nestle the pots in the gaps, fiddling with

Stunning pots like these are works of art in themselves. Artfully planted, they are like little moveable borders that can be shifted about the garden as needed. (Pots by Robert Jewett, plantings by Withey/Price Garden Design.)

their placement until they look natural. It often helps to curl a trailing arm from a nearby sprawler around the pot, or to allow a few leaves from a taller neighbor to overlap the pot edge. When all is right, *voilà*! The garden instantly looks revitalized and Gertrude would approve.

A Tea Garden for an August Noon

High summer is often a time of great floral strength, yet soaring or irregular summer temperatures often leave the border rather worse for wear. One corner of the garden, however, seems never to falter no matter how hot or dreary the summer. This is the tea garden, a sunny corner near my kitchen door which is also overlooked by the kitchen windows. Thanks to a backbone of evergreenery, including a good many Mediterranean subshrubs and herbs, this area looks well clothed in any season. In a difficult summer when other parts of the garden fail of their promise, the tea garden remains very much alive, overflowing with blossom and bees. Here, culinary herbs mingle closely with more strictly ornamental plants. Silvery, round-leaved horehound (*Marrubium vulgare*) and pink-flowered beauty mint (*Calamintha ascendens*) set off 'Water Witch' daylilies, lavender blue with a smudgy mauve watermark above a golden throat. Glossy purple trumpets of old-fashioned 'Mabel' lilies emerge between columns of bronze fennel. Cobalt blue borage flowers rise above explosive bursts of golden marjoram and yellow-leaved oregano.

The tea garden is not so much a place to take tea—though it is often used that way—but a place to make tea. In it, lavender and bergamot, rosemary and thyme bloom despite any vagaries of weather, their flowers attracting clouds of butterflies as well as an amazing variety of bees. All day, dive-bombing hummingbirds battle for nectar from red-flowered pineapple sage and violet anise hyssop (*Agastache anisata*). Each afternoon, tawny brown skippers cluster on the lavender's tall flower spikes, while at twilight, pale moths flicker above sticky, night-fragrant tobacco flowers (*Nicotiana alata* 'Fragrant Cloud'). These and other adaptable herbs thrive in dry, torrid summers yet take cool or rainy ones in stride. Though many herbs show a tendency to sprawl in wet summers, a good clipping will prompt a bushy second growth that remains tidy through autumn. Mounders like oregano and basil, mint and marjoram, savory and tarragon, dill and sage should all be sheared back in August. Woody herbs, too, such as rosemary, lavender, sage, and horehound, can be cut back a bit to tighten their texture and promote fresh growth. These, however, must be trimmed with a lighter hand, for if taken back to old (bare) wood, they rarely if ever refurbish. In every case, their mature leaves may be dried (indoors, if wet weather makes this necessary) for winter use as well as mixed into summer teas.

The teas themselves vary to reflect our moods as well as the weather. A warm, sunny morning might suggest a sparkling mixture of lemon verbena, orange mint, raspberry leaves, and a touch of chamomile. A cool, gray morning prompts a wake-up brew of minty anise hyssop enlivened with smoky bergamot and cinnamon basil. Rainy days are warmed by a zingy combination of mashed rose hips, lemon thyme, and a smidgen of lavender blossom. A relaxing evening cup might hold a sleepy blend of catnip, pineapple sage, red clover, and St. John's wort. On nights we plan to sit up late, perhaps watching the Perseid meteorites streak across the midnight sky, a refreshing spearmint and lemon verbena mixture keeps us calm but alert. Clearly, the teamaker's options are plentiful.

To build confidence and blending skills, begin with simple pairs of mildly flavored herbs. For a two-cup pot, try two teaspoons of fresh chamomile and five or six red currant leaves, or a small handful of lemon balm and several sprigs of spearmint. To create more complex mixtures, add new ingredients one or two at a time and in small amounts, altering them gradually as personal taste suggests. Flavor conservatives generally prefer clean, simple flavors, while those with consuming culinary curiosity have a lovely time experimenting with less common ingredients. (It's a good idea to check unfamiliar ingredients against a good herbal when experimenting, though, for sometimes one part of a plant may be edible while another is not. Rhubarb, for instance, has a mildly toxic leaf despite its edible stems.) In time, you may join the experts who employ dozens of herbs in a single blend, carefully balancing emphatic flavors with mellow ones, brightening a deep-toned mixture with a touch of brisk citrus or mint, or adding body and depth to light blends with a touch of culinary thyme or bitter horehound.

It is great fun to wander through the tea garden early in the morning, listening to the birds and enjoying the rising scents of leaf and blossom. Teapot in hand, I might toss in a bunch of chamomile flowers for my brew base, adding a snippet of fruit sage here, a handful of lemon balm there, a few stalks of spearmint, some cucumber-flavored borage blossoms, and a leaf or two of lemon basil. Top the mixture off with boiling water, let it stand, covered with a thick cozy, for some minutes—usually six to ten minutes, rather longer than one would steep black or green tea—and pour out a fragrant cup of summer. If making iced tea base, simply pack a large saucepot with herbs, fill it with boiling water, cover tightly, and let sit for fifteen or twenty minutes. (Four cups each of herbs and water make roughly enough infusion for eight to ten cups of tea.) Strain the tea through a fine sieve and taste—often such a blend is full bodied and flavorful all by itself, but some mixtures are improved by adding a bit of honey, mixed in while the tea is still hot. Stir well and chill until ready to serve the tea, diluted to taste with cold water, seltzer, or a flavored spritzer and garnished with a sliver of lime and a sprig of mint. Ice cubes made with limeade or lemon water add a cooling clink to the glass without weakening the tea.

Our tea garden is fairly large, extending over some 40 feet of border, itself 12 feet deep. Naturally, herbs in frequent use are ranged near the front of the border where they are easily got at, and the few taller plants that are placed further back have convenient (though hidden) stepping-stones at their feet to simplify access. Even so, we often wander farther afield, both to other parts of the border and even into the woods and meadows to gather wild rose hips or yarrow blossoms. However, gardeners whose space is limited can create practical and productive tea gardens in far smaller spaces. Dozens of herbs may be nestled about a tiny urban patio, grown between the flagstones of a narrow terrace or contained in pots on a balcony or deck. Wherever they are asked to live, nearly all herbs are united in appreciating plenty of sun and good, well-drained garden soil. Where winters are cold, the more tender sorts must be grown in pots and carried indoors in late autumn. If given a sunny windowsill to live on,

many will continue to reward the gardener with tasty leaves and flowers well into winter.

Though tea garden candidates are numerous indeed, a few are firm standards. The list of good mixers must be led by chamomile, a willing work-

Creeping golden oregano makes a handsome accent at the front of the border. A leaf or two adds depth and body to summer teas as well.

er that wants only sun and decent soil to produce an endless succession of tiny, starry flowers as long as you faithfully harvest them. Perennial or Roman chamomile (*Chamaemelum nobile*, Zone 4) is somewhat handsomer than the annual or German kind (*Matricaria chamomilla*), but neither is going to win any awards for style. Both are rather straggly but generous plants that dry well. Lemon balm (*Melissa officinalis*, Zone 4) makes a pleasantly mild tea base and its clean, sweet scent lifts the spirits. The type plant is unprepossessing and has a remarkable tendency to seed itself everywhere. The attractive form 'All Gold' is vividly yellow in spring, its foliage fading to old gold by midsummer. It is a less aggressive seeder, and a fair portion of its offspring will be similarly gilded. Spearmint and peppermint are both invaluable tea plants, while lemon, orange, and cinnamon mints are delightful palette extenders. The mints (*Mentha* species) are willing but rowdy and even in large gardens they are best confined to large pots. Set the pots on saucers or tiles to keep the thrusting roots out of the ground and divide the plants every few years to keep them lusty.

Culinary herbs earn a place in the teapot as well. Thymes come in an even broader range of flavors than mints. Specialty nurseries can provide thymes that smell and taste of lemon or orange blossom, of caraway seed or lavender, among many other things. Rosemary, both the flowers and the needlelike leaves, adds a sharp, pungent snap to a tea, as do peppery oregano and milder marjoram. Soothing dill tea has been used to lull teething infants to sleep for millennia. Fresh basil, fennel, and savory and cooking sage (*Salvia officinalis*) add an intriguing undertone to herbal teas, especially when used in tiny amounts. Tender sages such as the felt-leaved fruit sage, *S. dorisiana*, and pineapple sage, *S. elegans*, can be used more generously to add a high, citrusy accent to herbal blends.

Plants we are accustomed to thinking of as strictly ornamental may have ancestral connections with our teapot as well. Bergamot, or bee-balm (*Monarda didyma*), needs ample garden

Purple sage, *Salvia officinalis* 'Purpurascens', and bronze fennel, *Foeniculum vulgare* 'Bronze Form', are hard-working border plants as well as tasty tea ingredients.

space, but it rewards those who plant it with piquant foliage, the mysterious ingredient that lends character to Earl Grey black tea blends. On its own, the foliage makes a softly spicy brew our forebears called "Oswego tea." It is also a lovely blender with a potent floral fragrance that fills the kitchen. In the garden, bergamot boasts clustered, whiskery, red flowers that are prime favorites with hummingbirds and butterflies. The species is not a terrific-looking plant, but deep-toned 'Cambridge Scarlet', the copper-red 'Prairie Glow', or the clear pastel 'Croftway Pink' contribute to teapot and garden alike. Anise hyssop seed (*Agastache anisata*, Zone 6) is available from a number of native plant nurseries. This buxom late bloomer offers smoky violet flowers that are often combined in English gardens (where it is grown as a tender perennial) with rust and bronze chrysanthemums, slate-blue asters, and rosy Japanese anemones. We could easily do the same, and it would not protest a bit if we removed a few of its leaves for tea now and then. Indeed, pinching back its stems in early summer will cause it to be extraordinarily floriferous come autumn. Like many border beauties, this one appreciates moist soils rich with humus.

The rose family provides a goodly number of tea ingredients, from rose petals and ripe red rose hips to the aromatic leaves of raspberries, strawberries, blackberries, and red currants. Scented geraniums (*Pelargonium* species), with their thick, often velvety leaves, are also brewable and provide an even larger array of scent and savor, taking us past familiar flavors like apple or violet to exotics like nutmeg, coconut, and almonds. Unlike their hardy cousins, scented geraniums can't tolerate even a few degrees of frost and must retire indoors at the beginning of autumn, but they relish summers spent in the open.

If this sounds intriguing, you can start your own tea garden right now. Begin with trips to local nurseries that specialize in herbs (they are often listed this way in the phone book). Since many are small or family businesses, call first to check for open hours and directions, and ask about classes and workshops as well. If your area is low on herb suppliers, consult Barbara Barton's classic handbook, *Gardening by Mail* (see the appendix) for mail-order sources. You can also browse seed catalogs for less common herbs, for most, both annual and perennial, grow readily from seed. Pick a sunny, open site, improve the soil, and give your young plants a good start. Before long, you will find yourself in your own tea garden on an August noon, drinking in summer's essence.

Recycled Flowers

Practical Composting for Gardens of Any Size

Unromantic and often unlovely, compost is not one of gardening's glamour subjects. It is, however, among the most important, for few substances offer as many benefits to the garden. If you aren't exactly sure what compost is, you are not alone; despite extensive research, no one has yet been able to analyze, let alone duplicate, this gardener's black gold. Simply put, it is a blend of degraded organic matter. In nature, it makes up the organic portion (as opposed to the mineral elements) of soil, where it is known as humus. When we build compost and add it to our garden soils, we are increasing the humus content many times over, boosting both soil and plant health in the process.

Fortunately, we don't have to understand compost chemically to profit from it. Compost improves the texture of any soil, absorbing and retaining water in light soils, unlocking heavy clays to improve drainage and air circulation. Though low in nutrients, compost is a superb plant food, mild, long-lasting, and far more complex than any commercial fertilizer devised. It is the ideal nutritional supplement where slow, steady growth is the goal. It is a splendid soil builder, and as all gardeners know, healthy soils make for healthy, independent plants. Neutral in pH, compost buffers acidic or alkaline soils, bringing them closer to the neutral zone.

If the process of composting seems unpleasant, think of it not as rotting garden garbage but as recycled flowers. Compost is as natural as bread, and the enzymes and bacteria that transform dead plants into crumbly black humus are the equivalent of the wild yeasts that caused the first breads to rise. Recycling is exactly what composting is all about, returning vital resources to the garden.

To turn garden detritus into plant food, suitable materials are added to a compost pile or bin in layers, alternating green, or hot, materials—fresh grass clippings, leaves, and stems—and brown, or cool, ones—straw, dried grass and leaves. In order to rot nicely rather than nastily, compost, like plants or yeast, requires both air and water. Once a pile starts to work (or heat up; the term is the same for yeast), it should always be moist but never sodden. Too much hot stuff and the pile compacts and rots anaerobically, producing foul smells and slimy goop. Too much dry stuff and nothing much happens at all. When both green and brown materials are used in roughly equal measure, evenly mixed and moist and adequately aerated, the result is sweet-smelling garden gold.

Despite a zillion variations, there are really only two ways to compost. Slow, or passive, composting requires more time than effort and is most efficient where large piles can be built and left undisturbed for a long time. "Compost heap" is the usual term and a most descriptive one. Where space permits, one corner of the garden becomes the place where all garden gleanings are heaped up to rot at their leisure. Country gardens often hold serial heaps which provide a steady supply of compost for mulch, potting soil, or furnishing new beds. This method relies on size for success; piles less than a cubic yard are inefficient and may never heat up properly. Materials are layered on as they accumulate all year, each addition covered with a scattering of soil. (This soil layer conserves moisture, introduces soil bacteria, and reduces odors that may attract curious critters.)

All garden leftovers will break down sooner or later, but coarse, bulky plants like cabbages, Brussels sprouts, and corn stalks may take several years to degrade unless they are chopped up into smaller pieces. Large leaves may mat together and refuse to rot unless similarly reduced in size, and quantities of dry leaves should be mixed with fresh grass clippings and scattered over a pile rather than thickly layered alone. In spring, the entire pile should be turned over with a pitchfork, its contents remixed and mounded again. Six or eight months later, the inner portion will be ready to use. It may not look like picture book compost, but your garden won't care. If you do, rub the chunky stuff through a wire screen (often sold as a gardener's sieve) to get finer-textured compost. Larger chunks of uncomposted material may be set aside as the basis for another slow pile.

In smaller spaces, or where tidiness is important, hot, or active, bin composting is most practical. This requires greater human participation

Pink-flowered lemon catmint, *Calamintha citriodora,* has a complex, minty flavor and a sparkling citric scent. Our cats love to sleep beneath it, and it lends a relaxing, slightly soporific effect to summery iced tea blends. (Author's garden.)

Garden making begins with manure and ends in compost. These hard-working helpers supply my garden with a perfect blend of rabbit and chicken manure and composted straw.

but offers quick results. How quick depends on how much the gardener is willing (or able) to contribute to the process. Well-made hot compost really does get hot—a properly built pile can exceed 130 degrees Fahrenheit at its core. In hot composting, materials are added to the pile (or, more often, to the compost bin) in layers, but instead of waiting for nature to do the work, the gardener lends a hand by turning, or aerating, the compost at frequent intervals. Compost piles are most easily tossed and mixed with a pitchfork, but for small bins, compost wands are preferred. These are straight sticks with wing-shaped pro-

jections that fold flat when pushed in, then spring out when pulled back, leaving airholes behind. However it's done, aeration increases the available oxygen, feeding the bacterial fires that "cook" compost.

Hot compost is further accelerated by chopping or shredding coarse materials, since increasing their surface area also increases their rate of decomposition. It's great fun to slash away at precompost with a machete; like splitting wood, compost whacking lets off a lot of steam. Lawn mowers are also useful shredders—just run the Lawnboy over a pile of leaves a time or two and they are beautifully reduced. Garden trimmings tend to be of the green or hot persuasion early in the year, but by summer's end, a fair percentage will be browning off. To even things out, shred and add the greenest half to the compost bin, covered with a thin layer of dirt. Let the rest sit in the sun for a few days until it dries out, reducing in bulk and weight, then add it to the pile with another thin covering of dirt. Kitchen scraps can be reduced to slurry in a food processor, but bones or meat or any food with a high fat content such as cheese doesn't belong in the compost pile. Some will mold, introducing the wrong kinds of bacteria, while others produce ugly smells when they rot, often attracting animal scavengers.

To begin backyard composting, it is not necessary to buy an expensive bin; any topless, bottomless container that holds a minimum of a square yard will do. A good-sized garden produces a lot of clippings and groomings, so you may need several bins to contain the overflow. The most effi-cient home composting system is a series of three connected bins, each at least a yard square. Layer the first bin full of chopped wastes, sprinkling a little water if they seem dry, poking your compost wand in a few places if the mix seems too compact. Within a few days, the pile will heat up to the point where you can see steam rise from it on cool mornings. After a week or so, the pile will cool down. When it does, pitchfork its contents into the second bin, mixing well and giving it a few more pokes with the aerating wand. This pile, too, will heat up and cool down, at which point it is mixed and turned into the last bin, where it will make its final breakdown. After it heats and cools for the third time, any large, rough chunks are tossed back and the rest is ready to use in the garden. Start to finish, this method takes some six to eight weeks. Meantime, that first bin can be filled again, for the garden recycling process is as continual—and rewarding—as gardening itself.

SEPTEMBER

Big Picture Perennials

Standouts with Both Beauty and Character

For many gardeners, perhaps most, the pleasure of growing flowers one likes is ample repayment for whatever work may be involved. At first, all we ask from our plants is that they be themselves, delighting us in season. After mooning over fancy garden books, however, we begin to suspect that manipulating our flowers into memorable vignettes might be even more fun. Looking at colorful border combinations makes the concept seem quite a simple proposition; put a bunch of attractive, compatible plants together and stand back! It is a curious fact that the result does not always make a pleasing picture. There may be both framework—a backdrop of hedge or shrubbery—and frothy floral filling, yet the picture won't quite develop. When a garden group doesn't snap into focus, quite often it is because the plants involved are all of similar visual importance. Like a school group portrait, it lacks a centerpiece.

In or out of the garden, a striking picture always has a clear subject. Floral compositions are most often painted with perennials, which are lovely in bloom yet seldom definite enough in shape to stand out amid a blur of equally pretty

The huge seedheads of *Allium christophii* are often still resplendent in autumn, though the flowers have long since faded. (Garden of Steven Antonow, Seattle, Washington.)

The rugged, bronzed leaves of *Rodgersia podophylla* stand out dramatically amid smaller-leaved perennials. The golden globe flowers in the foreground are *Trollius chinensis*. (Garden of Eleanor Carnwath, Kirkland, Washington.)

size, shape, or coloring. Such assertive plants direct our attention, transforming visual chaos into satisfying pictures.

Several qualities contribute to showboat status. Stature, of both height and mass, often sets these plants apart. Large foliage is another plus, particularly if uncommonly shaped or colored. Eye-catching flowers are generally a strong asset. The biggest factor is harder to define but easy to recognize: showboat plants have presence. Whatever their qualities, they are distinctive and hard to overlook.

Wherever you live, there are plenty of potent perennials which can fill this vital role in your garden. Among the best are bear's breeches, several species of European perennial herb that have been pleasing the human eye for millennia. The big, leathery leaves of *Acanthus mollis* decorated the tops of ancient Greek columns and were a common motif in folk art and embroidery all over Europe. Several species make imposing garden plants some 4 feet tall and nearly as wide. *Acanthus mollis* (Zone 8, to 4 feet) offers glossy, deep-cut foliage some 2 feet long, punctuated by whorling spires of hooded, purple-and-cream flowers. The hardier form, *A. m.* var. *latifolius* (Zone 6 with protection, to 5 feet), has even more dramatic leaves, broadly oval and shallowly cut, while those of spiny bear's breeches (*A. spinosus*, Zone 6, to 4 feet) look like Martian ferns, each frond dangerously armed with spines. It produces generous quantities of mauve-and-ivory flowers on large spikes in midsummer. Though none are brilliant bloomers, their subtly colored spikes remain structurally potent for months, as does their magnificent foliage. All prefer sharp drainage, deep mulch, and some shade, especially in hot, dry regions, but accept nearly any good garden soil. *Acanthus mollis* is the better performer in cool

companions. Happily, there are a few perennials with pizzazz, plants which naturally assume pride of place. Put one of these showboats into an unsettled border scene and suddenly the other plants become pleasant subsidiaries. Instead of skipping restlessly over an indefinite mass, the eye is forcefully drawn to admire their strengths, whether of

summer climates, while *A. spinosus* and its extra lacy form, *A. spinosissimus* (Zone 6, to 4 feet), tolerate a broader range of temperature variations.

A culinary gem, *Angelica archangelica* (Zone 4) sends stalks of what looks like gigantic Queen Anne's lace 6 feet high, and its tremendous, coarsely divided, dark green leaves spread nearly as wide. An extraordinary Korean cousin, *A. gigas* (Zone 4, to 5 feet), has the same wide, rather ruffled leaves, but their sage green is veined in burgundy and their stems are richly wine stained. The flower umbels are similarly architectural but more compact, like gigantic pincushions stuck with a zillion pins, and they are colored midnight red, smoldering and ashy, rather than angelic white. Both are short-lived, ardently self-sowing perennials, rather like foxgloves, so allow some seedlings to mature each season in order to keep these plants in the garden. Both thrive in moist garden soils, taking sun or filtered shade in stride. *Angelica gigas* colors most dramatically in full sun, but its flowers last longer and its foliage looks better when grown in partial shade.

Both the outsized foliage and the ruddy, ribbed stems of *Angelica gigas* remind many people of rhubarb. In fact, some kitchen garden rhubarbs move as gracefully into the border as angelica, particularly those with red-backed leaves and feathery pink or cream colored flowers. Several exotic rhubarb species are grown purely for their delectable appearance. The most spectacular is the red cutleaf rhubarb, *Rheum palmatum* 'Atrosanguineum' (Zone 5). This stunning 6-footer can be grown from seed, though it may take three or four years for plants to reach their mature height. Sometimes 'Bowles' Variety', an especially good form selected by the famous English plantsman E. A. Bowles, is available from specialty nurseries; if so, snap it up and plant it where its fresh,

hot crimson leaves will sparkle against icy blue-green or old gold foliage. My father once waded into the border to breakfast off a Himalayan rhubarb, *R. australe* (Zone 5), which boasts elephant ear foliage and lusty, 7-foot bloom spikes. Though it's a beauty, I would not recommend serving this or other rhubarb relatives up with

Cousin to the culinary herb, gorgeous *Angelica gigas* is a standout in any company. Try it against the silvery gray foliage of arctic willow, *Salix glauca*, for a lovely contrast of texture and color.

strawberries and cereal, for the toxins that are concentrated in the foliage of the kitchen variety are present in all parts of some rhubarb species.

A big bruiser from Brazil, *Gunnera manicata*, and its slightly less robust Chilean buddy, *G.*

Plants don't have to be huge to have a lot of character. Yellow-flowered Jerusalem sage, *Phlomis samia*, is distinctive and statuesque, yet fits into small gardens with ease. (Northwest Perennial Alliance Border at the Bellevue Botanic Garden in Bellevue, Washington.)

chilensis (both Zone 7) are exceptional big picture plants. A tall man can stand without stooping beneath a well-grown gunnera, and there is no better antidote to suburban blandness than growing one of these outrageous giants in the front garden. Like many oversized plants, gunneras need a few years to reach their mature heights and in arid or starved soils they may remain dwarfed. Though often consigned to the waterside, gunneras thrive in any reasonably moist, good garden soil and can be successfully—and stunningly—grown in a large tub. Leaves the size of opera cloaks and bristling red flowers like Brobdingnagian chimney brushes create a highly exotic effect. In small gardens, these great plants promote the illusion of greater size and depth than actual space entails. In any setting, they effectively erase the harshest reminder of the ordinary world. Where winters are mild, their own great leaves, folded back on themselves to blanket their rugged crowns, are adequate frost protection. Elsewhere, they must be covered in late autumn with generous heaps of dry leaves and straw (throw in a handful of stinky mothballs to discourage nesting mice). I know of at least one garden in chilly Zone 4 where gunneras planted by a running stream are kept safe through long, hard winters with mountains of insulating bracken and branches. Not every plant is worth this much bother, but a well-grown gunnera can be the star of the garden.

Hardy and handsome, Jerusalem sage, *Phlomis samia* (also sold as *P. russeliana*, Zone 4, 3 to 4 feet) rises statuesque amid a rustling sea of simple bellflowers and daisies. This strongly formed plant boasts big fuzzy angel-wing leaves, massed in a whorling basal rosette, then mounting in arching pairs up the tall bloom stalks. In high summer, these are trimmed at regular intervals with round baubles like Victorian ball fringe, spiky with chamois yellow flowers, lipped, and tubular. To play up their form, surround Jerusalem sage with mounded 'Johnson's Blue' geraniums, strap-leaved, lemony daylilies, and ice-green dwarf poker plant, *Kniphofia* 'Little Maid'. Even after the flowers fade to a soft biscuit brown, the flower heads remain attractive and structural. In autumn, cut the stems back and groom away any yellowing foliage. Leave the tidy new growth in place and the plants will remain furnished through the winter. Jerusalem sage does best in full sun and any good garden soil that drains quickly.

A clumping sunflower, *Inula magnifica* (Zone 4), has broad, hairy leaves and mastlike, mahogany stems topped with hand-sized, yolk-yellow daisy flowers in August and September. Broad of beam and imposing in height (it can exceed 3 by 6 feet), this showboat needs ample room to develop. It consorts well with golden hops, purple hazel, or copper beech, and a single, well-grown specimen can anchor a large planting of less distinctive perennials with its solid, substantial good looks. Bigger and bolder (though rather coarser) is *I. racemosa* (Zone 4, 6 to 8 feet), which boasts stout sheaves of huge, elliptical leaves that can reach a yard in length at the crown's base. In bloom, these plants are pyramidal, for the leaves decrease in size as they scale towering stems like Christmas trees topped with a handful of stars. Finely cut petals give the flowers a light, fringed texture that offsets the heavy foliage and thick stems nicely. Though composites (sunflower family members) and ornamental grasses have become hackneyed partners, these giant sunflowers do pair attractively with pampas grasses or Chinese maiden grasses (*Miscanthus sinensis* forms).

These last two are good examples of large-scale plants that have a certain magnificence yet can scarcely be called knockouts. That distinction must be reserved for plants like bear's breeches and Jerusalem sage that have it all; great presence, good

form and habit, fine foliage, and attention-grabbing flowers. Browsing through any picture encyclopedia of perennials will turn up plenty of other big picture plants to try out. Choose a few, place them with care, and watch them effortlessly knit raveled borders back together. They do their work so well that it's tempting to pack the garden with these prima donnas. However, the impact of each may be diminished by the close company of equally powerful plants, especially in small spaces. Build clean compositions, surrounding a single focal point with appropriate secondary plants. Fiddle with their placement until they are just as you want to see them. All the fuss will be rewarded by remarkable vignettes that linger pleasantly in memory.

Leaves of Grass

Garden Grasses with Panache

Garden grasses quickly waxed and even sooner waned in popularity. A few years ago, they were all the horticultural rage, yet apart from a few majestic park plantings or a lone pampas grass decorating a trim suburban lawn, one seldom sees ornamental grasses in people's gardens. Perhaps this is because so many of those first highly touted plantings were intimidating in size and scope. Perhaps it is because few books illustrate grasses in beautiful and exciting garden combinations with shrubs and companionable perennials. Perhaps it is because so many second-rate grasses were introduced without accurate descriptions or thorough evaluation of their garden behavior. Whatever the reasons, among the masses of grasses are many undervalued plants which deserve to be better known.

Discard the encroaching and the weedy, the rank and the insignificant and what is left is a goodly host of handsome, mannerly garden grasses. Any experienced gardener's list of The Best will vary significantly from region to region, yet a hardy handful perform reliably under diverse and even difficult conditions all across the country. Quaking grass, *Briza media* (Zone 4, 2 to 3 feet), thrives almost anywhere, bringing interesting texture and graceful movement to border and bed. Its leaves are not especially luxuriant, but this one is grown for its dangling, gilded seed heads that resemble fat, braided loaves of wheat bread. They hold their looks for months in the garden and dry nicely for use in arrangements. Tufted hair grass, *Deschampsia caespitosa* (Zone 4, 2 to 3 feet), offers slim leaves in neat hummocks early in the year, then blooms in airy, shimmering veils that screen and soften all that lies behind. There are a number of fine garden forms with red, gold, or bronzed flower heads, any or all of which are worth growing. Hair grass is especially valuable for its tolerance of light, high, or partial shade, where its open, arching form and thready texture contrast wonderfully with unfurling ferns and bold hostas. Blue fescue, *Festuca glauca* (Zone 4, 6 to 12 inches) is an elegant edging plant, its densely whorled clumps of wiry, steel-blue foliage setting off bubbly little miniature 'Popcorn' roses or upright, needle-leaved rosemary. It, too, has excellent forms like 'Blausilber', appropriately silver blue with a pewtery sheen, or the lustrous, almost sky-blue 'Blauglut'.

Smaller grasses such as these work their way quite easily into combinations with perennials, bulbs, and dwarf shrubs. However, though bigger grasses look marvelous in parklike situations or borders built on the grand scale, they often seem less at home in small gardens. The trick to their proper placement is to treat substantial, heavy-looking grasses like feather reed grass, *Calamagrostis acutiflora* (Zone 5, to 6 feet), or Indian grass, *Sorghastrum avenaceum* (Zone 5 with protection, to 6 feet), as if they were shrubs, placing them firmly at the back of the beds where they can rise and later tumble without crushing all their neighbors. Lighter, airier grasses such as giant feather grass, *Stipa gigantea* (Zone 6, 5 to 6 feet), or tall moor grass, *Molinia caerulea arundinacea* 'Skyracer' (Zone 5, 7 to 8 feet), can be placed mid-border, where their flower stems arch like fountains of living water above massed perennials and border shrubs.

Among the best of the big are maiden grasses, a group of buxom beauties with multiple garden virtues. Hardy, adaptable, and easy to please, maiden grasses reward a minimum of care with surprising splendor. Like many large perennials, they will need to settle into a garden for a few years before they can fully develop their potential strength and beauty. Once mature, these gorgeous grasses bring potent silhouettes and delicate textures to the garden. Their architectural strength balances the soft, indeterminate shapes of many perennials. They change with the seasons, altering in size, shape, and color. Fresh and pretty in spring, they become powerful and handsome in summer, dramatic in autumn, subtle in winter, when their brittle, bleached leaves whisper with the wind.

Glorious and time proven, the striking Chinese maiden grass, *Miscanthus sinensis* 'Gracillimus' (Zone 4, 5 to 8 feet), fits gracefully

Golden strands of maiden grass, *Miscanthus sinensis* 'Variegatus', frame lesser celandines, *Ranunculus ficaria* 'Flore Pleno' in spring. (Northwest Perennial Alliance Border at the Bellevue Botanic Garden in Bellevue, Washington.)

A stunning striped maiden grass, *Miscanthus sinensis* var. *strictus* is still beautiful in October, and remains attractive well into winter. (Garden of Alice Lauber, Seattle, Washington.)

summer perennials. In autumn, the grassy fountains are topped by silken, red-gold plumes that echo the rust and copper of late chrysanthemums. In my garden, this grass is planted near an elderly white birch, and the slim strands of golden grass make a shimmering partnership with the clear yellow birch leaves for several months. Though it carries itself well, maiden grass slumps a bit as it ages, so give it stalwart companions that won't smother beneath its sagging embrace. Red-leaved *Weigela* 'Java Red', with pale red flowers in early summer, is an excellent candidate, as are stout hydrangeas.

Flame grass, *Miscanthus sinensis* 'Purpurascens' (Zone 6, to 5 feet), is a compact, finely textured plant, upright when young, softly cascading as a more mature clump. (Flopsy, rather shapeless forms that color poorly are sometimes sold under this name, so insist on getting the true plant, rather than some anonymous seedling with inadequate breeding. If in doubt, ask to see a mature plant, which should retain its elegance of form.) True flame grass remains slender and supple, its ruddy young foliage deepening all summer, then passing through a dazzling series of color changes that persist well into winter. By midsummer, its midnight green is tinged with burgundy. The wine red deepens to purple and brightens to bronze by summer's end, when each strand is streaked with sunset oranges, warm yellows, and hot reds. Flame grass remains glorious until hard frosts dim its brilliance to bronze and brown. Despite its height, this vertical grass works well near the front of a bed, breaking up a predictable stair-step planting of rigidly sized elements with unexpected zest. An early and abundant bloomer, flame grass sends up its long, silk-floss flower stalks in midsummer. Their airy texture and wheaten coloring contrast piquantly with red or green smoke bush (*Cotinus coggygria*), with round, coinlike leaves and soft clouds of floral smoke. Both foliage and flowers

into most garden schemes, formal or casual. Set at the back of a bed, it will rise in sparkling, silvery-green fountains to preside over spring tulips and

color well in any good soil and full sun, but regular moisture through the summer prolongs and heightens flame grass's autumnal performance.

A fast favorite with flower arrangers and small children is porcupine grass, *Miscanthus sinensis* var. *strictus* (also sold as 'Strictus'; Zone 5 with protection, 6 to 8 feet). This stunner is horizontally barred with buttery-yellow stripes that give big clumps the look of a duck blind. A small clump makes a delicious, sunny accent among perennials and dwarf shrubs, where its long lines and stiffly upright form contrast pleasantly with mounded or sprawling plants. Less tolerant of dry soils than some of its cousins, porcupine grass is most tightly vase shaped in moist, partially shaded situations. Indeed, though it adapts well to ordinary border conditions, porcupine grass enjoys wet feet and grows happily along streams or in boggy areas. Its flowers appear in autumn, looking at first like shocks of oversized corn silk, wiry and brown, then fluffing open to coppery rose feathers above buff-colored foliage.

There are dozens of delightful maiden grass forms in a good range of sizes, shapes, and colors. Lusty 'Goldfeder' (Zone 6, to 8 feet) is vertically striped with gold, while 'Zebrinus' (Zone 6, to 8 feet, often called zebra grass), carries tawny horizontal bars that make it look camouflaged. Compact little 'Cabaret' (Zone 6, to 6 feet) has broad leaves striped as gaily as a cafe awning in sage and cream. Daintiest of all is the glimmering, silver-frosted *Miscanthus sinensis* 'Morning Light' (Zone 5, 4 to 5 feet) which looks like a gigantic powder puff that might blow away were it not weighted down by companions like white hydrangeas and sea kale (*Crambe cordifolia*) with huge, cloudy blossoms. Specialty nurseries offer many others, both bold and diminutive.

Maiden grasses do well in any good garden soil, preferring open, sunny situations. Denied the summer heat they crave, late bloomers may not flower well in cool climates (such as the maritime Northwest), but are hardly to be shunned for this. Though many once established are tolerant of drought, all need regular watering as young plants and a few will flag in hot, sunny situations, preferring light or partial shade. Except in very poor

Big grasses make exciting winter bonfires for the adventurous in spirit, but be sure you have plenty of room (and a source of water close at hand) before tossing on the match. Here, *Miscanthus sinensis* and *Deschampsia flexuosa* are in their autumnal gold. (Garden of Doug Bayley, Seattle, Washington.)

soils, extra feeding, especially with strong commercial plant foods, is unnecessary. Indeed, overfeeding often forces the gardener to frequent plant division, a chore that ordinarily only needs to be carried out once every four or five years. When big grasses flop open at the heart, destroying their purity of line (and sometimes their hapless neighbors), it's time to cut them down to size. Left too long, division becomes a two-person job and the crown-splitting must be done with a sharp axe. Done in time, it's quite a simple task. Dig the offending plant up in late summer, split the crown in half (or quarters), then reset each piece in refreshed soil and water them in well. They will quickly develop new roots and by next spring they will be flourishing. An autumn mulch of compost and aged manure provides both winter protection and all the nourishment they need to rebound. If you don't get around to dividing overgrown grasses this month, hold off until spring or be prepared to lose young plants over the winter.

Though big grasses can be cut back hard when one tidies the garden in late autumn, it's a pity to do it then, for lovely as they are in summer, many acquire an extra degree of beauty in fall that lasts well into winter, when their understated color and whispering music are most welcome. If their seed heads are left for the birds, the winter garden comes alive with wings and twittering as they discover this interesting new food source. Cutting back the faded stalks is a pleasant chore for a mild winter afternoon; indeed, my family likes to welcome in the New Year by setting elderly garden grasses on fire, sending up wishes with the high-flying sparks (taking care, of course, not to let the fire spread, which it rarely attempts under damp winter conditions). The grasses refurbish unharmed with the approach of spring, when freshets of new leaves quickly mask last year's stubble. Ring their crowns with bulbs (but remember that the crown will increase, so leave plenty of breathing space) to play up the fresh green of young grass foliage. Midseason or late tulips are a good choice for grouping about maiden grasses, for when the bulbs bloom, the grass is filling out nicely, and when the tulips ripen and fade, the rising grass will hide their decaying foliage. To learn more about maiden grasses and their gardenworthy relatives, let John Greenlee's excellent book, *The Encyclopedia of Ornamental Grasses* (see the appendix), be your guide.

Late Bloomers

Extending Summer Color into Fall

The belated heat has finished off gardens that peak early, but those stocked with plenty of late bloomers are catching their second wind. Goldenrods and starry, asterlike boltonias fill the border back. Skinny pencil plant holds electric purple flower heads high mid-border, flanked by gaudy dahlias and flaming cardinal flowers. Obedient plant, that prim native, rises in tidy spires of rose or white. Austin roses (those new/old rose hybrids) are reblooming nicely, and hydrangeas are foamy with blossom. Though many a high summer beauty has faded away, plants like this are just coming into their own in September.

Goldenrods get a bad rap, but they do not cause hay fever. Perhaps if the F.D.A. would relabel them as hypoallergenic, more gardeners

Skinny pencil plant, *Verbena bonariensis*, hails from the plains of Patagonia, so it has no problem with hot, dry summers. Here it is paired with lemony daylilies. (Northwest Perennial Alliance Border at the Bellevue Botanic Garden in Bellevue, Washington.)

would try these splendid, late-flowering natives. They range in size from front-row dwarfs to feather-tipped towers, in color from ivory through lemon to old gold. Many are outstanding mixers, for their canary and citrus shades temper brassy golds, screaming reds, and harsh oranges. Seaside goldenrod, *Solidago sempervirens* (Zone 4, to 6 feet) is spectacular, rising in light, bright spears tipped with fluffy, softly golden flower heads that bloom through September into October. A daintier species, *S. bicolor* (Zone 3, 1½ to 3 feet), is called silverrod for its fluffy white flowers. Garden forms of silverrod tend to be compact and long blooming, starting in high summer and carrying on until hard frosts. Specialty nurseries often carry a few hybrids like 'Golden Mosa' (Zone 4, to 2½ feet), the gentle yellow of mimosa blossom, and warmer yellow 'Baby Gold' (Zone 4, 1½ to 2 feet). Goldenrods thrive in ordinary garden soils, preferring a lean diet, quick drainage, and full sun. Once established, most are drought tolerant and long-lived, sturdy independents that do very nicely without much help from us.

Boltonia asteroides (Zone 3, 3 to 6 feet) is native to southeastern meadows. Tall and sturdy, it never needs staking despite its fragile appearance. Boltonia's airy, filigree foliage and slim stems contrast pleasantly with bold hydrangeas and spiky globe thistles, and it grows happily in any good garden soil given a sunny situation. Starry white 'Snow Bank' is an excellent late summer performer, long-lasting both in the garden and as a cut flower. Pastel 'Pink Beauty' is similarly easygoing, also flowering from September well into October. It makes an elegant partnership with silvery artemisias and shocking pink Cape lilies, *Nerine bowdenii* (Zone 8, to 2 feet), or lavender autumn crocus, *Colchicum speciosum* (Zone 4, to 10 inches).

Pencil plant (*Verbena bonariensis*, Zone 6, 4 to 6 feet) has slim, bare stems that soar 3 or 4 feet interrupted by barely a leaf, topped with frizzy flower heads of saturated purple-blue. Like the statice they resemble, the flowers hold their color and form from high summer well into autumn. In my garden, a hazy scrim of *V. bonariensis* surrounds the creamy, yolk-yellow Austin rose 'Graham Stuart Thomas', while another great swale screens a big, marine-blue hydrangea to splendid effect. Though on the tender side, this ardent perennial seeds itself abundantly, so may be colonized as an annual in colder regions. In early winter, take the dried seed heads and tap them like magic wands all through the borders. Enchanting thickets of this attenuated plant will appear in spring, the seedlings as thick as weeds. Don't confound their narrow, tooth-edged pairs of new leaves for weeds, though, or you may lose the lot; they bitterly resent transplanting and once pulled can rarely be made to grow happily elsewhere. You can thin the seedlings if you like, but you needn't bother, for they are unobtrusive early in the season and harmless among larger plants. They elongate steadily as summer wanes, then come into glory as autumn arrives. Try them as companions for early bloomers such as alstroemeria, whose lanky stems get pulled soon after midsummer, leaving an unsightly blank in the border. Pencil plant is also stunning when grown with asparagus or copper fennel.

Cardinal flowers, *Lobelia cardinalis* (Zone 2, to 3 feet), blaze like living flames on shady eastern riverbanks. Their reputation for difficult behavior in the garden is probably due to their reluctance to be transplanted from the wild, for nursery-grown plants adapt willingly to garden life. Given humus-rich soil, consistent moisture, partial or filtered shade, and plenty of elbow room, small plants fatten up in a single season, putting on a prolonged display of flashy red flowers ranged on tall, sinuous spikes, from late summer into fall. A deep winter mulch of chopped straw or bracken brings them safely through hard winters, while frequent division (performed every three or four years) keeps cardinal flower vigorous and healthy. A German selection, 'Kompliment' offers big, scarlet flowers on outsized bloom spikes above crisp green foliage, a stunning complement indeed for purple and blue asters. White-flowered 'Alba' makes a quieter companion for late roses or chalky pink mallows such as *Lavatera* 'Barnsley'. Another eastern native, *Lobelia siphilitica* (Zone 5, to 3 feet), decorates its tall spires with ocean-blue flowers, lipped and fringed and touched at the heart with white seafoam. Flowering long and late, it associates delightfully with slumberous slate-blue asters or the darker periwinkle blue of *Aster* x *frikartii*.

A tender Mexican species, *Lobelia fulgens* (Zone 8, to 3 feet) lends its lustrous, red-black stems and leaves to a number of exotic-looking hybrids with maroon or near black foliage. Matronly 'Queen Victoria' holds up erect scepters trimmed with clarion crimson flowers above somber black foliage, as befits a mourning queen. She is ably championed by a stalwart bluebeard, the shrubby *Caryopteris* x 'Dark Knight' (Zone 6, 3 to 4 feet), whose sapphire-blue flowers set off the queen's rubies. The heraldic ebony and midnight red of *Lobelia* 'Happy Returns' (Zone 5, to 3 feet) contrasts excitingly with dusky *Gaillardia* 'Burgundy' (Zone 3, to 2 feet), the coppery New Zealand grass, *Carex flagellifera* (Zone 7, to 3 feet) and the peach-colored foam of annual *Alyssum* x 'Apricot Shades' (to 5 inches).

Obedient plant, *Physostegia virginiana* (Zone 3, 3 to 4 feet), is so named because the flowers,

The siren red of cardinal flower, *Lobelia cardinalis* 'Kompliment', is tempered by deep blue *L. siphilitica* and purple seedling asters. Both these lobelias are hardier than the black-leaved Mexican forms. (Author's garden.)

stacked in neat pyramids up tall bloom spikes, can be gently pushed to any angle you like and will obediently hold their new position, a boon for flower arrangers. This slim southeasterner snuggles easily between larger plants, hiding modestly early in the year, then emerging in a rosy glow at summer's end. The pinky-purple flowers mingle cheerfully with fiesta bright zinnias or pink and purple cosmos. 'Bouquet Rose' has deeper pink blossoms, most potent when mixed in with lavender and blue flowers against silvery or gray foliage. Those of 'Vivid' are a sparkling, light magenta, a clean and carrying color that looks wonderful against dark red or purple leaves. 'Summer Snow' flowers pristine white and looks very handsome surrounding the lemon and cream Austin rose 'Windrush', or banked in front of the dwarf shrub rose 'Seafoam'. Most striking of all, 'Variegata' has long, slim leaves streaked white in spring and tinting to pink and ivory in summer. By autumn, raspberry-pink flowers bloom against foliage stained with rose and purple, a wonderful sight when paired with purple cooking sage (*Salvia officinalis* 'Purpurea') or the rusty red florets of *Sedum* 'Autumn Joy'.

An oversized floral sage, *Salvia involucrata* 'Bethelii' (Zone 6 with protection) forms a shrublike column 4 feet high and 3 across, clothed in huge, furry foliage strikingly veined with fuchsia. Given plenty of sun and heat, it provides a long succession of bloom on sinuous panicles up to 18 inches long. The shocking pink flowers consort well with purples and blues as well as murky reds. It blooms long and late, a terrific companion for thundercloud blue asters and chrysanthemums in ruddy coppers and bronzes at season's end. Like all sages, this one appreciates well-drained but fertile garden soils and does best in full sun.

Japanese anemones (*Anemone japonica*, or more often *A.* x *hybrida*, both Zone 5, 1½ to 5 feet) are as silky and wide petaled as poppies and bring a curiously springlike note to the autumn garden. Rosy little 'Bressingham Glow' boasts warm pink, satiny semi-double flowers on 18-inch stems. An elderly American, 'Whirlwind', produced flurries of clean white, semi-double flowers some 3 feet high, while a salmony German selec-

tion, 'Kriemhilde', blooms double at the same height. Japanese anemones come in a good range of heights and colors, from clean white through a dozen pinks to deep rose. Sentinal tall, they remain upright without staking, despite buffeting wind or cold autumn rains. Once established, they are remarkably drought tolerant, spreading happily in any soil. Though they prefer open, sunny situations, they adapt well to shade, and in gardens where these lovely creatures make themselves all too much at home, a shady site will slow their traveling ways. Though Japanese anemones can be encroaching, it is hard to be cross with a plant which offers so much in return for so little. When they carry on without flagging from late summer through autumn, their space-absorbing ways are forgiven. Don't be disappointed if young plants don't achieve much display for a year or two; like many long-lived, tough plants, they expend a lot of energy establishing good root systems before producing flowers.

If your garden tends to fade away before you are ready to see it go, a rejuvenating infusion of late bloomers will extend its life and color well past Labor Day. Give these plants like-minded companions, so they don't bloom in forlorn solitude. A backing of evergreen shrubs will intensify the effect of their glowing flowers, as will placement that allows them to be backlit by the slanting sunshine of Indian summer. Try adding one or two such plants each year, and before long, your late-season garden will be gloriously ablaze instead of simply burned out.

Second Wind

Grooming for Renewal

High summer may have left the garden worse for wear, but don't throw down your trowel yet. The autumn equinox is the time to regroup, not give up. Sharpen up those clippers, haul out the grass rake, and do a few warm-up stretches, because it's fall tidy time. Tidying up may seem a waste of time with winter just around the corner; shouldn't we just have at the remaining perennials with a machete, reducing them to golden stubble, ready for winter? This makes sense if the garden is only usable for six or eight months of the year but in many parts of the country, gardens can remain colorful well into winter. Indeed, with careful plant selection and placement, most any garden anywhere can look attractive and be at least intermittently enjoyable all year long. Transforming a summer garden into a year-round one doesn't happen overnight, but the delightful process makes it easier to wait for fulfillment. Part of the process involves learning about hardy plants with year-round beauties. Part involves discovering which of those plants you like and how and where you want to use them in your yard. Part involves balancing the natural cycles of the garden year, and that's where grooming comes in.

A good grooming session gives the border an immediate lift and prepares the way for the coming glories of autumn. (If your garden isn't big on autumn glories, start making lists of late bloomers to add now for next year's performance.) Starry asters and fluffy chrysanthemums, gilded leaves, and flaming ones will shine far brighter against a tidy backdrop than a weary one. To this end, we go on border patrol, looking for trouble spots. Cruise the beds slowly, removing burned-out blossoms and fatigued foliage. Take spent stalks back to their base but leave any that still look vigorous. Gentle Indian summer often brings new life to tired borders and many summer bloomers will carry on until hard frosts arrive. Remember that we aren't putting the border to bed, but simply

renovating it. Don't remove everything with a touch of gold or brown or you may have very little garden left. Take only what's obviously finished with life and let the rest achieve graceful maturity.

Rose hips like these chubby charmers decorate many roses, including this rugosa, 'Frau Dagmar Hastrup'. (Garden of Steven Antonow, Seattle, Washington.)

Spent foliage and flower heads can go straight into the garden cart, headed for the compost bin. Snip larger detritus down to a compostable size as you add it to the cart or shred the whole load with

Deadheading is good for many plants, but if we get too tidy-minded, we will lose out on extraordinary treasures like these allium seed heads. (Garden of Steven Antonow, Seattle, Washington.)

a sharp machete to assist the composting process, which can slow down considerably as temperatures fall. Hang a bag on the side of your cart to hold rose leaves with black spot, peony foliage with botrytis, clematis with wilt—anything that looks diseased rather than merely ravaged by time. Anything of this sort should be tossed in the trash or burned, but never composted, for there it may spread garden troubles for years to come. If disease is really rife, add a jar of bleach and water to the cart so you can dip your clippers between cuts to avoid passing on infection to healthy plants. (A 1:3 ratio, or $\frac{1}{3}$ cup bleach to $\frac{2}{3}$ cup water, is an effective germicide but a few drops won't harm living plants.)

Yellowing strands of daylily or iris leaves can be detached with a firm, sideways tug from the base, leaving the remaining fans and sprays refreshed. Withering flower stalks from these two can be cut back to the ground, but waning lily stems need more time to ripen properly. The bulbs are still drawing nourishment from the green part of the stems to be stored for winter use, so trim stems bit by bit as they brown off. Check the leaf nodes for tiny bulblets, brown and glossy scaled, some of which may already be sprouting roots. Pot these little ones up or plant them shallowly 6 or 8 inches away from the mother stem to create an expanded colony of lilies. The babies take a year or two to bloom but are an inexpensive way to increase your holdings. Scatter a handful of soy or cottonseed meal over each bulb area (including dormant tulips, daffodils, and whatnot) to keep bulb roots well fed through winter, promoting fine future performances. Keep a bucketful of mixed compost and aged manure to scatter around the roots of any plant that looks stressed or hungry. Renew spent mulches as well, for a thick blanket of shredded bark, chopped salt marsh hay, or bracken will conserve moisture in a dry year, insulate against frost in a cold one, and keep early flowers clean in a wet, muddy spring.

If seedpods are trimmed as they form through the summer, many perennials will be stimulated to rebloom more or less continually. Ripening seed can drain plants' resources, and in general it is best to spare them the burden of production and remove all the seedpods in autumn. This redirects their energy toward building good roots or producing strong basal foliage. Roses are an exception, however, because the formation of hips signals the plants to harden themselves off in preparation for winter. Though many roses are in good rebloom in fall, leave their hips to ripen rather than trimming them to encourage still more flowers. Don't strip off their leaves yet (except those showing black spot or other difficulties); wait until winter approaches, usually the end of October or early November.

However, if you find fat seedpods ripening nicely on lilies, iris, or daylilies, you might want to remove all but one or two and let those mature. When the dry pods begin to split open, shake out the seeds and store them in labeled envelopes packed in a tightly closed jar. Toss in a packet of dry gel—the kind packed with film—or a spoonful of dry milk powder to keep moisture away from the seeds. In spring, sow them in flats or seed pans, rowing out the nicest in the vegetable garden when they get three or four true leaves. Many lilies, daylilies, and iris can be bloomed from seed in two years, with good care. Keep them watered and fed and before long you may be looking at a pretty crop of flowers that nobody has ever seen before. Unless you are growing just one kind of

Rusty-red *Sedum telephium* 'Autumn Joy' looks most attractive when frequently divided. Where winters are mild, it can be split and reset in fall, but elsewhere, save this job for spring.

lily, for instance, the seedlings may not look much like their mother, but many splendid border plants have been discovered this way. Raising a remarkable seedling is a distinct thrill and a lovely reward for the observant autumn tidier who did not let the seed fall unnoticed.

Glittering blue Lyme grass, *Elymus hispidus*, is a mannerly, non-running clump former that only needs division every five or six years. This one is backed by a California lilac, *Ceanothus* x 'Puget Blue'. (Garden of Barbara Flynn, Redmond, Washington.)

Long Division

Making Less into More

As you move through the fall garden, tidying tired perennials, keep your eyes open for plants that have outgrown their places. Sagging Siberian iris, flopsy colonies of tall *Sedum telephium* 'Autumn Joy', and bloated catmints are all good candidates for division. Overgrown plants not only threaten their neighbors' health but their own may suffer as well. Plants with crowded roots dry out quickly, are prone to disease, and bloom reluctantly. Cut down to size and given a fresh start in renewed soil, they will reward our attentions with healthy growth and lusty bloom. Indian summer drought may leave the ground too dry to contemplate much moving and shaking of roots right now, but as soon as autumn rains saturate the soil, it will be prime time for division.

As a rule, early and midseason bloomers like lungworts (*Pulmonaria* species), Jupiter's beard (*Centranthus ruber*), and delphiniums are divided in fall, while temperatures are still warm enough to encourage strong root growth. High summer and late bloomers like perennial sunflowers, phlox, and monkshoods are divided in spring, so they can recover their strength before flowering time rolls around again. Midsummer Day or the Fourth of July are traditional cutoff points; anything that flowers before then may be divided now. Perennials that flower after those dates are best left undisturbed until spring. Ornamental grasses, however, are most successfully divided in spring no matter when they bloom, for their young divisions are very prone to root rots and winterkill, particularly where winters are wet.

Division, the horticultural equivalent of surgery, may raise uncomfortable feelings for the inexperienced. The operation can, of course, damage or even kill plants if haphazardly performed, but by taking a few simple precautions, common perennials can be multiplied with ease. (Indeed, they are common precisely because they are easily grown and divided.) First, when digging divisible plants, take up as much soil as possible without harming the neighbors. The point is to avoid unnecessary root loss. Secondly, make sure your cutting tools—clippers, knife, and shovel—are very sharp. The vivisection you are shortly going to perform is more likely to be successful when roots are cleanly cut rather than roughly torn apart. Third, minimize root exposure to the air. In spring, warm air and sunshine can dry out tender roots in minutes. In autumn, cooler temperatures and moister air create a bigger window of opportunity before root stress occurs, but remember that they are still susceptible. Take as much time as you need to do a careful job, but until you gain experience and speed, keep freshly dug plants covered with wet burlap or newspaper whenever you aren't working on them. Treat new divisions the same way until you are ready to plant them. Fourth, be conscientious about aftercare. New divisions need protection from drought, wind, and heat (even the mild sun of Indian summer can wilt these shorn lambs). Water them in well, and keep their root zone moist. Be aware that if the soil around them is very dry, it can wick away available moisture. In warm years, a piece of cheesecloth or an old window screen can block sun and temper harsh winds. Armed with proper tools, materials, and these general guidelines, you can successfully divide almost anything. Ordinary plants that grow well in your garden will be most forgiving and make excellent tutors. Uncommon and/or very expensive plants may be slow to grow and reluctant to divide, so practice on your shasta daisies, not your rare hellebores.

The process of division begins with the organization of supplies. Fill the wheelbarrow with damp potting soil and compost, adding wet burlap or newspaper, a bucket of water, a bag for unhealthy scraps that need to be burned, and another bucket for compostable bits. Toss in pots of several sizes, labels, and marker pens, as well as a sharp garden knife (rose budding knives are very efficient) and secateurs or clippers. Small border spades reduce damage in confined quarters, while big, well-sharpened shovels are useful for splitting large, tough-rooted plants. The kind with a thin foot rest atop the blade makes it easy to bring your full weight to bear on a recalcitrant hosta or daylily. If that doesn't work, a very sharp splitting axe will whistle through woody clumps of Siberian iris or catmint.

The goal of division is to make several small, complete plants from one big one. To find out how to divide a specific plant, dig it up, shake or rinse off the dirt, and take a good look at the root system. Most perennials have two kinds of roots—plump storage roots and finer feeder roots. In autumn, the storage roots are fat with starchy reserves while the feeder roots, which serve during active growth, may be withering. Most plants still have leaves, so the growth points of the crowns are obvious. The majority of perennials, including primroses and daisies, have many small crowns above a network of storage roots and tangled masses of wiry feeder roots.

Strip away any dead roots (and fading foliage), trim feeder roots to 2 inches, then snap or cut the mass into pieces. Discard the hard, woody center of the mother plant, but each bit that has leaves (crown), storage roots, and feeder roots can be potted up or reset in the garden. Plunge potted divisions in the water bucket until the air bubbles cease to appear (to be sure the soil is thoroughly wetted down). Label each pot promptly, especially when working with several varieties of the same thing. It can be very hard to tell which is the pink phlox and which is the white after ten minutes, let alone the six months until spring planting time arrives. If you have a cold frame handy, it is an ideal place to winter over young divisions. Otherwise, they can be grouped in flats and heaped with dry leaves to shelter them from hard frost.

Divisions which are to be replanted should be heeled into damp soil or compost immediately. (The term "heeling in" means offering short-term protection to the root systems by heaping soil over them. The plants are often laid on their sides and packed quite close together. Most of the foliage may be exposed to the air but the roots are fully covered.) Replenish the garden soil with compost, digging as deeply as you can without disturbing the neighbors. Regroup the new plants in clusters of three or five—odd-numbered groupings are more pleasing to the eye, which tends to try and find formal patterns in evenly numbered plantings. To create attractively full clumps, space each small plant 12 to 18 inches apart, close enough that they read as a unit yet allowing plenty of room for expansion. One huge clump can become three good-sized clusters spaced throughout the bed. Such repeats become a strong design element, bringing coherence and unity to the plantings. Water each group in deeply, wetting the surrounding soil as well.

A large group of perennials, including daylilies, hostas, and tall sedums, varies in having multiple crowns that are actually small entire plants crammed tightly together. These plantlets can often be wiggled apart without cutting but elderly clumps of this type seem to fuse together, requiring radical surgery (catmints and asters very quickly fall into this category). The barren, woody core is surrounded by healthier satellite crowns which may be sliced off with a sharp knife and potted or reset as described above. A long-neglected plant can be a challenge to divide, and it may seem that there is more to toss out than to save. However, the leftovers will soon outperform the mother plant, which is generally in a sorry state, so the massacre is not in vain.

Iris roots, plump brown tubers with thinner white feeder roots, like their tops to rest above ground. Old clumps are quickly divided by snapping off fat, leafy pieces and discarding the old, shrunken bits. Any mushy or discolored bits should be burned and if the problem seems wide-spread, find a sunnier, better drained place to grow the divisions. Cut the foliage back by half and reset the new pieces in chevrons (each bit facing the same way) to make a handsome new clump. Pacific Coast iris can be divided now as well, but more gently, for they detest disturbance. Pull off all dead foliage and roots and cut back any leaves that are browning off, but leave those that look green and healthy alone, for many hybrids and species are evergreen. Don't divide evergreen *Iris foetidissima* in fall, or you'll forfeit the autumnal display of hot orange berries. Split up any overgrown plants in spring, discarding all dead roots and leaves, and you will reap a reward of extra flowers and even more of the showy seedpods next year. (If you want to dry the marvelous seedpods, pick them on long stems just as they begin to split open. Hang them upside down to dry or the stems will sag unattractively.)

If you aren't sure just how to tackle a certain plant, try several methods. Pull a few bits off, then cut some. Make a few divisions with plenty of roots and top growth and make some with smaller amounts of either. Record each set of variables on the plant label and note the results in your garden journal. Such specific information helps your garden grow, and the experience you gain helps you grow as a gardener. When in doubt, take a few risks. All gardeners have their failures and losses along with their successes; they are a necessary part of the learning process. The very best gardeners will freely tell you that they learn more from mistakes than from success. Besides, if you work carefully, keeping the needs of your plants in mind, chances are excellent that overall, you will increase your holdings. Before long, you'll be passing those excess plants over the fence to beautify gardens all over the neighborhood.

Most iris can be divided in autumn, but who would sacrifice the plump red berries of evergreen *Iris foetidissima*? This is another division to put off until spring.

OCTOBER

On Garden Making

Plants and People

If you close your eyes and say the word "garden" to yourself, what vision is revealed to your inner eye? Perhaps your secret garden is a warm place, sunny and alive with calling birds. Perhaps the air is full of drifting perfumes from roses, lilies, and mignonette. Probably flowers abound, scattered at your feet and arching above your head. Our dream garden is seldom sharply defined—it would be a challenge to reproduce it through a planting diagram. However, on that visionary level we all know exactly what we want from our gardens, how they should look in any season, and most important of all, how we want to feel when we are there. This last notion is probably the key to successful garden making, for a real garden is much more than the sum of its parts. A garden—a living, happy garden—is a synergistic relationship between plants and a person. If the gardener makes the garden, making a garden that stirs the heart also makes the gardener.

So what, then, makes a garden work? Loosely, anything that makes you—the maker—feel wonderful. For most of us, garden making is an open-ended

Cool October nights waken the fiery colors released by sugars stored in autumn leaves. Fallen leaves can be as decorative as flowers; unless they form smothering mats, leaves can be left where they fall to be enjoyed until their brilliance fades.

Chinese red bridges and gilded pagodas add a playful touch of fantasy to gardens. It is rarely appropriate or possible to recreate oriental gardens in this country, but we can emulate or refer to them by borrowing their traditional design elements, as in the style known as Pacific Rim gardening. (Kubota Gardens, Seattle.)

brilliant with fearlessly gaudy bloom. The graceful austerity of the Japanese zen garden or the red pagodas and golden dragons of the Chinese may capture our imagination. In years to come, we may find ourselves refining our work, coming closer each year to re-creating our inner garden. We may also end up endlessly experimenting, changing the known for the unknown, pushing past comfort to unexplored country, always looking for a new frontier. What matters is not that we achieve perfection with gardens of any style—indeed, that is an impossible (and unworthy, not to say silly) goal. What matters is that our gardens nourish us even as we nurture them.

As a general rule, the garden that delights its maker is as close to perfect as any garden needs to be. However, sometimes our desires outstrip our skills and we begin to lose our pleasure in yearning for picture book gardens. We must look to the same gardens that disturbed our peace for lessons in how to reclaim that feeling at home. There is no point at all in trying to copy somebody else's garden—it never works, for a garden is far more than a collection of plants in pretty combinations. There is, however, a great deal to be learned from any garden that knocks our socks off. No matter what kind of garden we want for ourselves, there are a few abiding principles that can assist us in our garden-making process. If we were to tour the world, looking at great gardens and asking ourselves what makes these places so wonderful, the first thing we would notice is that all of them are places to be in their own right. Most are enclosed in some way, whether with hedges or fences, woods, or walls. Sometimes the sense of enclosure is illusory, achieved with trellis work, screens, or visual baffles. Some of the enclosing elements may be borrowed—a neighbor's fence or hedge, majestic trees in a nearby park that lend themselves to the skyline, views of distant water or mountains

process; our gardens grow with us. A single bed full of cheerful, easygoing commoners can give us chills of joy when first we pick up a trowel. Later, as we travel further along the garden path, we may want more both for the garden and from it. Our original dreams may now be colored by English borders billowing with misty, pastel perennials, carefully graded by tint and tone. We may long for a sun-splashed cottage garden, gray with herbs or

glimpsed between tall shrubs or through the arch of a gate. Whatever their nature, enclosing elements make us feel that the garden is set apart from the world.

Any English garden designer could—and would—say straight off that most American gardens lack another necessity, which is structure. Quite often, the same things that enclose the garden also work to define the garden areas and frame its floral finery. Many a famous European garden is dominated by its structure—think of those French *parterres*, where plants are just bits of living color, or the Italian gardens in which plants are mere architecture. Both schools of thought are also represented in English gardens, but one of the enchanting things about the English is that they are so often plant-centered. Even at Sissinghurst, that bastion of structure (take a look at it from Vita's writing tower if you don't think so), we experience the garden as a series of plantings rather than as well-furnished garden rooms. When gardens don't work, very often it is because they either lack structure or suffer from an excess of it. The trick is to balance the architectural elements with what the English designers call "infill" but which many of us consider to be the main event—flowers.

Flowering plants may, of course, be as structural as any marble column, but in truth, the perennials to which many of us are passionately drawn do tend to be indefinite in shape. The fact is that flowers are most potent and pleasing when seen in a supportive context. The same border can be made to look splendid or scrubby, simply by adding or removing its backdrop. A great border with no backing will look insignificant next to a mediocre border with a hedge or wall. A handful of tulips or daffodils dotted or strung in skinny ribbons about the border have very little impact. The same handful become smashing when tucked

together into the bay between two rhododendrons and given the company of a spotted pulmonaria and some primroses or sweet violets.

This leads up to the third great principle: Plants like company. In nature, the only time we find plants growing in isolation is where conditions are exceptionally harsh. In the garden, plants look and grow best when interlayered harmo-

Plants, such as this Japanese rhubarb, *Rheum palmatum* 'Red Strain', can be every bit as architectural as structural elements like columns or gates—things designers call "hardscape." In naturalistic settings, living architecture often looks more at home than man-made objects. (Author's garden.)

niously, small trees sheltering shrubs encircled by colonies of perennials and annuals, interwoven with bulbs and ground covers. Plants set a careful yard or two apart, up to their necks in beauty bark, cannot look or act naturally. Once your garden framework is contrived, fill it generously, for abundance is its own reward. Celebrate diversity, using plants of all kinds arranged in nature's tiers. Where space is limited, choose plants that will remain appropriate in scale for years: dwarf or slow growing trees and shrubs, demure perennials, and moderate ground covers. Enthusiasts that increase relentlessly may work wonders where a wilderness needs taming, but remember that elsewhere they can destroy the garden in their zeal to multiply. Drape the garden walls with vines and let them romp through the trees and shrubs. Arrange your flowers in sociable profusion. Let the garden be a place of comfort and freedom for your plants and you will experience it that way as well.

This underlines a basic difference between those great gardens of Europe and our own humbler versions. By and large, our gardens are not intended to be formal showplaces but genuine living spaces. We want gardens where we can comfortably put our feet up and enjoy a cup of coffee and a good book. We want to sit quietly and tell a child a story, observe butterflies feeding from a butterfly bush, watch baby chickadees hatch and fledge and fly away. More than that, we want our garden to be both a refuge from the world and a powerful connector to the earth. In it, we rediscover natural cycles and rhythms, patterns that are hard to discern in the busy fret and roar of the larger world of humanity. From it, we gain peace for ourselves, our families, our friends. We garden in part to heal the earth, practicing good stewardship of whatever land lies under our feet. What feels better than taking on a battered, abused piece

of city and healing it? By dint of compost and mulch and with the help of a few good worms, we can make sour, starved dirt into moist and nutritious soil. Dig in and discover that peaceful strength that pours up from the earth, passing through our fingers into our hearts.

Rewarding as garden making is in countless ways, patience is perhaps its most valuable lesson, one we get to learn and relearn, over and over in a cycle almost as enduring as the rolling tide of the year itself. Give it time, take your time. It takes time and an accumulation of shared experience to make a garden, just as it does to make good friends. Over time, small plants grow, visions mature, skills sharpen. Over time, the garden shapes itself; even with the advantage of mature trees and shrubs, it takes about five to seven years for a garden to come into its own. This time is not passed in fruitless waiting, for it has fulfillments of its own. Grooming and weeding are not bothersome chores but vital connectors that literally put us in touch with our plants. Through such work, we get to know their needs and appreciate each stage of growth into maturity. Making the garden and keeping it together keeps us together as well. We make gardens not just to embody our dreams but because our spirits are uplifted each time we touch the earth.

Astonishing Asters

American Natives that Bloom Like Stars

Autumn is supposed to arrive in a blaze of glory, but after a hot, dry summer, or when the gardener loses interest by Labor Day, the garden's floral fires may gutter out early. If your garden generally burns out by fall, give it a supplementary boost by adding plants that gain energy as the year slides away. Asters, those bright-eyed daisy relatives, are

Fluffy fringe and sunny centers give asters a cheerful appearance, although they herald summer's end. Rich periwinkle 'Opal Blue' is a long-blooming mounder that will soften the edge of raised bed or border.

stellar late bloomers that need very little encouragement to light up the autumn garden. Aster is the Greek word for star, and the best of the garden asters definitely rank among the stars of this golden season. Though rank is something these graceful weeds are emphatically not, like so many of our native flowers, asters had to leave home to get respect. After spending several centuries touring the Continent and attending European finishing schools, their offspring are returning to these shores in quantity and to general acclaim. Sporting new names, great variety of form, and a wide array of colors, these European hybrids of our roadside weeds are both gardenworthy and utterly respectable.

New England field asters, *Aster novae-angliae* (Zone 4, 3 to 5 feet), are tough, hard-blooming beauties that adapt to almost any conditions with panache. There are dozens of them, mostly single or semi-double in form, their bright golden buttons trimmed with fine-cut fringe in half a rainbow of shades, beginning with white and passing through pinks and reds into lavenders, blues, and purples. Tall 'Treasurer' (to 5 feet) is among the deepest toned, its midnight purple contrasting beautifully with the coppers and bronze-reds of perennial sunflowers like *Helenium* 'Moerheim Beauty'. Sizzling, hot-pink 'Alma Potschke' (to 3 feet) looks smashing amidst a haze of slim purple *Verbena bonariensis*, while softer, satiny 'Harrington's Pink' (to 3 feet) mirrors the rose and cream hollyhock flowers of *Lavatera* 'Barnsley'. Icy 'Herbstschnee', crisp white with a citrus-yellow eye, combines well with sunny *Rudbeckia*

Native to New England meadows and woodlands, the white wood aster, *Aster divaricatus*, is a good neighbor in mixed borders. Let it tumble over a border edge or lean companionably into a nearby plant, as here with southeastern native *Polygonum (Tovara) virginianum* 'Chevron Form'.

crowding quickly into big colonies. These need rigorous thinning (the removal of every third shoot usually suffices) each spring but reward the gardener with abundant and long-lasting bloom at a time when the garden is rather thin of company. Towering 'Climax' (to 6 feet) is an exception to the size rule, and its bottle green columns topped with lilaclike clusters of big, Wedgwood-blue blossoms brighten the border back well into October. 'White Climax' (5 to 7 feet) is similar in style, an excellent companion for pale, porcelain-pink 'Priory Blush' (to 5 feet). On the other end of the scale, siren-red 'Alert', sparkling blue 'Royal Opal', and frosty 'Snowball' (all 8 to 12 inches) spread along the border front, so thickly set with flowers that their leaves are nearly invisible. Gentle sisters, powder-blue 'Marie Ballard' and rosy 'Patricia Ballard' (both to 30 inches) make a delicate froth of color beneath hydrangeas and late roses.

Perhaps the very best garden aster is a Swiss hybrid between a European and Himalayan species. *Aster* x *frikartii* (Zone 5, to 3 feet) has justly been named as one of the ten best plants all over the temperate world. Few plants are as obliging and long blooming as this one, and fewer still have its ineffable style. The cross yielded a handful of good seedlings, the best and bluest of which is 'Monch' (2 to 3 feet). Its siblings are similar but more relaxed in form; 'Wonder of Stafa' is periwinkle blue while 'Jungfrau' is a deeper lavender-blue. All the *frikartii* asters are reliable in difficult conditions and outstanding in better ones.

The parent species of remarkable hybrids are often not wonderful garden plants in themselves, and this is true of both the above families. However, a number of species asters which seem unprepossessing in the meadow are Cinderellas-in-waiting. Invite them into the garden, give them light and room and good soil, and they will

'Goldsturm' and gilding maiden grasses. New England asters insist on well-drained soils, but other than that, sunshine and elbow room are all they require, for these sturdy independents hold their own without staking or grooming.

New York asters, *Aster novi-belgii* (Zone 4, 3 to 4 feet), prefer moister soils and will even grow in frankly wet situations. They tend to be lower growing and more compact than their cousins,

reward your kindness with style. Like Cinderella, these species asters are less in need of a radical makeover than of simple recognition. What looks plain and undistinguished in a raggedy meadow plant is revealed under better conditions as elegant simplicity. Properly treated, several species are as lovely and long blooming as any hybrids. Indeed, they age even more gracefully, remaining handsome in winter, when their furled brown seed heads become favorite observation posts for small birds.

The multiple branching arms of blue wood aster, *Aster cordifolius* (Zone 3, 3 to 4 feet), carry generous sprays of clear lavender flowers, small but liberally produced. Long popular in England both as a garden flower and for cutting, its selections, 'Silver Spray', palest pink with a soft, old gold eye, and 'Blue Star', larger and deeper toned than the species, are most widely grown. Though good-sized plants, the blue wood asters are inclined to slump unattractively. They cannot be staked without ruining their graceful lines, but they do very well when given a companionable shrub to spill through. Heath asters, *A. ericoides* (Zone 3, to $2\frac{1}{2}$ feet), look very similar but have much better posture. Sturdy and healthy, heath asters can grow happily for years without division, as handsome in leaf and seed head as in flower. The bushy plants carry hundreds of twiggy stems, each tipped in autumn with masses of starry little flowers, white with twinkling golden eyes. Variable in nature, it has several delightful forms, among them the diminutive, satin pink 'Esther' (to $1\frac{1}{2}$ feet) and the taller 'Pink Cloud' (to 3 feet). Most unusual of all is the pearly, grayish-pink 'Ringdove' (to 3 feet), its flowers as softly opalescent as a dove's feathery breast. All of these will charmingly accompany late roses or mingle with rusty tall sedums and glossy-leaved bergenias.

White wood aster, *Aster divaricatus* (Zone 4, 1 to 2 feet), is used extensively in English country gardens, where its tumbling clouds of bloom soften the hard line of boxwood hedge or foam over the lip of a wall. We can take a tip from such treatment, for this delicate, filigree woodlander is incurably floppy, yet adamantly resists all attempts at staking. It blooms from late summer into autumn and its brittle network of black stems and bronzed seed heads holds its looks well into winter. White wood asters have small crowns that fit neatly into constricted spaces (they look smashing in window boxes, with miniature roses, for instance) and they will share limited space comfortably with ground covers and small bulbs.

Each region of the country boasts aster species of its own, many of them marvelous garden plants. Specialty nurseries offer dozens of mannerly species as well as countless hybrids, so with very little effort, one can have asters blooming from midsummer until autumn's bitter, chilly end. Once you have them, you have only to treat them according to their modest needs and they will repay your efforts many times over. As a clan, asters do best in ordinary, well-drained soils. Many willingly tolerate poorish soils if offered supplemental humus and mulch at planting time. Nearly all asters prefer full sun but many species, including the wood asters, will bloom nicely in light or partial shade. However, even the most upright forms may need staking in shadier situations, for their stems tend to get lanky without direct sunlight. The tallest asters can be supported with English border hoops set on trios of wire legs, or the central stalks may be bound lightly to bamboo stakes. Asters that flop even in full sun can be given tall, four-tiered tomato cages, set in place in late May when the plants are pinched back. (This involves pinching out the growing tips of each shoot and snipping off the top two pairs of leaves with your thumb and forefinger to encourage bushy plants with loads of buds.) All but naturally dwarf forms will be most shapely and floriferous when pinched back in late spring or early summer. Plants that flower in August and September should be pinched in April and May, while later bloomers can be left until late May or early June.

Clumps that look crowded should be divided in mid-spring as well. Cut the mother plant into pieces, each with several leafy stems on top, some thicker storage root and fine-textured feeder roots below. Though certain species, like heath asters, are natural thicketers which can persist for years without disturbance, most named forms bloom best as young plants, becoming woody and reluctant to divide within a few seasons. Should your asters falter, split them up next spring and give them a fresh start with humus-enriched soil. Come fall, your beds and borders will be aglow once again with glimmering galaxies of floral stars.

Garden Aflame

Foliar Fire Keeps the Garden Glowing

Most years, Indian summer, with its warm days and sunny skies, keeps the garden alive long after Labor Day, the traditional time to throw in the trowel. By October, a few drenching rains have renewed our parched plants and the last, late perennials bloom against an increasingly vivid backdrop as cool nights and warm days awaken fading foliage to brilliance. Leaves once green are now old gold and brass, mahogany and scarlet, tawny orange and rhubarb purple.

Those who admire the extravagant splendors of the New England woods in autumn may find that anything less seems rather flat. Fall foliage colors may indeed look relatively subdued elsewhere, but all across the country, regional palettes of fine colorers are rich and varied. Even where summers are cool, a host of shrubs and small trees will color brightly and reliably. (Fall leaf color depends on a number of factors, including stored sugars and significant day/night temperature differences, but accumulated summer heat is among the most critical.) As a child in Massachusetts, I thought nothing more magnificent than a stand of sugar maples in October. Later, the red sourwoods (*Oxydendrum arboreum*) of Ohio, Colorado's gilded cottonwoods, and Nevada's burnished aspens seemed just as breathtaking in their own ways. Here in the maritime Northwest, burning bushes (*Euonymus alata*) blaze rocket red, katsuras (*Cercidiphyllum japonicum*) burst into gold and crimson fireworks, and sweetgums (*Liquidambar styraciflua*) become upright columns of foliar flame in yellow and orange and fire engine red, despite our modest summers.

Such showboat plants as these can overwhelm a small garden, but plenty of smaller border shrubs are just as dependable. What's more, you don't need to pack the borders with hotshot shrubs to keep the color coming. A couple of stellar foliage plants set among quieter ones will bring long-lasting excitement to the autumn garden tapestry. Though flowers are relatively few, fluffy asters and spidery chrysanthemums may be joined by dangling fuchsias, gay coneflowers, and sunny black-eyed Susans. If a little tatty upon close examination, the garden remains a visual feast for the near-sighted, who savor the fading border in soft-focused overview, the bits and pieces of color blending together to maintain the illusion of a harmonious whole.

Some of the hottest fall foliage is flaunted by garden sumacs. The best of these boast large, divided leaves like oversized ferns which lend an exotic, tropical look to the border. Fragrant sumac, *Rhus aromatica* (Zone 4), is a sprawling shrub some 3 to 5 feet high which thrives in dry, well-drained soils, however poor. 'Low Grow', an almost prostrate 2-foot version, is often used on sloping hillsides and banks, where it puts on an astonishing display of screaming red leaves from September into November. Its dangling clusters of little red berries persist from midsummer well into winter, more attractive to humans than birds. The foliage releases a pungently spicy fragrance when crushed, and dried leaves look and smell terrific when worked into flowery wreaths. The lanky laceleaf staghorn sumac, *R. typhina* 'Laciniata' (Zone 4, 10 to 15 feet), is a good-looking, multi-trunked shrub with character all year round. In late summer, its softly furred stems are tipped with bunches of fat red berries that linger until spring. In autumn, its long, deeply cut leaves turn to glowing ruby lace before falling to reveal velvety brown stems and a striking winter silhouette. Both shrubs sucker freely, especially when their roots are disturbed (which happens easily in small gardens), but adapt readily to root containment, even growing happily in tubs or big planter boxes where space is limited.

Several members of the witch hazel family provide two seasons of beauty, greeting spring with fragrant flowers and fall with flaming foliage. The shapely little shrub *Fothergilla gardenii* (Zone 5, 3 to 5 feet) is native to the southeastern woods but very much at home in gardens across the country. In early spring, its slim, up-reaching stems are tipped like silky bottle brushes with masses of whiskery white flowers. The big, boldly rounded leaves deepen in fall to desert sunset tints of burnt orange, sandstone red, and thundercloud purple. A compact form, 'Blue Mist', has smaller,

Flaming red burning bush, *Euonymus alata*, calls out the hot sparks in Chinese maiden grass (*Miscanthus sinensis*) seed heads. When green is scarce, golds, buffs, and cinnamon reds make ideal backdrops for fiery autumn foliage. (Garden of Doug Bayley, Seattle, Washington.)

oval leaves with a blue-gray sheen which develop equally smashing late color. Largest of the bunch,

A clambering purple grape vine, *Vitis vinifera* 'Purpurea' winds its way into a white river birch. Its companion is the lemon-belled *Clematis serratifolia*, which will have turned pale gold by October's end.

F. major (Zone 5, 6 to 8 feet) enriches the back of the border to similar effect, while a selected form with exceptionally large leaves and flower clusters which is usually sold as *F. monticola* grows very slowly to 4 feet. These graceful plants appreciate good garden soil enriched with extra humus, and though tolerant of dry situations, they grow and color best when helped through long droughts with supplemental water. They are unusual in coloring nicely even when grown in light or partial shade, where autumn tints may continue over several months. In shady, wooded gardens, a Japanese cousin, *Disanthus cercidifolius* (Zone 6, 8 to 10 feet), colors with remarkable intensity. Its great, heart-shaped leaves contrast pleasingly with those of both conifers and broad-leaved ever-greens, and they ignite to a black-tinged ember red which increases from late summer throughout the fall.

Certain spring bloomers experience a second wind in autumn when their leaves rather than flowers catch the eye, though the strength and length of their performance vary both regionally and from garden to garden. Chinese *Forsythia suspensa* (Zone 6, 8 to 10 feet) was the first of its family to be grown in America. This casually weeping shrub opens its gentle yellow trumpets very early in spring, then announces the arrival of autumn in clarion reds and muted gold. It makes a stunning backdrop for the sea-blue, ruffled blossoms of the twice-flowering clematis 'Lady Betty Balfour' and a long-blooming rose, 'Charles

Austin', toast pink with a good deal of cinnamon in it, that highlights the coppery tints of the forsythia. Other spring bloomers that color nicely come fall include the shrubby dogwoods, notably the newer hybrids which tend to hold their colorful leaves for weeks on end. *Cornus florida* 'Cherokee Daybreak' (Zone 4, 20 to 40 feet), softly variegated in pink and cream in spring, becomes a roaring inferno of reds in fall, while 'Cherokee Sunset' begins as a lemon-lime blend and ends up a heady mixture of terra-cotta, copper, and rose. Sargent crab apples, *Malus sargentii* (Zone 4, 8 to 12 feet) color with especial luster, while a weeping crab, 'Red Jade' (Zone 4, to 15 feet), turns strawberry blond in fall and retains its fat little apples well into winter.

Not only shrubs but plants of all sorts can brighten the autumn garden. A good number of species grape vines will drape tall trees with swags of gladsome gold or can cheerfully disguise funky garage walls and ugly chain-link fences with red and purple banners. Claret vine, the purple wine grape (*Vitis vinifera* 'Purpurea', Zone 6, 8 to 20 feet), is lovely in spring, when its big, hand-shaped leaves unfurl burgundy-black and slightly furry. They turn flat green in summer, warming to hot shades of red and purple as summer wanes. The long, slanted autumn light transforms them into glowing translucencies that shimmer against a backdrop of pale, gilded birch leaves. Amber maples look like liquid butterscotch behind thick ropes of shield vine, the Japanese grape, *V. coignetiae* (Zone 5, 20 to 50 feet). This one has huge, sculptural leaves that contrast excitingly with steely blue spruces or towering, ink-green firs.

Perennials, too, join the party with confetti-colored leaves as well as late flowers. Bowman's root, *Gillenia trifoliata* (Zone 4, 3 to 4 feet), becomes a sheaf of beaten gold by late September,

while the last balloon flowers of *Platycodon grandiflorus* (Zone 4, to 1½ feet) look radiantly blue against the citrus yellow of their leaves. Dwarf leadwort, *Ceratostigma plumbaginoides* (Zone 5, to 12 inches), holds sapphire-blue florets above luminous maroon leaves. Dozens of garden grasses become incandescent in autumn, notably the tall, shimmering switch grass, *Panicum virgatum* 'Heavy Metal' (Zone 5, 4 to 5 feet), the dwarf fountain grass, *Pennisetum alopecuroides* 'Hameln' (Zone 6, 1 to 2 feet), and ruby-red ribbons of blood grass, *Imperata cylindrica* 'Red Baron' (Zone 6, 1 to 2 feet).

Once you begin to seek them out, autumn beauties both brazen and subtle will appear at every turn. Welcome them into your garden and give them like-minded companions. Rather than closing up shop when Labor Day arrives, keep the garden beds in reasonably good trim. Before long, you will find yourself regarding the end of summer as merely the beginning of the fall bonanza.

Pure Potential

Planting Spring as Chilly Winds Blow

I love the tail end of autumn, when the leaves are nearly gone. Stark tree branches shine gray against the pearly sky, their lines both strong and delicate, like dancers. At ground level, the last of summer's decaying muck is cleared away and a comforting blanket of mulch spread over the sleepy roots. This year, the whole garden is getting a thick layer of washed manure—gorgeous, fluffy stuff—from a local dairy farm. When modern milking barns are washed clean each day, the manure goes into deep holding pits. The liquid leachate is returned to the fields as fertilizer and the composted manure is sold to blissful gardeners, who value it as a lovely soil conditioner. Once the fall tidy is finished, I dig out my rubber kneeling mat, gather up the bags and boxes of bulbs that clutter the back porch, and head for the borders to plant pieces of spring as chilly winds blow.

Most bulbs are frumpy little objects, lumpy and misshapen. Who would guess that such unprepossessing lumps of latent plant could become gossamer anemones, satin tulips, or gilded, trumpeting daffodils? Homely as they might appear, these dim bulbs are merely hiding their light, for they are truly the prepackaged essence of spring. Tulips and daffodils, hyacinths and Dutch iris, fritillaries and anemones, all are held in stasis, awaiting the burial that recalls them to life. Here is a miracle that requires neither sainthood nor skill, promising a garden aglow with effortless blossom, from the first snowdrops to the last of the autumn crocus.

Moreover, bulbs give their goodness to anyone who asks, for they are among the least demanding plants in the garden. Their needs are simple—decent soil, plenty of sunshine, and good drainage—yet their gifts are unstinting and abundant. Such astounding plants would be worth any price, yet many of them are as cheap as their humble kitchen counterparts. This state of affairs—these days due to industrious Dutch field growers as well as laboratory tissue culturing, rather than unscrupulous wild collection—is entirely fitting, since these bulbs and tubers are just as necessary to the garden as onions and potatoes are to the larder.

Since bulbs offer so much for so little, it seems curious that one so seldom sees them excitingly used in ordinary gardens. Perhaps we are in part influenced by catalog illustrations that show bulbs in parklike settings, massed as bedding plants or marching in military rows, rather than ornamenting little, personal gardens. Though generosity is one key to getting a really good display from bulbs, planting them in unrelieved blocks or sheets does not answer in a home garden, where the highly artificial results are only partially softened by traditional bulb partners like forget-me-nots or pansies.

In home gardens, it works much better to cluster the larger bulbs, things like border tulips and narcissus, in informally shaped groups, tucked gracefully between established shrubs and emerging perennials. In smaller gardens, each group might hold ten or twenty bulbs, while greater expanses require groups of fifty or a hundred. If most bulbs in each group are concentrated in the center of their area, with a few spaced further apart at each side, such groups look relatively natural rather than sternly regimented. The shrubby backdrop puts the bulbs in context and increases their visual impact manyfold.

To link them more closely with their surroundings, each group of large bulbs can also be laced with lower growing minor bulbs. This gives a finished look to each grouping, and when bulbs of both sizes are planted with a liberal hand, the effect is like finding frilly, lace-edged bouquets all over the garden. Starry windflowers (*Anemone blanda*, Zone 3) in pink or blue or white, swirl in little galaxies around pastel tulips or creamy daffodils. Plump, navy-blue and sky colored spikes of grape hyacinths (*Muscari latifolium*, Zone 3) contrast delightfully with the diminutive bronze

A close look at bulbs reveals their fascinating variety of form. Turkish tulips from frigid mountain passes have tight-fitting jackets lined with tufts of grayish fur. Several tiny species are as hard and brown as hazelnuts, while many hybrids have the soft, plump look of an opulent Edwardian beauty.

Perched on sinuous stems, their petals as fringed as feathers, the parrot tulips look astonishingly exotic amid the usual spring bloomers. This sensual confection is 'Blue Parrot'.

unsightly browning off stage will be masked by fast-rising perennial companions. Strong, carrying colors that may be a bit much at close range are splendid choices for such background positions. Try the stunning Darwin tulip 'Daydream' (Zone 3), which opens the same warm yellow as the nodding cowslips, *Primula veris* (Zone 5, to 8 inches), a pretty combination further enhanced by the broad blades of Bowles' golden grass, *Milium effusum* 'Aureum' (Zone 5, to 14 inches). As it ages, 'Daydream' deepens to a rich, coppery orange that picks up the softer orange of Welsh poppies, *Meconopsis cambrica* (Zone 6, to 16 inches), and is echoed in the thready strands of a brunette New Zealand grass, *Carex flagellifera* (Zone 7, to 18 inches), all good back-of-the-border plants. The exotic split-cup *Narcissus* 'Palmares' (Zone 3, to 14 inches) is wedding-white touched with gentle tints of pink and peach, too delicate to carry across a distance yet too obtrusive in its old age for front-row placement. Put this one a few feet back, nestled between clumps of silvery *Artemisia absinthium* 'Valerie Finnis' (Zone 3, to 4 feet), which will set off the delicious 'Palmares' flowers, then expand to mask their dreadful death.

Middle-sized bulbs look wonderful when lavishly arrayed beneath the skirts of garden shrubs, whether deciduous spring bloomers like forsythia and quince or evergreens like rhododendrons and mountain laurels. Glossy Oregon grape, *Mahonia aquifolium* (Zone 5, 4 to 6 feet), opens its lax clusters of intensely fragrant, sun-yellow flowers in March or April, just in time to greet the jonquilla *Narcissus* 'Pipit' (Zone 4, to 1 foot), a delicate reverse bicolor with a chalky yellow corona around an ivory cup. Encircle the whole ensemble with white wood anemones (*Anemone nemorosa*, Zone 4, to 8 inches) and pale yellow primroses (*Primula vulgaris*, Zone 3, to 8 inches) for a charming and long-lasting display. The oval, leathery leaves of

bells of botanical tulips, *Tulipa batalinii* 'Bright Gem' (Zone 3) or banana-yellow dog-tooth violets, *Erythronium tuolumnense* 'Pagoda' (Zone 4). Cobalt clumps of Siberian squill (*Scilla siberica*, Zone 3) glow like puddles of fallen sky in the spring garden, setting off rosy tulips or buttery daffodils to perfection.

The largest bulbs and groups belong at the back of beds and borders. There, sheltering shrubs can support their floral effects, while their

mountain laurel (*Kalmia latifolia*, Zone 5, 15 to 30 feet) set off their own icy white, eight-sided cups to a nicety. The red-veined, pink-budded blossoms pleasantly echo the pink-and-cream-striped leaves and flagrant red flowers of 'Cheerleader' tulips (Zone 3, to 16 inches), which are all further emphasized by a ruffle of white grape hyacinths (*Muscari botryoides* 'Alba', Zone 3, to 1 foot).

Smaller and earlier blooming bulbs can go toward the middle and front of the border, for their leaves will have returned to the earth by the time the summer flowers arrive. Front line clusters might include baby daffodils like miniature *Narcissus triandrus* 'Ice Wings' (Zone 4, to 14 inches) or the tattered double, yolk-yellow flowers of 'Rip van Winkle' (Zone 4, to 10 inches), and cheerful sprays of such wild Turkish tulips as the creamy *Tulipa turkestanica* (Zone 3, to 8 inches). Carpets of snow crocus, perhaps hot yellow *Crocus ancyrensis* or sunny *C. chrysanthus* (both Zone 4, to 5 inches), can spill over the border front into the lawn to spangle the new grass with glowing cups of gold. Little bulbous iris like *Iris reticulata* 'Harmony' (Zone 5, to 6 inches), a bright blend of blues, ripen their long, skinny leaves very early, and their charming flowers, often strongly fragrant, merit a front-line position. Try threading porcelain white *I. reticulata* 'Natascha' (Zone 5, to 6 inches) among clumps of black mondo grass, *Ophiopogon planiscapus* 'Nigrescens' (Zone 6, to 1 foot), and send running ribbons of tiny, lipstick-red *Tulipa linifolia* (Zone 4, to 6 inches) between the ruddy leaves of coral bells like *Heuchera villosa* or *H. micrantha* 'Palace Purple' (both Zone 4, to 2 feet) at the border's edge.

However they are used, bulbs need thoughtful placement if they are to deliver of their best even once, let alone for many years to come. Their needs are simple but strong: Give them plenty of sun and room to develop and multiply. Choose their sheltering companions, whether woody or perennial, with discretion, so the ripening bulbs are not smothered as they approach summer dormancy. In heavy soils, many bulbs are prone to rots, so mix fine gravel or coarse sand into their planting soil to ensure quick drainage. In lighter soils, additional humus will be appreciated. In any soil, an enriching layer of manure should be spaded into the planting hole, mixed well and covered with topsoil. A planting pad of fine gravel can add years to bulbs' lives, as can planting large bulbs (such as crown imperials, *Fritillaria imperialis*) at their sides to prevent water from collecting in their soft neck pockets as they ripen off.

Where mice, gophers, or voles are active during the winter, deep planting holes can be lined with fine wire mesh or horticultural barrier cloth topped with soil and amendments. A handful of smelly, naphtha-based mothballs blended into topsoil and mulch will also discourage these pests. When chipmunks and squirrels insist on swapping stale peanuts for precious fritillaries or minor bulbs, mix ground pepper and more mothballs into the fresh fall mulch (this also dissuades cats from disgracing themselves in the borders). In some areas, crocus are an especial favorite of mice, but *Crocus tomasinianus* and its various named forms are evidently less tasty than others, and are such strong multipliers that any winter losses are usually made up by spring. Last of all, mark the outline of each bulb planting with short bamboo canes or small, unobtrusive rocks to jog inconstant memory; the best planting care is wasted if you then spade up the slumbering bulbs to plant something else in what seems to be an empty spot.

Though big tulips and daffodils are just expensive annuals in many parts of the country, well-placed, well-planted, and well-fed groups may persist for several years under favorable conditions. The various species known as botanical tulips may even multiply, especially when their foliage is allowed to ripen off naturally. Bulbs sold as "Perennial Tulips" are usually long-lived selections of single early and cottage tulips, which are among the most persistent in garden settings. Fancy peony-flowered tulips are perhaps the most fleeting, sometimes returning as single—and not very nice—blossoms for a year or two before dying out. Regular feeding, whether with a moderate (10–10–10) general-purpose commercial fertilizer or a homemade mixture (I use manure, kelp meal, and alfalfa pellets in both spring and fall) can also be surprisingly life prolonging.

Minor bulbs, on the other hand, are likely to reward ordinary care with several—even many—years of loyal service. Should your minor bulb groups falter after a few years, they may have become overcrowded. Dig up the entire group; if they appear healthy but cramped, replenish their soil and reset half of the original group, placing the rest elsewhere. If instead you find signs of rots or mold, discard any soft or moldy bulbs and remove the soil completely. (To renew diseased soil, expose it to heat or strong sunlight, then mix it into a hot, fresh compost pile). Replace the old soil with aged compost and gritty sand before replanting anything and consider resettling the bulbs in a more congenial spot, substituting perennials that like heavy clay.

If you aren't sure which spots will be best for bulbs, experiment with small groups in various locations. Where bulbs look stunted or lean lanky to the sun, don't fight facts; grow your ornamental bulbs in pots or find another place to put the garden. On the other hand, where tulips or narcissus rise tall and sturdy, plant them by the hundred. With some experimentation and practice, the sweet spots where bulbs will thrive can be discovered in any garden. Treat them right, make appropriate choices, and you may enjoy their beauty for many seasons to come.

When planted in well-amended soil and fed at appropriate times, tulips can be surprisingly long-lived. The key to long-term success is to permit the foliage to ripen fully. (Northwest Perennial Alliance Border at the Bellevue Botanic Garden in Bellevue, Washington.)

NOVEMBER

Skeletons and Garden Bones
Structure from Plants

Early winter is upon us, and though the garden is stripped of all its summery delights, its essential shapes and patterns are laid bare for us to admire and critique. Without the eye-catching distractions of rapid growth and change, what we see in these quiet months is the garden's skeleton. Gardeners often carry on like medical students about skeletons and bones, but what they are really talking about is garden anatomy. This means the combination of architectural plants—hedges, mature trees, evergreen shrubs—and hardscape—walls and patios, arbors and paths—that frame and divide the garden. Just as a photogenic person is said to have good bones, photogenic gardens have striking architectural features. Some gardens have more and better bones than others, but fortunately, it doesn't take a plastic surgeon or even a professional makeover to give a spineless garden a little more backbone. What it does take is time (for plants to grow) and attention (yours).

To assess your own garden in terms of form and structure, stroll through it during the off season. Visit at various times of day, pausing here and there to

Silvered by frost or hazed by morning mist, the garden gains a quiet magnificence as its winter death approaches. (Northwest Perennial Alliance Borders at the Bellevue Botanic Garden in Bellevue, Washington.)

absorb fuller, more detailed impressions. Begin your critique by taking notes, emphasizing not only what's wrong but also what works. Though snowy grass, sodden shrubs, and naked trees may elicit something closer to criticism, a kindly critique is really more useful. After all, the point is not to drive ourselves to despair over the garden's shortcomings but to help nudge both gardens and gardeners further along their chosen paths. If the winter garden feels shapeless, look for places where evergreen trees or shrubs could form effective barriers, or consider building a trellis or an enclosing fence. Should unwanted views obtrude themselves without the summer screen of greenery, make notes about the placement, size, and shape of the gaps in your garden boundaries. You can then spend the worst part of winter figuring out which plants will fill them most satisfactorily. If there are lots of gaps, or more gaps than shelter, concentrate on the most annoying visual holes. The rest can wait, and some may even resolve themselves (remember, plants grow larger while you aren't looking) before you are ready to address those minor trouble spots again.

Take notes about off-season ambiance as well. If the garden still has presence and character in December, if it feels like a place to be in its own right, congratulations! Your thoughtful work is paying off nicely. If, on the other hand, the garden seems to have vanished with summer, it may be time to increase its structural components. Since garden structure can come from various sources, both man-made and natural, which kind you choose to employ depends entirely on your personal taste. Most books on garden design are rooted in architectural values. Nearly all begin the design process with hardscape, reshaping the lie of the land, placing the paths and walls, and so on before a single plant is mentioned. This is an eminently sensible way to go about things, and indeed it is the easiest way to make a structural, visually strong garden. However, most of us begin to garden because we love plants, not pergolas. Architects may start by creating places for plants, but the plant-obsessed gardener will plant a vine first, then look for something for it to climb on. Our plants join the garden community as we discover them, and those that originally appeared on the master plan soon have more company than we bargained for. When we finally recognize that our wonderful garden is overstuffed and losing its shape, it's a bit late to rectify matters the professional way. Small, heavily planted gardens and earth-moving machinery—not to mention crews of large-footed workers—do not mix.

Fortunately, the things that hardscape provides—definition, enclosure, privacy—can also be achieved with plants. It's certainly quicker to erect a fence than to wait for a shrub to become an effective visual barrier, but if your garden has only a few bothersome gaps and you prefer green architecture, you have plenty of excellent options. Architectural evergreen plants such as Portuguese laurels or slim, columnar junipers become as structural a design element as anything made of wood or stone. Whether grouped as hedges and screens or used individually to plug up visual gaps, such plants can be used to direct eyes and feet where you want them. Groups of medium-sized shrubs, both evergreen and deciduous, can be massed behind beds and borders to frame floral displays, and grouped along the property line to define the shape of the garden itself. Smaller clusters of dwarf evergreen shrubs give solid backing to early bulbs and summer perennials. Deciduous dwarves with bright berries or handsome bark can be mingled attractively amongst the little evergreens, their contrasting colors and textures making the beds and borders more interesting to look at in winter.

Once you have identified places within the garden that need more definition, enclosure, or interest, the fun begins. Curl up on the couch, surround yourself with reference books and nursery catalogs, and search out plug-in plants that could correct your garden's most regrettable deficiencies. Next, write the most expensive ones on your holiday wish list so you can give a dear one the happiness of making you happy (the thoughtful generosity of gardeners is legendary). Savor the possibilities, always considering plant and placement together. Perhaps the glossy-leaved, self-cleaning pink *Camellia* 'Donation' would be the perfect plug for the awkward spot between the garage and the garden. A sculptural rhododendron from the hardy David Leach series would build into a stabilizing mass behind the perennial bed. Feathery, upright 'Wichita Blue' junipers could frame the entry gate or disguise the garbage can holding area.

When selecting likely candidates for each position, there are several factors to keep in mind. The first, of course, is hardiness, but don't just rely on catalogs or reference books for your information. Check with other local gardeners, ask at good nurseries, and seek out other regional resources, whether botanic gardens, university programs, or county extension agency Master Gardener programs, to develop a good overview of the possibilities open to you. Visit as many gardens, public and private, as you can, and make notes about which architectural plants look healthy and attractive. Make notes, too, about their mature size, for this can be hard to visualize, despite the label information, when you buy a hopeful young tree or shrub. As mentioned earlier, some growers list the plant's height at five or ten years, not at maturity. This seems deceitful, but it has been explained to me by several growers as reflecting the actual life span of most woody

Repeated elements, whether rugged tree trunks or man-made objects, create a satisfying sense of rhythm and flow within the garden. Here, Western red cedars rise above a pale sea of sweet woodruff (*Galium odoratum*) in restful yet potent combination. (Garden of Bobbie Garthwaite and Joe Sullivan, Bainbridge Island, Washington.)

plants in garden settings. Apparently we either kill them off ourselves or move away and leave them to the mercies of nongardeners with dependable regularity. In any case, it is as well to know what could happen in ten or twenty years so you can plan and choose accordingly.

Ask yourself, too, exactly what each plant candidate offers your garden. Evergreens obviously bring solid shapes, a comforting mass, and a year-

Rough, strongly textured fir bark gives this living column a sculptural quality. Architectural plants anchor their companions to their setting and make visual links between the intimacy of the garden and the larger scale of the house and its neighborhood.

scale of your plantings for many years. These are worth buying as larger, older specimens, even though they will be expensive. Faster growing evergreens are usually correspondingly coarser in form and texture but may be just the ticket where you want a quick solution and there is plenty of room for plants to sprawl.

Deciduous plants can also qualify as architectural, particularly those with shapely skeletons and lovely bark. A good number also produce berries or fruit—certain crabs hold their charming little apples well into the frostiest winter, for instance—and a few, like the autumn cherry (*Prunus subhirtella autumnalis*, Zone 4, 20 to 40 feet), may bloom all winter in mild years. The dogwood clan is particularly full of plants with off-season attractions, and many of the choice, compact Japanese garden maples are strikingly handsome when naked. Indeed, winter is a good time to wander through the back lots of nurseries, noticing which plants retain their charms without their clothing leaves. When you get home, you can compare all these notes, distilling from them a short list of essential plants with backbone to spare. Even if budget constraints mean you can only add one or two of them a year, before long your garden will be improved in looks and character. Even a slow infusion of bone plants will transform a spineless garden into one with spirit and strength. Each year, as young plants mature and you make more thoughtful additions, the garden within the garden emerges, more definitely itself and more clearly a place where dreams have come true.

Garden Carpets
Ground Covers with Rewarding Ways

For most gardeners, the subject of ground covers rivals only dirt as the ultimate dull topic. If the

round presence, but some could be considered self-pruning while others will require constant vigilance. The self-pruners are those with tidy or at least appealing natural shapes, while the renegades lose their balance over time, dropping crucial branches or responding to being cut back by producing quantities of off-shoots. Many of the best are slow growers which preserve the balance and

term conjures up a stultifying sweep of vinca or a blank expanse of ivy, try thinking instead about garden carpets. Why not break up those blah green rugs with clusters of seasonal bulbs and clumps of contrasting foliage plants? Make stylish, magical carpets, decorated with imaginative detail. And why must a ground cover be green? Roll out a rich red carpet of *Ajuga reptans* 'Burgundy Glow' (Zone 2, to 8 inches) to add pop to a pastel planting. Pour sparkling 'White Nancy' lamium (*Lamium maculatum,* Zone 2, to 8 inches), with whitewashed foliage and clean white flowers, beneath a dusky purple smoke bush (*Cotinus coggygria* 'Royal Purple').

We often assume that ground-cover plants are intrinsically boring, fit only for a life of servitude. Happily, mental habit, not horticultural law, demands that they be homely or inconspicuous. Escape the constrictions of conventional wisdom by ignoring routine choices like pachysandra or St. John's wort in favor of equally hard workers which are delightful in their own right. Similarly, we may profitably rethink their expected garden roles. Ground covers do indeed suppress weeds, yet they also perform other vital tasks willingly and well. In spring, they protect bulb blossoms from rain-splashed mud. Through the growing season, they conserve moisture, reducing evaporation and shading shallow-rooted perennials. Repeated groups of theme ground covers can unify complex border plantings, leading the eye gracefully while subtly linking disparate areas. Evergreen ground covers can make permanent place holders for ephemeral plants or act as the stage for a succession of "sandwich" plantings, interlayered bulbs and perennials that chase each other through the year. They also provide winter interest while insulating borderline tender plants from deep ground frosts. As for the prime directive, the best ground covers suppress weeds artfully, creating a neutral zone between warring colors, softening primary colors or emphasizing secondary tints.

While every garden holds numerous niches which are best filled by cooperative ground covers, we need not use the same plants over and over again. Rather than perpetuating those drab, impersonal stretches of plain ivy or pachysandra that give ground covers a bad name, try a new approach. Plant each niche individually, employing a full range of plants with foliage and flowers in uncommon colors or subtle shades. Try lacy, prostrate beach wormwood, *Artemisia stellerana* 'Silver Brocade' (Zone 3, to 2 inches), under 'Black Joker' pansies and vivid red roses. Surround ashy blue *Iris sibirica* 'Summer Skies' and deep purple trumpet lilies with the crinkly rosettes of black bugleweed, *Ajuga reptans* 'Metallica Crispa' (Zone 2, 4 to 6 inches). Loop swirls of sheep bur, *Acaena* 'Blue Haze' (Zone 6, to 4 inches), around salmon and apricot daylilies. Circle a creamy pink miniature rose with tidy tweed sheets of pinky purple *Sedum spathulifolium* 'Roseum' (Zone 5, to 3 inches). Let a treasury of golden piggybacks, *Tolmiea menziesii* 'Taff's Gold' (Zone 6, to 1 foot), glow like lost sunshine beneath leathery rhododendrons.

By now, you may be wondering whether we are talking about plant combinations or ground covers. The point is to think about both. One clump of golden piggyback under a canary-yellow *Rhododendron* 'Hotei' is a combination (or at least the start of one). An encircling crowd of golden piggybacks becomes ground cover. Their circle need not remain unbroken, of course; it might be punctuated by clumps of ostrich ferns, daffodils, and blue summer onions (*Allium azureum*). Similarly, that creeping wormwood,

'Silver Brocade', that spills over the path edge can also crawl back into the border, accentuating gray 'Krossa Regal' hostas and hazy catmint. Blue sheep bur (*Acaena* 'Blue Mist') can both surround and echo glittering clumps of steel-blue oat grass (*Helictotrichon sempervirens*) and quivering, blue-leaved meadow rues like *Thalictrum glaucum*. The ruddy sedum might play host to purple crocus in spring, set off the pleated, silver-green leaves and rosy flowers of pink clover (*Oxalis adenophylla*) in summer, then play backdrop to the tiny, fragrant annual violet cress, *Ionopsidium acaule*, from autumn well into winter.

When they perform as intended, ground covers can be the busy gardener's best friend, but if they exceed their commission they may rank among our worst enemies. Essentially, we are asking plants to grow where we want them and not where we don't, which is rather like explaining to the cats that they are welcome on the couch but not on the computer keyboard. To reduce conflict, be chary in your choices. This necessitates self-education, for the more you know your conditions—dry, sandy soil in full sun, heavy acid clay in half shade—the better you can create a list of plants that will grow in those situations. Next, find out how each of your candidates behaves in your part of the country. This matters, since a plant that acts demure in North Carolina may turn rowdy in my maritime Northwestern garden (which nominally enjoys the same Zone 8 climate) or vice versa. It also underlines another important point: If your experience differs markedly from that of gardeners in other countries or counties, or from information offered in gardening books, don't feel that either you or they must be wrong. Many environmental factors can significantly influence plant growth and behavior, causing the same plant to act very differently in different places. Overall, the experience of gardeners and nursery folk in your region will often prove more practically helpful than English garden books, or even North American ones intended for a general readership.

Since ground covers are by definition plants which readily carpet the ground, unfamiliar candidates for garden placement should be handled with caution. Play it safe and give experimental selections—especially natives—a trial season or two in a nursery bed to prove themselves before unleashing them in your favorite border. This is an especially recommended practice when dealing with plants from families with bolting tendencies, like mints and campanulas. Rampant spreaders often act deceptively meek for their first season, and only the following year do you discover what their roots have been up to underground. This doesn't mean that there is no place in the garden for strong, aggressive carpeters; some situations are best served by garden thugs. However, knowing in advance what to expect from your ground covers can save a lot of hard work and heartache.

When choosing candidates, remember that ground covers don't have to be flat or tiny; any plant that suits the style and scale of the planting and fulfills your requirements for a designated area can do the job. If you aren't sure where to start looking for replacements for insufferably dull old standards, check their family connections, for many of them have cuter cousins. Periwinkle, or

Sedum x 'Ruby Glow', daughter of the famous *Sedum* x 'Autumn Joy', spills in lax tumbles over the pleated leaves of lady's mantle, *Alchemilla mollis*. Both are hard-working border perennials that double easily as ground covers, either singly or in partnership.

creeping myrtle (*Vinca minor*, Zone 4, to 5 inches) is much prettier when painted with gold or silver variegations as is the case in the cultivars 'Variegata' and 'Argentea'; and delicate, airy 'Miss

Golden creeping Jenny, *Lysimachia nummularia* 'Aurea', stitches itself over and through bigger companions in brilliant embroidery. Here, it accompanies black mondo grass, *Ophiopogon planiscapus* 'Nigrescens', in full sun, but it is even more useful for bringing its golden light into shady places.

Jekyll's White' is a collector's plant. Ordinary bugleweed is a weed indeed but buxom, blue-spiked *Ajuga reptans* 'Catlin's Giant' and the richly textured 'Purple Brocade' (both Zone 2, 12 to 14 inches) are knockouts. Our eastern native Allegheny spurge, *Pachysandra procumbens* (Zone 4, to 1 foot), is attractive enough to plant as a specimen, with its bronzed and marbled foliage and fluffy ivory flowers.

Certain creeping herbs make gorgeous garden rugs, especially the prolific mother-of-thyme (*Thymus serpyllum*, Zone 3, to 1 inch). The species is variable, producing sheets of tight-textured green foliage smothered from late spring well into autumn with tiny flowers of purple or lavender. It boasts numerous named forms such as white 'Albus', clear red 'Coccineus', 'Pink Chintz', and 'Reiter's Red'. The most enticing form, woolly thyme (*T. s. lanuginosus*), spreads in soft gray rugs over any light or open soil, wanting only full sun and quick drainage in order to thrive. Golden marjoram (*Origanum vulgare* 'Aureum', Zone 3, $1\frac{1}{2}$ to $2\frac{1}{2}$ feet) forms low, cascading tussocks of rounded, banana-yellow foliage before sending up thickets of taller stems tipped with frizzy purple flower heads. This strapping form (often sold at specialty herb nurseries) is a willing worker in larger-scale settings, but where space is limited, you might prefer the choicer 'Norton's Gold', a dwarf mounder some 5 or 6 inches high, its mild pink flowers held on 12-inch stems. A good many other marjorams and ornamental oreganos are worthy of consideration where you want ground covers to be both lovely and luxuriant yet tough and drought tolerant. All grow well in hot, dry situations, doing nicely beside heat-reflective staircases, sidewalks, and driveways as well as swimming pools.

There are many diminutive forms of favorite border plants as well, such as prostrate baby's-breath, *Gypsophila repens* (Zone 3, 4 to 6 inches), a ground-hugging mat that foams with white froth (or pink, in the case of 'Rosea') from late spring through midsummer. Like its larger cousins, creeping baby's-breath prefers sun and open, limy soils, sulking or dying away in heavy, acid clays. Several mat-forming veronicas are enchanting carpeters, including the very dwarf *Veronica pectinata* (Zone 2, to 3 inches), with toothed, silvery leaves crowded in summer with short spikes of sky-blue flowers. An even grayer version, 'Rosea', has warm, blushing pink flowers that accord nicely with peonies and old roses. The slightly larger *V. prostrata* (also sold as *V. rupestris* or *V. teucrium*) has little leather-green leaves and vivid, purple-blue flowers softer in the form, 'Heavenly Blue', and rosy in 'Mrs. Holt'. A daintier, golden-leaved version, 'Trehane', has sea-blue flowers (all Zone 4, to 8 inches). All the veronicas like full sun but prefer moister soils than the hardy thymes.

Whether you choose traditional or uncommon ground covers for a given setting, it is vital to balance plant and situation with vigor and scale. Where a good deal of ground needs to be covered, perhaps beneath mature trees and shrubs, our carpeters must be determined but not outright thugs. Running comfrey, *Symphytum grandiflorum* (Zone 5, to 1 foot), weaves an evergreen tapestry of coarse, hairy leaves trimmed from spring into summer in dangling clusters of ivory bells tipped with china blue in 'Hidcote Blue' or pastel pink in 'Hidcote Pink'. A chalky blue-flowered form with leaves handsomely streaked in buttery yellow and cream is called 'Variegatum'. It makes a wonderful, stippled flooring for a sun-dappled woodland, consorting well with shrubby dogwoods (*Cornus* species) and flowering currant (*Ribes* species). Among big, bold plants like hostas, rodgersias, and tall ostrich ferns, we need understory plants that can hold their own without overpowering the

This diminutive perennial, *Veronica prostrata* 'Trehane', is a lovely and efficient carpeter for sunny borders. It's an especially appropriate natural ground cover choice for yellow, blue, and white color schemes, but also works well with blues and purples, blended with old gold and chartreuse.

main events. A vigorous, white-flowered carpeter, *Houttuynia cordata* (Zone 5, 1 to 1½ feet) is an aggressive traveler in damp soils but more restrained in drier, wooded gardens. Its pretty variegated form, 'Chameleon', is more moderate in growth, and its heart-shaped leaves (which smell like marmalade) are cheerfully splashed with copper pinks and bronzed reds. It will fill in between the crowns of larger perennials or shrubs while adding depth and finish to the planting. In a modest border, ground covers like the above-mentioned veronicas and bugleweeds will be hearty enough to compete successfully amongst taller plants, yet never overwhelm. In a tiny urban courtyard, restraint and long-term company manners are musts, and diminutive alpines will be the ground covers of choice. An orchestrated group of evergreen border shrubs could be fronted down with prostrate rock plants, sheets of choice thymes and ornamental oreganos in sun, or a glossy evergreen native like *Galax urceolata* (Zone 5, 1 to 1½ feet) and thick club mosses in a shady situation.

Clearly, our choices are many, which makes plant selection more fun than ever. Chosen well, these garden workhorses are not only helpful but harmonious, enhancing, even exciting. If we carpet the garden as thoughtfully as we do our living quarters, choosing ground covers with an eye both to practical functions and to intrinsic beauties, the results will be anything but dull.

Winter Wraps

Preparing for Hard Times to Come

I always wait too long to do the final autumn chores, feeling that to rush things when the air has any lingering hint of warmth is to declare the death of summer. The result, of course, is that I end up in late November draining and coiling stiff, half-frozen hoses, muttering curses as I shake out their heavy, muddy lengths to free them of remaining water (and ice). This job is so easy to do on a breezy day in October, when the autumn

sun is still warm enough to make the rubber supple, that it just doesn't make sense to put it off. Once they are drained, coil them up and hang them on a stout peg in the garage, or pile them neatly on a basement shelf. Don't leave them in heaps on the floor, for if hoses should freeze, they become quite brittle and can crack under pressure. All hoses last far longer if properly stored over the winter. Hose attachments like sprinkler heads and oscillating sprinklers should be gathered up and cleaned off for storage as well. Most have a small rubber cap on the end that does not attach to the hose. Pull this off and drain out any water, then poke a toothpick or a darning needle into each drip or spray gasket to push out any dirt that might clog the little nozzles. Hang them from hooks to keep them undamaged until spring. All this may sound finicky, but it really only takes a minute and can prolong the useful life of even an inexpensive sprinkler for years.

Retiring the lawn is a trickier proposition, for though its growth rate slows down in summer, it picks up again in fall and it won't actually stop growing until the first hard frost. I soon lose track of how many times I perform the ceremonial last mow of the season, but often the true last time is somewhere around Thanksgiving. It's worth keeping up with the grass for several reasons, for not only does it give the garden a tidier look, but short, smooth turf makes for pleasanter walking in winter (though this is less evident if snow carpets the ground early). Most important, short grass shows off the spangling of spring crocus better than raggedy, tangled grass, yet a late winter mow is apt to slice the emerging tops off the bulbs

Autumn leaf fall signals the beginning of the great fall garden cleanup. However, in certain places, it is more rewarding to let the foliar confetti linger until the colors fade.

before they are up enough for me to notice when the roaring Lawnboy drags me in its wake.

In late fall, when all the leaves have fallen, clean up the garden access paths and stepping-stones that run through the beds and borders, for otherwise their coating of rotting leaves and slug slime can prove lethal to the unwary. Step-stones set under dripping trees that may get slicked with

Clay pots, especially the tender rosy Italian terra rossa containers, need protection from harsh frost. (Garden of Barbara Flynn, Redmond, Washington.)

ice during the winter should receive a dusting of coarse sand to give booted feet better traction. Gardens that are never visited might not need such attentions, but once you have planted areas to hold winter interest, you naturally become interested in watching their progress, so it pays to keep the garden paths clear.

Though much of the sleepy garden has been tidied already, the latest bloomers should now be groomed as well. Cut back a spent aster here, cut down a sagging sunflower or faltering chrysanthemum there, readying each for the long winter's nap ahead. Their beds should be readied as well, cleared of soggy stems and leaves that could smother hopeful shoots and wanted seedlings over the winter. Where tired soil needs renewal, don't spade everything up, but layer on a thick coverlet of compost and mulch and let the worms do the underground mixing for you. Thin, exhausted summer mulches should be topped off again with chopped leaves, straw, or shredded bark. Heap mulches especially high around tea roses and marginally hardy perennials. This includes any that are barely cold hardy in your climate zone, as well as recent transplants and divisions of hardier things which may not have settled in properly yet. All such plants must be coddled a bit if they are to come through hard winters unscathed, so if the ground is very dry, water the plants well and scatter on a bit of compost or cottonseed meal before mulching. When you mound mulch around the base of any plant, toss in a handful of stinky naphtha-based moth balls to discourage mice from making a winter resort in the mulch heaps. (Moth balls are also effective rodent deterrents where you have been planting bulbs.)

Gardeners who like to push the limits of their climate are accustomed to taking summer and autumn cuttings of borderline tender plants, but the resulting youngsters don't really make up for the loss of, or serious damage to, the mother plant after a hard winter. For on-site protection, I have come to appreciate greenhouse umbrellas, clever gadgets which work like portable, miniature cold frames. These are dome-shaped umbrellas of thick gauge, clear vinyl, set on a spiked (rather than curving) handle. When unfurled and pushed into the ground, each covers a space $2\frac{1}{2}$ feet high and $2\frac{1}{2}$ feet in diameter. Placed over tender plants, they create a warm environment that offers the equivalent of up to a full climate zone of protection. These umbrellas are ideal for winter vegetables as well, creating a terrific sheltered microclimate for salad greens, broccoli, and leeks. Even in extraordinary winters, high winds do not dislodge the umbrellas, and snow slides right off the steeply curving sides. The worst problem I have with them is that cats love to get inside and bask in the warmth, which can be hard on young divisions or cuttings. A half-dome of chicken wire set on top of the plants protects them from being crushed, though it doesn't discourage the cats much. Timing is critical with these umbrellas, for if they are put in place too early, the protected plants can be tempted into precocious growth that is very susceptible to winterkill. On the other hand, if you wait too long, the ground freezes and you can't insert the spikes adequately deep. Figure out exactly where you want to use them, then set them up when the first frost warnings are heard. (If you can't find garden umbrellas locally, they can be ordered from the Solar Garden Company, Box 909, Cherry Hill Cottage, Stockbridge, Massachusetts, 01262, phone: 1-800-477-GROW.)

Small pots and ornaments should be gathered in for the winter now, lest they be damaged by hard frosts. Large containers made of clay or terracotta should be carried (or rolled, in the case of big pots) under cover in the shed or garage. Clay planters and birdbaths should also be drained and stored out of the weather. My biggest clay pots winter over in an unheated sun porch, where they get just enough protection that they don't freeze solid. Left outside, soft materials like clay may splinter and flake, and if it gets cold enough, full pots may crack or shatter when the wet dirt inside them expands and freezes. If the plants are left inside the pots, I give them a topcoat of rich planting mix topped off with mulch. While in storage, an occasional light watering—perhaps monthly—will keep the dormant occupants alive. Next spring, as soon as new shoots begin to appear, you can start regular watering, adding a low dose of liquid fertilizer each time. When the weather settles and you roll the big pots back into place in the garden, the plants will be ready to leap into fresh growth. Similar treatment will bring fuchsias in hanging baskets through the winter. Cut them back to 4- to 6-inch stumps, then hang the baskets in the cellar or any dim, dry place where they can rest quietly. Let the soil dry out slowly and keep it barely moist all winter. When new leaves appear in spring, begin regular watering with a fertilizer boost. Repot them in fresh soil, and they will perform better than ever next year.

Where winter snows are generous and apt to arrive early, plants often sleep snugly beneath their fluffy white blanket. If snows are late and scanty, icy wind and frost heaves can cause a good deal of harm to dormant plants. It helps to have a good supply of chopped brush and twiggy branches on hand to heap over the beds as winter begins. This is a great way to recycle the Christmas tree as well, for the worst storms often arrive with the new year. Trim off the side branches and pile them lightly over vulnerable or new plantings. This gives a few degrees of frost protection and cuts off drying winds as well. When bitter Alaskan fronts are predicted, we go a step further and drape all the broadleaf evergreen shrubs with sacking. Here in Seattle, where coffee is queen, burlap coffee bean sacks are easy to come by. Elsewhere, you could use woven feed sacks or flour bags, or buy plain burlap yardage. In a pinch, old sheets and

In real life, our toolsheds don't have to look like a designer's dream, but they should be tidy enough to be functional. When tools are adequately cared for and accessibly stored, every garden job becomes much easier to carry out.

shower curtains are effective frost baffles, though certainly far from scenic. If the whole job is done with brown burlap, the result looks less like a tornado has dropped the better part of a rummage sale in your backyard. Though any protection is better than none, the garden is plain enough in winter without adding insult to injury.

All these tasks may be carried out over the next few weeks, weather permitting. Once they are done, you can sit back by the fire, garden books at hand, and enjoy the onslaught of winter without guilt or worry, confident that the garden is also enjoying a well-earned rest.

Implements of Construction
Working Tools and Their Care

The oblique afternoon light slopes across the garden, emphasizing its tattered, dingy grandeur. Magnificent even in decay, it still offers glimpses of lost glory. Scarlet Virginia creeper scales a silver blue spruce, while cinnamon pink 'Charles Austen' roses nod amongst amber and bronze forsythia leaves. A few *Crocus zonatus* spangle the grass beneath the pear tree, their periwinkle goblets dangling on rather weak white necks. Though the last brave asters and the white daisies of feverfew are still going strong, the browning borders are quiet now, slumped and slumberous. These are the days that divide fall from winter, and in them, we can still safely divide and move spring and early summer bloomers. It's time to tidy up the garden and work areas, to carry tender plants back indoors for the winter, and to get new plants still in their nursery pots into the ground. Such work can be carried out until hard frosts threaten, but as rains get colder and mud squelches chilly underfoot, the idea becomes less enticing. If the slanting sun still speaks of summer, its warmth is waning daily. As surely as rain turns to sleet and soil turns to mud, autumn is turning to winter.

When the last chore is done, it's tempting to celebrate by tossing the tools in the shed, abandoning wet wellies in a grimy heap, and settling in by the fireside with an armload of garden books saved up from busier seasons. Both you and your tools will benefit if you resist that temptation. Rather than leaving them to rust through the winter, give all tools a quick once-over before putting them away. Rinse off the mud, chipping off caked dirt deposits with a stick. Some gardeners swear by those little rectangular blocks of wood called "woodmen," sold for this purpose, but a piece of kindling works just fine for me. Dry the blades and handles well, and touch up rusty spots on the metalwork with fine sandpaper, rubbing firmly until any trace of black is gone. Next, they need a protective coat of oil. We use 3–in–1 or light motor oil on carbon steel and linseed or similar wood protection on wooden handles.

This is a good time to sharpen the blades of shovels and spades as well. (Do this before you oil the tools, however.) Few people are aware that shovel blades do not come presharpened, or even that shovels should be sharpened at all, yet having sharp tools makes a very big difference to the tool user. I find it easiest to rest the shovel head on a low fence post, so that it is about chest high. You can straddle the handle, which helps keep the blade steady, or work from one side. Take a medium-fine metal file and run it away from yourself, up and off the end of the blade, working in slightly rounded arcs that move from the center of the blade outward. Usually, just the bottom quarter inch or so of the blade is beveled, and a few firm strokes in each spot are enough to renew the edge.

Stainless steel blades may only need a very light touch-up, like a well-set knife blade, to regain their cutting edge. If, however, the bottom of the blade is badly pitted and worn, you may want to extend the sharpened area deeper, perhaps an inch or so up the blade. When you're done, oil both blade and (wooden) handle lightly. It doesn't take long once you have the hang of it, and it is a lovely treat come spring to have sharp, clean tools all ready to hand.

Tool storage is also worth reconsidering if your idea of putting tools away is to jumble them anyhow into the shed or garage. Fortunately, it isn't necessary to have a designer toolshed, with each scrubbed and pristine tool artfully arrayed by size along a tastefully rustic wall—indeed, I always use such tools with a nervous sense of desecration. It is, however, worth spending a few minutes to contrive a practical way to store your garden things, not just for their long winter's nap, but all year round. Pegs or racks from which the tools hang flat against the wall keep those blades sharp (they get dull quickly on the floor). I have seen a large barrel used like an oversized umbrella rack for shovels, and an overhead array like a kitchen pots-and-pans holder (though all those handles hanging over my head made me uneasy). Anything that keeps tools upright and out of the way will help to eliminate those sudden encounters with a rake handle that can be so very painful on a dark winter's afternoon. Besides, after going to the trouble of cleaning and sharpening them, one gets a proprietary interest in one's tools. This is good for the relationship, which otherwise tends to be somewhat cavalier; the bigger the investment, the greater the attachment and responsibility one feels. So tuck those tools neatly out of the way of sleds and garbage cans or car

Shovels and spades are primary tools that can become beloved life companions, so take time to explore the possibilities before choosing. It's always worth spending more for well-crafted tools, but remember that the most expensive aren't always the best.

One shovel. The best are sturdy enough to use as pry bars when moving trees and shrubs, but light enough not to exhaust the user. Most shovel blades are carbon steel, which is strong and holds an edge fairly well but will rust over time unless cleaned and oiled periodically (this can mean once or twice a year) to prevent rust. Stainless steel is more expensive but lighter in weight, and it won't rust. Teflon-coated blades are silly, because the coating wears off almost immediately. Shovel handles also present choices: fiberglass handles do break, regardless of claims to the contrary, and are not appropriate for tool abusers (also defined as people who like to push their tools to the limits). Metal handles are heavy, and they, too, can break if used hard. Wooden handles are also heavy, but good ones take a lot of strain and are kind to the hands in cold weather. All come in varying lengths, from 26 to 28 inches up to 38 to 40 inches, so try several to see which feels most comfortable. Swing each a few times, and don't worry about looking eccentric in the store. When you're back in the garden working happily with a tool that truly suits your needs, you'll be glad you took the time to check everything out carefully.

One spade. Spades are smaller than shovels, often quite narrow bladed and shorter in the shaft. A spade is used when digging planting holes and for moving plants or moderate amounts of soil in crowded beds and borders. Its compact blade makes it easier to avoid disturbing the roots of neighboring plants. Border spades have flat, rectangular blades with a curved bottom (which should be sharpened like a shovel blade). Poacher's spades have long, slim blades, often slightly rounded, which make them very useful in tight quarters and in rocky soils. The same handle fac-

wheels, to wait patiently for the return of spring. As you do so, take inventory, so you can add anything you are lacking to your holiday wish list. The list of absolute necessities is short, so get the best available, choosing professional models whenever possible. Here's what each active gardener should have:

tors should be considered here, though spades are rarely worked as hard as shovels. Spade handles generally have hand grips, or hilts, as well. D-shaped cap hilts, which sit on the handle top, are great for people with small hands, while elongated or oversized T-shaped hilts suit those who need more hand room. Y-shaped hilts look much like the D's, but because they are made by dividing the handle, they can fracture under stress.

One border fork. These are the short-handled, square-tined, blunt-tipped forks used to lift and divide plants or harvest potatoes, blend in soil amendments, and break up soil lumps in the beds. Gardeners who build large compost heaps will also want a long-handled, round-tined, sharp-tipped fork for turning their heaps. These are often sold as manure or hay forks, and they are indeed useful for moving both of those important substances. In either case, choose solidly constructed forks in which both the neck or socket that fits the handle and the tines are made from a single piece of metal. Those made in two parts and joined at the neck can't stand up to serious garden work. If all else is comparable, choose the fork with the longest neck, for short-necked tools often part company with their handles.

Two rakes: one metal, one bamboo or plastic. Metal rakes are good for smoothing and leveling planting beds, working out lumps, and fishing out clumps of grass and roots left in the wake of shovel or tiller. They are essential for preparing a fine-textured seed bed. Heavy-backed flathead rakes look a bit like straight combs, with thick, short, blunt tines set along a straight bar, at right angles to their handles. Short (2-foot) models with 12 to 14 teeth are best for small spaces, while the 3-foot,

16- to 20-tine models cover a lot of ground fast. The best flathead rakes have long, strong necks so they won't come off their handles; these are almost indestructible. Lighter bowhead rakes have a finer-toothed comb set beneath arching, bowed arms that hold the teeth at a wider angle to the soil. Bowhead rakes are fine for small, less strenuous jobs. Grass or leaf rakes are fan shaped, their long, flat blades spreading gracefully out from the handle, which can be very light wood or metal. Bamboo rakes last best in dry climates, but rot readily in wet ones (especially when left outdoors repeatedly). Plastic ones work well anywhere, indefinitely. Their hollow metal handles can fill up with stagnant water if uncapped, so these are best stored upside down.

One set hand tools. Each active gardener should have a wide-bladed trowel, a narrow transplanting trowel, and a hand fork. Stainless steel or aluminum blades will not rust, while carbon steel tools must be kept oiled. (Even those with paint or plastic coating should be checked now and then, for these usually wear off along the working edge, exposing the metal to damp.) These sets come in many styles, with all shapes and sizes of hand grips, which may be made from wood, plastic, or metal. Gardeners with arthritic wrists or carpal tunnel syndrome often favor tools made of solid cast aluminum with rounded pistol grips that rest easily in the hand and warm up almost instantly in cold weather. Once you discover your own preferred style, buy yourself hand tools of the best quality you can find. These are garden workhorses, and nothing is more annoying than dealing with shoddy equipment on a daily basis. The best hand tools don't cost much more than the worst, but if price is an issue, buy these tools one

From late winter into spring, and again in fall, gardeners' hand tools are in constant use. It's important to find ones that you enjoy working with for hours at a stretch, especially if you have physical limitations like arthritis or carpal tunnel syndrome.

at a time, starting with the wide-bladed trowel. This one is used for planting out bulbs, potted plants, and divisions. The narrow-bladed trowel is useful for planting tiny bulbs or six-pack plants, and is a favorite with rock gardeners. Hand forks are used for prepping small areas, loosening heavy soils, weeding, and digging small plants.

One pair of clippers or secateurs. Only the best clippers will do, for cheap ones which mangle stems instead of cutting them cleanly are not called "the nurseryman's friend" for nothing (dead plants mean more sales). Again, there are many kinds available, with all manner of blades and hand grips. No matter which you choose, buy scissor-cut clippers, rather than those with crushing anvil-cut blades. It has been years since I used anything but Swiss Felco clippers, which are excellent and long-lasting tools. Every single part is replaceable, from the blades and handles down to the springs and screws. Those with big hands usually prefer the #2 or the ergonomic #11 model, while #6 is popular with the small handed, and lefties love the #9. I am a heavy user, and find the #8 (which is just like the professional nursery model, #7, but without its rotating handle) to be easiest on the hands and wrists. (No, I don't own stock in the company—but I wish I did.) Use your clippers to cut back perennials, prune and deadhead roses, and trim shrubs.

One hand knife. Actually, my own basket holds several knives, but the best of the bunch is sold as a hari-hari, or Japanese farmer's knife. Cast iron with a wooden handle, its wide blade is toothed on one side and smooth on the other. It is the best tool going for weeding, but also functions quite nicely as a transplanting tool, or for taking small divisions off less sensitive plants like daylilies, pulmonarias, and iris while the mother plant is still in the ground. I also use a very sharp, strong Japanese rose budding knife. Made of carbon steel, it comes in its own wooden sheath, and like so many Japanese tools, is very beautiful. A good strong knife like this is perfect for slicing divisions off crowded clumps of catmints or hostas. I also use it to cut twine and stretch ties when I can't find the scissors, and occasionally use it on recalcitrant weeds (though that is not especially good for the blade).

One folding pruning saw. Not strictly necessary, but these little saws are small enough to be used effectively in cramped spaces—like at the base of overgrown shrubs—without damaging stems you want to leave in place. This is a finesse tool, not a chain saw, and can't be expected to take out tree trunks, but works very well on anything up to 3 to 4 inches across. It cuts on the pull stroke, rather than the push, so can be used when lying prone beneath a twiggy lilac without enough room to put oomph in your stroke.

One pair heavy scissors. These are endlessly useful for cutting twine, plastic ties, and thin wire. Also fine for cutting flowers when somebody else has your clippers.

One basket. It can be a fancy trug or a plastic utensil tray from the five-and-dime; all it needs to do is hold your hand tools and a few other choice items. Mine also contains twine, labels and marker pen, envelopes for collecting seed, and a few plastic bags to hold cuttings or small divisions while I work.

That's really all an ornamental gardener needs, besides soil and plants, of course. There are the bigger tools, like wheelbarrows and carts, as well as things like hoses and sprinklers, that every garden also needs. There are also masses of specialized tools like bonsai trimmers, which you will accumulate along with each new enthusiasm. However, these are enough to get you started and keep both you and your garden going strong and healthy.

DECEMBER

Developing Garden Style
Adapting Lessons and Skills

When we first begin to garden, our concern is almost wholly with the plants themselves. We gradually discover which plants we really love and how to make them thrive, moving past the automatic thrivers which gain our immediate affection to those that need understanding or coaxing to give their best. This first stage may take years or pass quickly, but once we know how to grow plants well and how to combine them attractively, the process of garden making seems to accelerate. The next stage is one of joyful exuberance in which the garden almost makes itself, the breathless gardener hastening to keep up with the booming plant communities. Wonderful things can happen when we let our gardens develop willy-nilly, yet at some point, desire to create a specific kind of garden may awaken. That is when we begin to consider the question of garden style.

The decision to make the garden formal or casual is rarely difficult, for everything from the architecture of our house and neighborhood to our own taste and proclivities will feed that initial choice. The next step, however, requires more introspection. What kind of style do we want to evoke? Do we want to try

Even when winter closes in early, making armchair gardening the order of the day, we can bring some of the garden's fruits indoors with us. The well-stocked garden offers a splendid variety of ingredients for seasonal arrangements and decorations.

Like painting or sculpture, gardening is a visual art. It is a lively art as well, based on the flow and change of living things. By trusting your own taste, you'll develop a garden style that is both personal and generally pleasing. (Little and Lewis Water Gardens, Bainbridge Island, Washington.)

the patterns of paths and lines of beds. Indeed, gardens made to generic patterns or according to standard rules may be a sight to see without ever becoming a place to be. They may be made in a style without having any style of their own. To gain individual style, a garden has to be somebody's beloved child, the fruit of an ardent imagination. Style is not just external, but an expression of taste. A stylish garden has a distinctive appearance. It has a recognizable character, as will its maker. Ideally, your garden could never be mistaken for mine or anybody else's, because it is so very obviously the representation of your own pleasures and propensities.

Naturally enough, our taste informs our chosen style. Some of us love formal green rooms, others adore sheer color in casual profusion. Our dominant themes may be early rococo or late suburban. Our gardens may hold plastic flamingos and gnomes or faux stone heads and reproductions of European cherubs and chimney pots. None of these are inherently better or worse choices. The important thing is that they be our own genuine choices. Too often, we allow glossy magazines and seductive picture books to dictate what is or is not good taste. We let Martha or Ralph become the arbiters of taste, and we grow addicted to their advice. When we do that, we lose confidence in our own spontaneous choices. As our choices lose sincerity, their power to please us is reduced. Lifestyle books and magazines leave us with an uneasy double message, a feeling of mingled resentment and envy. Why don't I have time to lacquer little acorn cups for my children's tea parties, time to make wonderful gardens and keep them immaculate, all the while serving up endlessly stylish meals on incredibly decorated tables in a fabulously decorated house? What's wrong with me?

The worst problem with lifestyle publications is that they diminish the natural world. The

our hand at a specific school of garden making, reproducing perhaps a billowing English cottage garden, a tidy French parterre, or a Japanese zen sand garden? Might we rather create something more individual while still conjuring up the feeling of an English country border or a French impressionist garden?

Garden style is often assumed to be dependent on design, yet design alone can't help us here. Developing a garden style involves far more than

underlying message is that nothing is good enough as it is. Plain reality is simply not acceptable. The ungilded lily is worthless, and the natural must be rearranged or controlled or manipulated to qualify as art. Let's be clear: that isn't art, it's artifice, artificial. This is not to say we can't indulge in a bit of whimsy, or incorporate attractive objects into our gardens, but we cannot, must not lose sight of the essential reality of the garden itself. In so many ways, we allow ourselves to be removed, almost sealed off from the natural world. Insulated in homes, offices, shops, and cars, we can choose not to experience weather or seasonal change, wearing the same clothing summer and winter if we like. We can eat strawberries any day of the year, if we can afford them. Darkness can be banished at the touch of a switch. Through television and video, we can experience a thousand realities without leaving home. We can hear and see so much excitement, beauty, and physical perfection of all kinds that plain old day-to-day life can seem dull in comparison.

Gardeners, however, have a peculiar resistance to the lure of such sirens, both imaginary and material. Constantly renewed contact with the earth, with physical dirt as well as weather and seasonal fluctuations, keep us firmly connected to the most ancient cycles of life. Recent studies show that people who can see trees and green plants from their office windows have lower blood pressure, better overall health, and greater resistance to disease, while those who see only artifacts—other buildings, streets, and endless streams of cars—will suffer more from stress and malaise. What's more, people who have living plants in their work areas actually produce more endorphins (pleasure-producing hormones also stimulated into being by laughter and chocolate) than do those who are divorced from contact with plant life. Humans have a deep, archaic relationship with plants, and

when we forget to renew that relationship, we become less well.

While stylish gardens can be tremendous fun, a source of pleasure to all who visit them, it is vital that the elements of style never overbalance those of substance. Living gardens are places where things happen, where change occurs, where there is room for serendipity. They are not poison neat, like a stiff New England front parlor. Always

If you want your handiwork to be found unfailingly tasteful, simply plunk together a potful of prim pastels. But it's far more fun to play off plants with dynamic shapes, textures, and colors to get distinctive, memorable results. (Garden of Barbara Flynn, Redmond, Washington.)

changing, never done, gardens are the life force embodied, and if they are a bit out of control now and then, that should neither surprise nor shock us. Our attitude toward the natural world is already overly control oriented, but control is not the issue, life is the issue. Our gardens don't need to be as tidy as our living rooms (and our living rooms don't need to be as tidy as those in magazines and movies). Life is a messy process, and real, living gardens will always have messy times, messy areas, and that is right and proper. When I was a schoolgirl, my teacher told us that when Margaret Fuller, one of the American transcendentalists, declared stirringly, "I accept the Universe" while reading an essay to the club, Ralph Waldo Emerson muttered (carefully, loud enough to be overheard and repeated), "Well, she'd better." We, too, had better accept the worth of substance over style, the value of green leaves and well-rotted manure over gold, or we stand at risk of losing touch with the very roots of our racial sanity.

A Garden in Winter

Planting for Cold Season Pleasure

Winter, with its dark mornings, short days, and early, endless nights, is hard on gardeners. Haunted by thoughts of green, growing things, we wander out to the chilly garden, seeking signs that spring is indeed just around the corner. Instead, we are apt to find the border furnished with sodden shrubs, the beds unpromisingly icy and carpeted with rotting leaves. Should we want to pause a while to drink in the atmosphere of the winter garden, we discover that all the available seats have been taken by heaps of snow. The air is dank and chilly, the plants are naked, dripping, and depressing. When the poet tenderly

queries, "Oh wind, if winter comes, can spring be far behind?" we answer shortly, "Yes." Pots of forced bulbs and forsythia twigs on the windowsill do help to break winter's deadlock by offering a firm promise of spring to come, but for many of us such artifice isn't really satisfying. Those lucky enough to have a greenhouse can find a good deal of solace there, but if that is not possible, there is still at least one practical option for plant-hungry gardeners.

After years of trying to ignore or struggle against it, I finally realized that the best way for a gardener to appreciate winter is to make the best of it. To this end, I walked the soggy garden again with a new goal in mind. This time, I was looking not for immediate satisfaction but for a corner of the garden that would catch whatever midday sunshine winter affords. Here I would gather together plants with true winter beauties, creating a little garden that would be at its best from November into March. Ideally, it should be protected from morning light, which can burst frozen buds that handily survive slower thawing. It should also be sheltered from the bitter north wind, and if there were a covered area where I could watch the rain or snow without getting soaked, so much the better. I set out plastic garden chairs in several possible sites in order to evaluate their potential. The whole family got involved, trying out each one, offering opinions and suggesting wonderful (if improbable) additions to the basic plan.

Eventually, after much consideration, we settled on an angled corner between the kitchen and the sun porch. The walls provide a fair amount of shelter right away, and because it faces southwest, this little area actually feels warm on sunny winter days, even with snow on the ground. Since it isn't already furnished with evergreen shrubs that offer winter beauties of berry and twig, I am adding them a few at a time, as the budget allows. Next summer, we will pave part of the angle, making a small terrace to keep our feet dry during the wet months. The boys are designing a covered seat to heap with waterproof cushions (these will be stored inside), which they will build for a winter project. With a picnic rug to blanket cold knees, insulated mugs to keep tea or mulled cider hot, and warm boots, personal comfort is soon established. Warm, dry, and mellow, we will be ready to enjoy what winter can offer.

So what does winter offer? Even in gardens where no thought has gone into planting for winter delight, there may be some surprisingly beautiful things. Dogwoods reveal graceful branches and glowing lavender bark in winter, while many small maples gleam scarlet or shrimp pink. To learn which other small trees are similarly attractive in the nude, visit nurseries in the off season and look for good lines, great silhouettes, and bright bark. Winter fruits are plentiful, not only from the obvious candidates: certain crab apples will hold their ice-coated fruit past New Year. English holly, *Ilex aquifolium* (Zone 6, 15 to 75 feet), and the native *I. opaca* (Zone 4, 15 to 45 feet) bear fat clusters or red berries in winter. Tough, healthy *Pyracantha coccinea* (Zone 6, 5 to 8 feet) and the lustier *P. crenulata* (Zone 6, to 12 feet) are also heavily decorated with pretty berries, not just red but also in shades of orange, yellow, and white. The twigs of beautyberry, *Callicarpa bodinieri* 'Profusion' (Zone 5, to 10 feet), are smothered with beadlike lavender fruits in winter, while those of the more compact *C. japonica* (Zone 5, to 5 feet) are bright purple. The chunky berries of *Pernettya mucronata* (Zone 6, to 3 feet) may be pink or purple, rose or white, and persist all winter. Our native snowberry, *Symphoricarpos rivularis* (Zone 3, to 8 feet), has

Take time to wander through the winter garden, seeing the beauties of bark, branch shape, and silhouette. Look, too, for a sunny spot which might make a cozy place to sit, despite frost and snow.

a delightful opalescent hybrid, 'Mother of Pearl', as well as a frosty pink one called 'Magic Berry.' Many species roses provide profuse displays of hips in many shapes and ruddy tints from red to salmon and coral. Some of the best are the seaside rose, *Rosa rugosa* (Zone 2, to 8 feet), which offers flowers in many colors, followed by big red or orange hips for tea making, and *R. moyessi* (Zone 5, to 10 feet), with small, ruby-red flowers and elongated, tomato-colored hips.

Some broadleaf evergreens will provide our corner with extra shelter, and winter bloomers deliver both color and fragrance. Among the hardiest are the rhododendrons hybridized by David Leach, such as 'Lodestar' (Zone 5, to 10 feet), its flowers a froth of whipped cream and lemon, dusky red 'Sumatra' (Zone 5, to 2 feet), or buttery-yellow 'Hong Kong' (Zone 5, to 10 feet). Sweet-scented winter daphne, *Daphne odora* (Zone 6, to 6 feet), and its yellow-variegated form, 'Marginata', are good candidates where hardy, as is *Viburnum tinus* (Zone 7 to 8, 10 to 20 feet), which blooms from November through March. Winter honeysuckle, *Lonicera fragrantissima* (Zone 5, 6 to 10 feet), blooms from February through April in mild years, its small, ivory flowers as sweet as the name suggests. This one tends to be rangy (though it responds well to pruning), but dapper, neatly tiered *L. pileata* (Zone 5, 2 to 4 feet) brings good form and structural support to any garden composition. Native Sierra laurel, *Leucothoe davisiae* (Zone 5, 2 to 3 feet) and coast leucothoe, *L. axillaris* (Zone 6, 3 to 6 feet), are graceful evergreens, their drooping arms trimmed with pairs of elegant, tapered leaves that turn vivid shades of copper and red-bronze in winter. Though leucothoe doesn't bloom until summer, leathery little sweet box (*Sarcococca hookerana* var. *humilis*, Zone 5, 2 to 3 feet) blooms in mild winters from January on, smelling like honey and vanilla. Deciduous wintersweet (*Chimonanthus praecox*, Zone 7, 8 to 12 feet), which blooms with the snowdrops, and witch hazel (*Hamamelis mol-*

lis, Zone 5, 15 to 30 feet) are also intensely fragrant from February well into spring.

Needled evergreens bring splendid variety of shapes, color, and textures to the winter tapestry, and many trim their branches with little cones. There are dozens of dwarf and compact border forms of junipers, for instance, some with a blue or lavender cast to the fine-textured foliage, others silvery or gray, sunny yellow or old gold. Be aware, however, that too many will give the winter corner a stiff, prickly look, and create uncomfortable root competition for smaller plants. These may be added as liberally as climate allows.

A surprising number of perennials have at least some degree of winter charm, and though they may look unhappy when hard frosts arrive, they perk up, often flowering during the thaws of midwinter. My winter corner also holds several clusters of cold-hardy perennials, from evergreen autumn ferns, *Dryopteris erythrosora* (Zone 4, to 2 feet) to glossy, round-leaved *Bergenia cordifolia* (Zone 3, to 20 inches), which sends up fat, frilly stalks trimmed with pink or red or white bells in late winter. Christmas roses (*Helleborus niger*, Zone 3, to 18 inches), and their cousins the Lenten roses (*H.* x *hybridus*, also called *orientalis*, Zone 4, to 18 inches) ring out their wide bells in many colors, from purple to white (or in the case of bearsfoot or stinking hellebore, *H. foetidus*, Zone 6, to 18 inches) in mid to late winter. Indeed, by shopping at plant society sales and specialty mail-order nurseries, one can assemble a selection of hellebores that will flower from November into March. Kaffir lilies, *Schizostylis coccinea* (Zone 6, to 2 feet), bloom during every warm spell, their lax foliage punctuated by swoop-

Well-placed, shapely evergreens can be treated as structural elements in the garden. They gain particular importance in winter, especially when given supportive companions. (Garden of T. R. Welch, Bainbridge Island, Washington.)

ing, gladiolalike flower stalks. 'Oregon Sunrise' flowers are soft but saturated pink, while 'November Cheer' blooms cherry red. Both mingle well with evergreen herbs like rosemary, lavender, cooking sage, and blue rue, and fit nicely between little evergreen shrubs, which lend them the firm support they need to look their best. Arrange whatever combination of these plants best suits your fancy, sprinkle in some crocus and snowdrops, carpet the whole with a tidy ground cover such as the dwarf evergreen *Vinca minor* 'Miss Jekyll's White' (Zone 4, to 5 inches), and you have created a winter treasure.

Where snows arrive early and lie deep all winter, such a corner may seem but a pipe dream. However, the addition of some extra shelter may enable you to create at least a modified version of the winter garden. Perhaps an open arbor could be partially enclosed in winter, with one or two sides left open, the top covered at least in part. In this protected nook, you can array whatever winter wonders your climate allows, screening the smaller plants with larger, bulkier ones. As the year draws to a close and the garden lies quiet, wander out and see it with new eyes, looking for a place to create a winter haven. Make some sketches of possible locations, watch where the light falls and the winds blow over the next few months. If nothing leaps to mind, think about what might be cleared away to create a protected little place where you can start to make friends with winter.

Joyful Junipers

Needled Evergreens that Decorate House and Garden

Each year, my family takes great pleasure in filling our elderly farmhouse with greenery gleaned from the garden and the woods beyond. Since we celebrate the solstice as well as religious events during this season, our decorations generally have a natural rather than a specific holiday theme. All over the house, arrangements fill squat teapots and tall glass jars, their stiff sprays of evergreen foliage enlivened by ivory snowberry and red holly, coral and tawny rose hips, ruddy barberries, and citrus orange and yellow pyracantha fruit. Swags, wreaths, and Advent candle rings deck every possible surface, their basic fir-and-cedar green threaded with feathery blue juniper and golden teardrop false cypress, tasseled Atlantic cedar, and whirling wolf pine.

Most of this richesse comes from what I call the "wreath border," a long hedge forming along the north side of our property line. Its purpose is twofold; it shelters and screens our garden from the neighbors and also provides a variety of colorful ingredients for holiday decorations. Though the wreath hedge is a mixed one, containing both evergreen and deciduous elements, the bulk of it consists of junipers, one of my favorite evergreen families. Despite being scorned by plant snobs and treated like disposable trash by careless landscapers, junipers survive neglect with aplomb. Perhaps this hardy clan gets no respect because it is most often represented by boring rows of planted juniper tams or the ubiquitous Pfitzers, plopped into a sea of ground-up bark. Though any of these plants can be quite lovely if well placed and well supported, they are generally neither, so it's not surprising when their quiet beauties are overlooked. What is surprising is that although this clan holds dozens, perhaps hundreds, of fascinating forms, only a handful of junipers are really common, and these are neither the prettiest nor the most appealing varieties. Gardeners who care to explore the possibilities will discover a host of highly attractive junipers, varied in form, texture, and color, all ready to surprise us most pleasantly if given half a chance.

Winter is a good time to assemble an interesting assortment of needled evergreens, for you can see how the plants will look during the off season. Many take on winter tints of purple, copper, or gray, and though the majority of evergreens really are green, they illustrate a thousand shades of nature's favorite color, from palest celadon to the ink green of the midnight forest. A good many evergreens have silver threads or golden needles, whether warm and brazen or cool and citrusy. Dozens more offer blue foliage in every shade between pewter and white-capped ocean, including turquoise and lavender.

If you have a hedge to plant or a slope to cover with evergreens, take time to investigate your options before automatically ordering *Thuja* 'Pyramidalis' or juniper tams. Reflex choices, made because everybody makes them, are often boringly predictable. Those usual suspects can be an unprepossessing lot, especially when rowed out like sullen delinquents in a police lineup, but no horticultural law dictates their constant use. We can choose amongst scores of handsome needled evergreens, combining them to emphasize their individual qualities and strengths. Why dot a hillside with fifty identical tams when we can weave an intricate, colorful tapestry that delights us all year round? Such a tapestry is great fun to create and even more fun to admire, especially since it needs very little help to remain beautiful. Indeed, if you already have a juniper plantation out front, consider replacing half the plants with others radically different in form, whether upright, creeping, or eccentric. In gardening as in cooking, wonderful ingredients can transform a simple idea into a stunning showpiece. Don't just settle for what's on sale at the big garden center; choose plants in combinations you will actively enjoy looking at for years to come.

Like many backbone plants, junipers are more attractive in combinations than *en masse*. Even ordinary plants are revealed as beautiful when properly paired. Partnerships of plants with strongly contrasting shapes set at irregular intervals make a plain planting visually intriguing. A wide carpet of sprawling, blue-green 'Bar Harbor' juniper (*Juniperus horizontalis*, Zone 3, 1 by 6 feet)

In house or garden, ivory snowberry and red holly, coral rose hips, and tawny and citrus-colored pyracantha fruit are set off to perfection by a backdrop of feathery junipers.

Arranged in artful partnerships, junipers and other needled evergreens are far from boring. In this Pacific Rim garden, they mimic clouds and rocks and flowing water. (Kubota Gardens, Seattle, Washington.)

'Obelisk' (to 8 feet) and broad mounds of *J. c.* 'Sulphur Spray' (3 by 5 feet).

Since few junipers can be considered garish, whether alone or in combination, it's hard to go wrong in terms of color coordination. Despite their variations, all have some shade or other of green in their makeup, which creates visual ties between even the brightest and least similar forms. Thus, vividly contrasting color forms can emphasize the brilliance of one partner without diminishing the subtlety of the other. To see how this works, play around at the nursery, putting together pairs or trios of good-looking junipers. Watch how the intensely yellow, young tips of *J. horizontalis* 'Mother Lode' (Zone 3, 1 by 4 feet) accentuate the metallic, steely blues of *J. squamata* 'Maxi Star' (Zone 4, 2 by 4 feet), while the saturated Irish tints of *J. communis* 'Wintergreen' (Zone 2, 15 to 20 feet) lend luster to the gentle *J. chinensis* 'Old Gold' (Zone 3, 4 by 5 feet).

One of my favorite partnerships is handsome at all times, but especially effective in the snow. Tightly columnar *Juniperus communis* 'Sentinal' (Zone 2, 5 to 10 feet) is as slim and upright as the name suggests, though it can get a bit potbellied in time (as after forty or fifty years). In the short run, it remains skinny and densely textured, its foliage dark and lustrous. On either side are plants of *J. chinensis* 'Gold Coast' (Zone 3, 5 by 8 feet), a sturdy, reliable shrub that holds its gilding nicely (many golden junipers turn a depressing copper-yellow in winter). Its branches build in frothy layers that look like frozen sea spray, for their gold has in it both the grayish greens of prairie sage and the murkier green of the deep forest.

Slim as a sword against the sky, our native hillspire juniper, *J. virginiana* 'Skyrocket' (Zone 2, 10 to 15 feet), is the color of cold-pressed steel. It works wonderfully in formal plantings, holding its

sets off the tight texture and formal shape of a green columnar form like *J. chinensis* 'Spartan' (Zone 3, to 18 feet) or the perfect globes of *J. c.* 'Pfitzeriana Nana' (to 4 feet). Smooth, rounded *J. c.* 'Globosa' (to 6 feet) makes a calming counterpoint to the tufted, twisting turrets of Hollywood juniper (*J. c.* 'Torulosa' or 'Kaizuka', 10 to 20 feet). Tall fountains of *J. c.* 'Hetzii' (10 to 15 feet) are balanced by the ruffled pyramids of *J. c.*

amazingly narrow profile in maturity, and also works to balance billowing or informally shaped shrubs. Its sibling, *J. v.* 'Manhattan Blue' (to 20 feet), is rather broader at the base, but tapers quickly into a whirling, heavily frosted cone that can bind the airy hybrid *J.* x 'Blue Cloud' (Zone 3, 4 by 6 feet) or the glittering, arctic blue *J. squamata* 'Blue Star' (Zone 4, 3 by 5 feet) down to earth.

Few plants are more lastingly lovely than the pyramidal Rocky Mountain juniper, *Juniperus scopulorum* 'Wichita Blue' (Zone 3, to 18 feet). Open and rather coarse in texture, it has feathery branches decked with glowing, ice-blue needles. This kingly creature will preside majestically over a group of smoke-colored *J. virginiana* 'Grey Owl' (Zone 2, 3 by 6 feet), a plumy, wire-textured shrub that carries heavy crops of its silvery, berrylike cones in winter. (These are used to flavor gin, as well as certain native stews and soups.) The pale aluminum blue of 'Wichita Blue' sets off nearly any other color, especially rich reds, purples, and lavenders. In one of my favorite plantings, it emerges from a swirl of creeping junipers, low growers that form dense, rippling carpets over time. The brightest of its companions is *J. horizontalis* 'Blue Chip' (Zone 3, to 1 by 6 to 10 feet), which spreads in pools of sparkling stream blue in summer, turning hazy lavender-blue in winter. Finer textured and more ruffled in form, *J. h.* 'Lavender Chip' (to 1 by 6 to 8 feet) has feathery tips that undulate in rolling breakers. Next to it, the stunning *J. h.* 'Turquoise Spreader' (Zone 3, 6 to 12 inches by 6 to 8 feet) pours in glimmering, blue-green wavelets, shot through with shifting sea tints that deepen to copper and purple in winter.

If all these blues and grays leave you cold, you can warm up with sunny golds and summery greens. Broad-based, rather fluffy columns of *J. communis* 'Gold Cone' (Zone 2, to 12 feet) counter heavy, earthbound plantings nicely, while the slimmer, tightly conical *J. chinensis* 'Aurea' (Zone 3, to 10 feet) lends drama to smaller-scaled beds of slow-growing, diminutive shrubs. Windswept, forest-green *J. c.* 'Hetz's Columnaris' (to 15 feet) has a whirling texture that draws the eye upward, so its stocky columns seem light rather than stolid. It makes a sturdy contrast to the splendidly plumed *J. c.* 'Armstrong' (4 by 6 feet), which builds in soft, shaggy sprays of rich, dappled green that look like living water. If more color power is needed, *J. c.* 'Mint Julep' (6 by 8 feet) is tighter in texture and a few shades brighter in color.

This lengthy catalog by no means exhausts the possibilities of the junipers, let alone other evergreens such as yew (*Taxus* species) and false cedars (*Chamaecyparis* species) which add their own particular charms to any hedge planting. Since reference books provide a bewildering variety of plants, not all of which may be available or appropriate for your region, start hunting out exciting junipers at garden centers. If you can't find much of interest locally, check Barbara Barton's inimitable guide, *Gardening By Mail* (see the appendix), for appropriate specialty nurseries in your region and try to arrange a few visits. You can also send away to several of the listed nurseries and while away a wet day or two browsing through their catalogs. Though few small nursery catalogs offer splashy illustrations, they are often gold mines of specific information, gained through direct and personal experience, which is often more useful than the generic information presented in bigger, all-purpose catalogs (or reference books).

Once you have made your selections, prep the planting area as usual, removing sod and turning the soil to remove weeds and rocks. However, unless it is absolutely impoverished, the soil won't need as much amendment as it would for perennials. Indeed, junipers prefer lean soils to rich ones, so mix in tilth improvers like aged manure, compost, or shredded leaves but leave out the nitrogen boosters like bone or soy meals. To fully enjoy these plants in garden settings, it's important to respect their modest but inflexible needs. Given full sun, well-drained soils, and plenty of room, your junipers will reward you richly, returning healthy good looks in exchange for occasional weeding and an annual soil-conditioning mulch (sawdust and compost or aged manure and shredded bark work wonders).

The most common cause for juniper failure is excess water. Naturally, new plants will need to be watered regularly until they are established, yet supplemental water can be fatal to mature plants, particularly those planted in heavy, clay-based soils. Except in persistent, severe droughts, mature junipers should not receive routine waterings. Root rots, tip burn, and persistent browning off from the inside of the plant are all symptoms of overwatering. If your soil is very heavy, add a good helping of coarse grit or builder's sand to each planting hole, and plant on sloping ground whenever possible. Repositioning automatic lawn and garden sprinklers to avoid the junipers can add years (and the gloss of health) to their life.

A second very common problem is whiplash, damage caused by weed whackers that score bark, causing dieback and browning off of branch tips. This situation can be avoided altogether, simply by placing plants properly. Be aware of the mature size of each variety before you plant, and position it accordingly. It is perfectly acceptable practice to overplant a bed so that you don't have to wait six or eight years for it to look luxuriant. However, if you plan to do this, use inexpensive and less wonderful plants as filler. When sacrifice time rolls around, it won't be a painful process (for you, anyway). The extra plants can be transplanted to another area, if you prefer it; junipers are not good movers in general, but if you are both fast and careful, you may save a good percentage of them.

Pruning should not be necessary, except when plants are damaged by dogs, storms, or something of the sort. However, if low branches do overhang a path or sidewalk, reach under the plant and

Slim and shapely, these sentinal junipers are clipped to emphasize their charming curves. Left fluffy and natural, such a hedge would grace an informal setting with similar strength. (Garden of T. R. Welch, Woodinville, Washington.)

remove the entire offending section from the bottom rather than hacking away at the end of the piece that protrudes. Junipers are easily wounded and will not grow back when pruned to old wood. Since they look unsightly when butchered, place these plants where harsh controlling measures will not be necessary. Respect their needs and you can freely enjoy their multiple beauties. Choose your junipers with an eye to their glories and they will combine in joyous concert to gladden your heart and lift your spirits all through the year.

The Year in Review

Performance Assessment for
You and Your Garden

As winter pulls its creamy curtain over the sleeping garden, the gardener retires to the warm house to review results and plan next season's revisions. Notes and pictures will assist us more than memory here, for many gardeners share a curious skill; the ability to envision the garden as a collective impression of all-time bests. When in December I sit by the fire and recall the garden, I see in my mind not the sere and thirsty garden of late summer '92 (thank goodness), nor the half-drowned one of '93, but the peerless roses of '86, the ebullient perennials of '88, the first annuals I ever grew—everything at its peak or prime, all assembled into one seamless garden of perfection. I am not alone in this tendency, for others say the same; they never dream about balled, fungal roses or stunted annuals, not crowded perennials or mangled shrubs, but only about quintessential plants. It is as though we envision our plants' archetypes rather than remembering their garden reality. Perhaps this is why the gardener is an eternal optimist; if so, it is a lovely gift, pulling us past failure toward the never-ending dream. Okay, so this year's border wasn't perfect, but surely *next* year....

The nicest thing about this drive for garden perfection is that despite its strength, most of us are fairly easily pleased. Only rarely does it spawn the kind of critical perfectionism that spoils our pleasure in what we have by constant mental contrast with what we wanted.

Winter is when we can weigh what we wanted against what we got without any loss of pleasure. It is the time to ponder and study, to explore new ideas or learn new techniques that help us more closely approximate those gardens of the inner eye. One of the best ways to do all this is through books, garden guides that can take us a bit further along our chosen paths. Some of us see our gardens as living art. Some of us garden for a living, or live to garden. All of us are hoping to improve our skills this time around, dreaming of creating the perfect garden. Whatever our goals, the best books for our needs will not only increase our knowledge and broaden our plant palettes, but will encourage us to be relaxed and playful about gardening, to accept and even provoke change, and to allow nature to intrude.

Perhaps the most valuable book any of us can own is a garden journal in which we record notes about weather patterns and plant performances, chores done and undone, garden problems and solutions, successful or otherwise. The best of these are undated, divided into four or five sections for each month, with space for several years' notes on each large page. It's a good idea to include a few snapshots in your journal, to visually record the triumphs of each season. Through these records, you can spot trends, both favorable and not, and gain an invaluable sense of progress. It really doesn't matter what kind of record book you use—even a looseleaf notebook will do—so long as you use it frequently. Personal garden journals become more valuable the more you use them, eventually forming a repository of specific information and experience that no generic book can begin to match.

Many people are daunted by the thought of writing such journals, but the notes can be as lean as a grocery list and still prove quite useful over time. Your writings don't have to be of earth-shaking importance or exquisitely literary, just informa-

When we envision our plants during the off season, we recall them in the perfection of their archetypes. Perfect lilies, intensely fragrant, against a backdrop of spotless sea kale—never a slug in sight, nor any trace of disease or neglect to mar their beauty. (Garden of Peggy VanBianchi, Kingston, Washington.)

tive. Mine, for instance, include high and low temperatures for each month, general weather patterns ("very warm and wet, lots of wind mid-month"), and observations about which beds or areas look specially good (or bad). I record outstanding plant performances, combinations successful or otherwise, and any cultural care that seems effective. Problems, both persistent and unusual, get a fair amount of attention, as do the various solutions I try out, along with their results. I also keep running lists of things in bloom, with general notes about how long key plants stay in bloom, when rebloom occurs, and for how long. Though my records are often incomplete (I am not especially patient or thorough), a surprising amount of information gets itself compiled anyway, and nearly all of it proves useful at some point.

Our journals can demonstrate and speed our progress in other terms as well. If we missed staking a few things, perhaps we stocked up on peony hoops and tall tomato cages. Even better, we can make notes right now, writing ahead so that next spring we will find pointed reminders to put the new gear in position at the right time, before the need is obvious. If the garden ground is hungry and our plants flagged early this year, we can budget for a bulk buy of manure and alfalfa pellets to layer on the beds in spring. Tomorrow, we can start another compost pile, making a reminding note to spread its goodness generously come March. If only half our careful color schemes came off properly, we can devise new companions and new placements, basing them on our notes about bloom times and durations. The plants necessary for these refinements can be added to our wish list, which helps keep our heads clear when the catalog deluge begins. In such ways we refocus goals and projects, refine ideas, and create new directions to guide our garden making over the coming year.

While reviewing your notes, you may find that your ideas have changed along with the garden. The goals you began the year with often shift, subtly or radically, as both you and the garden grow together. This doesn't necessarily mean that you have gotten off track; it may well mean that you have come further along the garden path and are ready to attempt more ambitious and challenging projects. If many combinations need rearranging, perhaps your ability to conceive artful ensembles has matured. If unhappy plants must be moved to better locations, you have learned how to recognize and alleviate distress. Whenever you improve an unsatisfying vignette, you hone your visual editing skills. Garden making is a lengthy process, one which lasts the lucky a lifetime, and there is no hurry about it but the natural impatience of the smitten to see plants bloom before they are even bought, let alone planted. Take this time not to criticize but to congratulate yourself for whatever good your garden has brought you this year.

My favorite time for journal review is between the dark end of the old year and the bright beginning of the new, the traditional time in which to examine the past and plan for the future. As the great seasonal tide of the year turns, plants and people alike feel the change. From now on, every day will be a few minutes longer. After this long night passes, buds begin to swell on shrub and tree, while underground, root and bulb start to stir. The return of the light brings a renewal of spirit to the gardener as well, reawakening our desire to create, to make, to achieve. Leaving the garden in slumberous peace, we can retire to a comfortable, well-lighted place to review our garden journal notes, old plans, and planting diagrams. We are looking not for shortcomings (many though there may be), nor for failures of

Good journal keeping helps hone garden editing skills. Just as in any other lively art, we need to revise and refine our border work on an ongoing basis to incorporate new thoughts and experiences. Left unrecorded, our observations and dreams are too often lost. (Garden of Peggy VanBianchi, Kingston, Washington.)

accomplishment or intent, but for progress, however modest.

To complete your year-end review, you must consult your feelings as well as your notebooks. To analyze your progress in garden design terms, walk the quiet garden, looking at shape and form in beds and plantings, latent as they may be. Ask the same questions you did when you were start-

ing out: Does the garden as a whole have a clear, definite shape? Are the shapes of the beds pleasing, generous, in scale with the house and lawn? Are evergreen and architectural elements harmonious and balanced? Do they dominate other plantings? Are they too recessive and indefinite?

When many answers aren't wholly satisfactory or positive, it is easy to get discouraged. To counteract this, remember that in the garden as elsewhere in life, most important changes are incremental. This is where those snapshots will be very helpful, reminding you of how far you and the garden have come, as well as how far you still have to go. I like to compare notes with myself, rereading what I wrote in my journal this time last year. As I mentally check off the tasks and projects that I did complete, and mark the progress made against longer-term goals, my mood swings up to one of satisfaction and pleasure. This struggle, one many of us engage infrequently, may be a peculiarly American one, representing the tensions between our work ethic and pleasure principles. We seem to want to live out the slogan of the Minnesota Twins; we should work hard, play hard, then get out there and by golly win! If we don't fully succeed in making the garden of our dreams, for whatever reasons (surely a year is plenty of time), we feel at fault and our pleasure in the garden itself is diminished.

The garden, however, is one place we can be free of the relentless pressure to perform. Here, if nowhere else, we can actively enjoy ourselves, taking satisfaction in every blossom and bud and accepting failures philosophically, knowing that they are a necessary part of the total picture. We can certainly learn from our difficulties, but since we can't control weather or nature, we can't accept their vagaries as our personal responsibility, either. Though the pangs of loss (or loss of control) may

ABOVE: Long-necked *Crocus zonatus* blooms in November and December, both a promise and a reminder that winter really does lead directly back to spring.

OPPOSITE: Wait until deciduous and ephemeral plants bow out before assessing the garden's winter bones. A frost-bitten hydrangea reveals unexpected beauties of texture and form even in decay, making a solid case for not being too tidy too soon.

be severe at first, they grow less over time. This is not because we grow callous or learn to care less, but because with experience, gardeners come to recognize that both success and failure are cyclical, intertwined, and inevitable. We know, too, with utter certainty, that every step, however small, takes us onward and upward along the garden path. Endless and ever changing, full of unexpected turns and twists, the path leads us to plants and places as yet unknown and only dimly imagined. That, too, is part of the joy, for change and surprises are the only constants. Onward we go, in haste or at our leisure, in gentle pursuit of the new plants, new combinations and new ideas that are always waiting just around the next corner.

A p p e n d i x

Books for Further Reading

Those who want to delve deeper into a given topic will find a bewilderment of books before them. Following are some of the most useful to the novice garden maker. A few, like Barbara Barton's *Gardening By Mail,* are worth a whole bookshelf in themselves. Others, like Penelope Hobhouse's *Colour in Your Garden,* are specialized, yet still of general interest. Not all of these books are in print, but they are worth seeking out, whether from second-hand bookstores or through book-searching services. Capability's Books carries the largest selection of in-print garden books in the country. For a catalog, call 1-800-247-8154. Booknoll Farm, a wonderful mail-order book service started by the late Elizabeth Woodburn, carries a large selection of new and used garden and horticulture books. For a list, write to: Booknoll Farm, Hopewell, New Jersey 08525.

Regional knowledge is always invaluable to the gardener, so local authors are also worth seeking out. It is a good idea to check regional libraries and local universities as well as county extension services for reliable sources of specific, regionally appropriate information.

Armitage, Allen. *Herbaceous Perennial Plants.* Athens, Ga.: Varsity Press, 1989.

Balston, Michael. *The Well-Furnished Garden.* New York: Simon & Schuster, 1986.

Barton, Barbara. *Gardening By Mail.* Boston: Houghton Mifflin, 1994.

Beckett, Kenneth. *Growing Hardy Perennials.* Portland, Ore.: Timber Press, 1982.

Bloom, Adrian. *Winter Garden Glory.* New York: HarperCollins, 1993.

Boisset, Caroline. *Gardening in Time.* New York: Prentice Hall Press, 1990.

Brookes, John. *The Book of Garden Design.* New York: Macmillan Publishing Co., 1991.

———. *The Garden Book.* New York: Crown Publishers, 1984.

Chatto, Beth. *The Green Tapestry.* New York: Simon & Schuster, 1989.

———. *The Damp Garden.* London: J. M. Dent & Sons, Ltd., 1982.

———. *The Dry Garden.* London: J. M. Dent & Sons, Ltd., 1978.

Druse, Ken. *The Natural Garden.* New York: Clarkson N. Potter, 1989.

Ellefson, Connie, Tom Stephens, and Doug Welsh. *Xeriscape Gardening.* New York: Macmillan Publishing Co., 1992.

Ferguson, Nicola. *Right Plant, Right Place.* New York: Summit Books, 1984.

Fish, Margery. *A Flower Every Day.* London: Faber & Faber, 1981.

———. *Cottage Garden Flowers.* London: Faber & Faber, 1981.

———. *Gardening in the Shade.* London: Faber & Faber, 1981.

———. *Ground Cover Plants.* London: Faber & Faber, 1981.

Harper, Pamela J. *Designing with Perennials*. New York: Macmillan Publishing Co., 1991.

———, and Frederick McGourty. *Perennials: How to Select, Grow and Enjoy*. Los Angeles: Price Stern Sloan, 1985

Hayward, Gordon. *Garden Paths: Inspiring Designs and Practical Projects*. Charlotte, Vt.: Camden House, 1993.

Hobhouse, Penelope. *Colour in Your Garden*. Boston: Little, Brown 1985.

———. *Flower Gardens*. Boston: Little, Brown, 1991.

———. *Garden Style*. Boston: Little, Brown, 1988.

Jellito, Leo, and Wilhelm Schacht. *Hardy Herbaceous Perennials* (2 volumes). Portland, Ore.: Timber Press, 1990.

Keen, Mary. *The Garden Border Book*. Deer Park, Wis.: Capability's Books, 1987.

Kennedy, Des. *Crazy about Gardening: Reflections on the Sweet Seductions of a Garden*. Vancouver/Toronto: Whitecap Books, 1994.

Kourik, Robert. *Drip Irrigation for Every Landscape and All Climates*. Santa Rosa, Calif.: Metamorphic Press, 1993. (This can be ordered for $16 post-paid from Drip Irrigation Book, P.O. Box 1841, Santa Rosa, CA 95402).

Lacy, Allen. *The Garden in Autumn*. New York: Atlantic Monthly Press, 1990.

Lawrence, Elizabeth. *A Southern Garden*. Chapel Hill, N.C.: Duke University Press, 1991.

———. *Gardens In Winter*. Baton Rouge, Louisiana: Claitor's Publishing Division, 1977.

———. *The Little Bulbs*. Chapel Hill, N.C.: Duke University Press, 1986.

Lima, Patrick. *The Harrowsmith Perennial Garden*. Camden East, Ontario: Camden House, 1987.

———. *The Harrowsmith Illustrated Book of Herbs*. Camden East, Ontario: Camden House, 1987.

Lloyd, Christopher. *Christopher Lloyd's Flower Garden*. New York: Dorling Kindersley, 1993.

———. *Foliage Plants*. New York: Random House, 1973.

———. *The Adventurous Gardener*. New York: Random House, 1983.

———. *The Well-Chosen Garden*. New York: Harper & Row, 1984.

———. *The Well-Tempered Garden*. New York: Random House, 1985.

Lovejoy, Ann. *The American Mixed Border*. New York: Macmillan Publishing Co., 1993.

——— (ed.). *Perennials: Toward Continuous Bloom*. Deer Park, Wis.: Capability's Books, 1991.

Malitz, Jerome. *Personal Landscapes*. Portland, Ore.: Timber Press, 1989.

McHoy, Peter. *Pruning: A Practical Guide*. New York: Abbeville Press, 1993.

———, with Tim Miles and Roy Cheek. Edited by Alan Toogood. *The Complete Book of Container Gardening*. North Pomfret, Vt.: Trafalgar Square, 1994.

Obritzok, Robert A. *A Garden of Conifers: Introduction and Selection Guide*. Deer Park, Wis.: Capability's Books, 1994.

Osler, Mirabel. *A Gentle Plea for Chaos*. New York: Simon & Schuster, 1989.

Phillips, Roger and Martyn Rix. *Bulbs*. 1989.

———. *Perennials* (2 volumes). New York: Random House, 1991.

———. *Roses*. New York: Random House, 1988.

———. *Shrubs*. New York: Random House, 1989.

Sabuco, John. *The Best of the Hardiest*. Flossmore, Ill.: Plantsmen's Publications, 1990.

Sackville-West, Vita. *Vita Sackville-West's Garden Book*. New York: Atheneum, 1983.

Schenk, George. *The Complete Shade Gardener*. Boston: Houghton Mifflin, 1984.

Solomon, Steve. *Van Patten's Organic Gardener's Composting*. Portland, Ore.: Van Patten Publishing, 1993.

Thomas, Graham S. *Perennial Garden Plants*. Portland, Ore.: Timber Press, 1990.

———. *Plants for Ground Cover*. London: J. M. Dent & Sons, Ltd., 1984.

———. *The Art of Planting*. Boston: David R. Godine, Inc., 1984.

Verey, Rosemary. *The Art of Planting*. Boston: Little, Brown, 1990.

———. *The Garden in Winter*. Boston: Little, Brown, 1988.

Whitehead, Jeffrey. *The Hedge Book*. Pownal, Vt.: Storey Communications, Garden Way Publishing, 1991.

Whiten, Faith and Geoff. *Creating a New Garden*. New York: W. W. Norton & Co., 1986.

Wilder, Louise B. *Adventures with Hardy Bulbs*. New York: Collier Books, 1990.

Woods, Christopher. *Encyclopedia of Perennials: A Gardener's Guide*. New York: Facts On File, 1992.

Wright, Michael. *The Complete Handbook of Garden Plants*. New York: Facts on File, 1984.

Wyman, Donald. *Wyman's Gardening Encyclopedia*. New York, Macmillan Publishing Co., 1986.

Index

Page numbers in *italics*
indicate photographs.

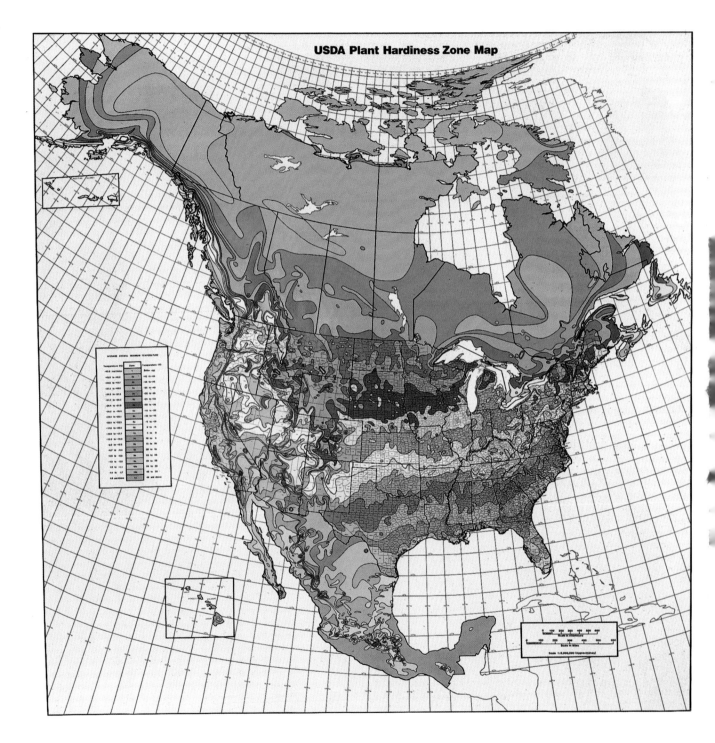

USDA Plant Hardiness Zone Map